COLLECTION MANAGEMENT

11/05	18	10/05
2/06	0-1	
9/09	10-1	6/09
5-12	12-1	7-31-10

100 Old Roses
for the
American Garden

100

OLD

ROSES

for the

AMERICAN

GARDEN

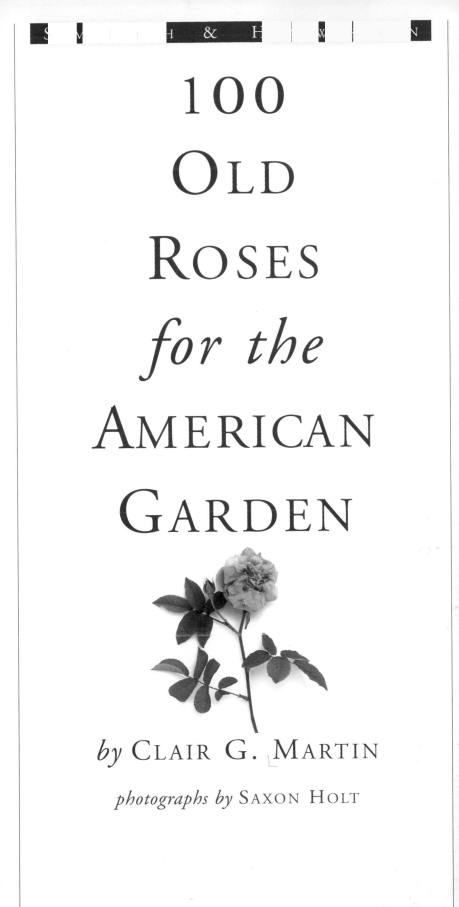

by CLAIR G. MARTIN

photographs by SAXON HOLT

WORKMAN PUBLISHING · NEW YORK

Acknowledgments

I particularly want to thank my partner, Jeff Cameron, who has acted as my personal copy editor and proofreader. Jeff has devoted so much time and energy reading, making suggestions, and contributing substantially to the overall spirit and tenor of these books—to say thank you does not even come close to expressing what I owe him.

I also want to acknowledge my garden volunteers, without whom I could not have focused so much energy on writing and lecturing. Over the years, the Huntington "deadheaders" have inspired and encouraged me with so much love and positive energy that much of what the garden has become is due to them.

Over the past few years, a number of people across the country have corresponded with me, sharing their knowledge and love of Old Roses. Their invaluable assistance has been most appreciated. Among those networkers I need to thank are Terri Campbell, Bill Christensen, Ron Chronister, Candy Craig, Patrick Cullen, Crenagh and David Elliott, Sandy Gaal, Paul and Anne Graber, Kreg Hill, Ruth Knopf, Glenn Mackie, Jackie and Don McElhose, Judy Miller, Brian Rice, Bunny Skran, Sharon Van Enoo, Leah Watterberg, and Tina Weakly.

Much gratitude goes to the editorial staff at Workman Publishing, most notably Sally Kovalchick and Mary Wilkinson, as well as my agent, Charlotte Sheedy, for their attention to every detail, not to mention their regular positive reinforcement and their genius and foresight in taking on an unknown writer.

Finally, I have to thank you, the reader, for supporting what we're trying to do here. I hope you derive as much pleasure and insight as you read this book as I did in writing it.

Unless otherwise noted, all photos are by Saxon Holt, except those on pages 6, 11, 23, 25, 30, 48, 57, 67 by Clair Martin; page 12, by Syl Arena; and page 26, The Granger Collection, New York.

ISBN 0-7611-1341-X
THE CATALOGING-IN-PUBLICATION INFORMATION FOR THIS
TITLE MAY BE OBTAINED FROM THE LIBRARY OF CONGRESS.

WORKMAN PUBLISHING COMPANY, INC.
708 BROADWAY
NEW YORK, NY 10003-9555

MANUFACTURED IN CHINA
FIRST PRINTING
10 9 8 7 6 5 4 3 2 1

CONTENTS

APPENDIXES

A Personal Note from the Author

A life as a professional rosarian was not one I had envisioned for myself, but the possibility opened up when I began volunteering in the Rose Garden at the Huntington Library. I was attracted to the garden because of the comprehensive range of roses grown there, and the opportunity to use the institution's fantastic research library.

A lifelong love of history led me to new discoveries as I learned where roses had come from and soaked up the wonderful stories ensconced in their names and places of origin. Eventually I faced the daunting responsibility of taking over the garden, which had a long history and tradition of its own. That was two decades ago. We at the Huntington now face many new challenges as our core structure shifts, a new visitor center/office complex is built, an improved nursery compound is created, and new gardens are being considered for the first time in decades. These projects will hopefully add to the distinctiveness of this eminent institution, all while my garden's 100th anniversary brings me face to face with the new millennial century.

As the future races to meet us, I find it especially fitting to stop a moment and acknowledge those who have made this book and its older sibling, *100 English Roses for the American Garden,* possible.

Thanks especially to all the following: The Huntington Library, Art Collections, and Botanical Gardens; John and Louise Clements of Heirloom Old Garden Roses; Joyce Demits of Heritage Roses of Tanglewood Farms; Mary Brosius of Descanso Gardens; and Greg Lowery of Vintage Gardens. I thank them all for allowing Saxon Holt and me into their gardens and collections to gather and photograph the flowers you see in this book.

—CLAIR G. MARTIN
Pasadena, California
November 1999

Paradise Regained

It never fails to amaze me how visitors to my garden react to the variety of flower shapes, forms, and fragrances displayed within its beds. The average sightseer doesn't seem to have a clue that roses might have any form other than that of the typical, high-centered, commercial Hybrid Tea. Their entire experience with roses begins and ends with an urbanized, homogenized product that is the florist's rose: tall, pointed buds on long stems that hopefully open to fully petaled, classically shaped Hybrid Tea Roses that, if one is particularly lucky, also impart a smidgen of fragrance. They have no idea that roses come in a myriad of shapes and forms, from the simple, unadorned elegance of an ancient, five-petaled Species Rose to the rococo complexity of a flat, quartered Bourbon Rose. The public's familiarity with one style of flower form is due more to a lack of exposure than anything else.

Nurserymen have long catered to, and indeed have instigated, the popular tastes of the masses, refraining from introducing roses that don't fit into a mold they themselves create. The rose-growing public of the eighteenth and nineteenth centuries were not so limited in their experiences and certainly not so amalgamated. Their multifaceted conception of "rose beauty" had not yet crystalized into what we have been brainwashed to believe is the "perfect rose." In those times, growers regularly introduced cultivars displaying a broad range of flower types and forms, and gardeners were eager to experiment and plant this eclectic abundance.

Today's gardeners cut their teeth on the readily available

Hybrid Teas, learning and honing their skills as they discover the more popular and ubiquitous classes of Modern Roses. Eventually, though, some gardeners want more, and with a little investigation, they find there's an entire universe of color, fragrance, and shape to be explored.

They might first discover the simple, unadorned beauty of single, five-petaled roses—blooms the way Mother Nature conceived them. This breakthrough comes as something of an epiphany for these budding rosarians, and they begin to move farther afield, opening themselves to all possibilities of flower forms and shapes. Heretofore unknown and unappreciated roses become desirable, and then suddenly, gardeners can't find enough space to house all the plants they want. For most suburban gardeners, finding enough space to accommodate an ever-expanding collection of Old Roses means less and less grass and a much broader horticultural medley of plant materials than the archetypal suburban garden of lawn, shade trees, and foundation plantings.

Gardeners are asking themselves, If the Hybrid Teas are a class of roses with barely one hundred years of history, what came before? The answer is, quite simply, Old Roses. Gardeners today can partake of this extravagant inheritance and experiment with the same truly ancient roses that once graced Empress Joséphine's garden outside Paris or President Jefferson's beloved Virginia plantation. We can plant a rose that grew in a medieval monastery, enjoy roses that Shakespeare immortalized, and experience the seductive perfume of a rose that Romans harvested for religious festivals solemnized in temples on the Seven Hills. We don't even have to settle for copies—we can actually plant a piece of the original. Scholars and book collectors rely on photocopies of rare manuscripts, but we clone our antiques so that every piece is a genetic descendant of the original.

Each season, more nurseries are discovering that the demand for Old Roses is not just a fad— the gardening public is actively seeking out and planting them. More and more specialty growers are springing up, providing local gardeners with an ever-increasing variety. Even major national growers have jumped on the bandwagon and include them in their slick-and-thick, shop-till-you-drop color catalogs. Never in our lifetime have there been as many Old Roses available to the public as there are right now.

Isn't it strange that in our search for the "perfect rose," we have come full circle and are once again giving serious consideration to flowers that were dismissed and discarded only a few short decades ago? And as more of us have gained knowledge about the fine garden qualities of these long-lived, hardy, and in many cases, extremely disease-free shrubs, a new age in rose growing has dawned—one filled with exquisite beauty and intoxicating fragrances that were almost lost forever.

WHAT MAKES *a* ROSE . . . OLD?

We live in an age of constant change and rapid obsolescence; "accelerated decrepitude," as a sci-fi movie character once put it. The computer purchased yesterday is replaced today by a model half the size, many times faster, and with scads more memory. Particularly since the end of World War II, Western culture has had to become inured to an ever faster pace of turnover from the old to the new.

Nowhere is this progression from archaic to innovative more evident than in the field of commercial roses. Should you wish to create a new garden bed of nothing but award-winning roses from the past fifty years, you would find it nearly impossible to do so. This is primarily because large numbers of such modern medal-winners are already out of commerce or extinct. Many of these have disappeared from catalogs not merely out of neglect but because they were just not good roses and failed to flourish even with the best of care.

By the middle of the twentieth century, only a small minority of people worldwide still cared enough to maintain collections of what were coming to be known as "Old Roses." Cultivars once so popular as to seem ubiquitous were rapidly dropped from suppliers' catalogs, a trend mirrored by their disappearance from gardens both public and private. One large civic rose garden went so far as to discard its entire collection of award-winning, gold-medal honorees— just dumped them into the waste bin, replacing them with the latest roses from that year's catalog lists.

Some years back, a group of friends got together to see if they could form a local club for the study and preservation of Old Garden Roses (OGRs). Inspiring the group to assemble was not difficult; dedicating the group to the study of OGRs was easy; but getting the group to agree on a name for their new organization—now, that was almost impossible. After

*L*uxuriant, deep red–purple blossoms of 'Cardinal de Richelieu' create a dramatic contrast in the spring garden when interplanted with soft grasses and other perennials.

what seemed like endless hours of discussion and heated argument, one venerable lady shook herself loose, rose slowly to her feet, and announced in a hoary voice, "I don't care what you name this club, but I will not be called an ANTIQUE ROSARIAN!"

In her own roundabout way, my articulate friend was correct. Age is a key component defining Old Garden Roses, but it is certainly not everything. Old Roses are old, but they also come with a story. The myriad of roses available today did not just appear like Athena from the head of Zeus. Someone cultivated them through a long, laborious birthing process. They have a name or series of names relating to their place of origin and the interests of that

time. In other words, they have acquired the patina of history.

My own first recollections of roses were of those growing in the southeastern Kansas garden of my stepfather's mother. The rather large extended family spent many holidays in the small home, so there was always lots of noise and bustling excitement, but I remember most a long hedge of climbing roses bordering a side street along one side of the property. All I remember of their color is that some in the hedge were red and some pink. I have very strong memory images of their perfume, hanging sweet and rosy in the hot, humid midwestern summer's afternoon. I have no idea what they could have been—maybe 'Paul's Scarlet' for the red and 'New

Dawn' for the pink—but whatever they were, I recall rather strongly the deep, rich black loam soil, a legacy from the tall grass prairie that the first settlers encountered when they broke sod for their new farms a century earlier.

OLD ROSES BY CLASS

GALLICA. Also known as French Roses and the Rose of Provins, these are among the most ancient of all roses, although there is little historical documentation left to trace their ancestry definitively.

On the whole, Gallica Roses are short, compact plants that have a strong propensity to spread out into massive thickets when grown on their own roots. The canes tend to be thin and wiry, and are covered with a myriad of prickles that vary in shape and size—the most delicate resembling hairs, the rest graduating to substantial, needlelike structures. Generally, the foliage is

WHAT DO WE CALL OLD ROSES

A contentious lot, rosarians still can't agree on an acceptable official name for this group of roses. Will we ever come to a consensus on Antique Roses or Heritage Roses, Heirloom Roses or simply Old Roses, as I have done here? Beginning in the 1930s, much of the splendid horticultural diversity of historic roses was rapidly being lost. Lucky for us, a few writers and dedicated collectors took up the challenge to collect and identify this colorful legacy. The term "Old Garden Rose" was coined to differentiate these cultivated Old Roses from the other group of truly Old Roses—the Species, or Wild Roses. Throughout this book, I have used the two short forms for this diverse group of Old Garden Roses: "Old Roses" or "OGRs."

In this book, Old Rose refers to any rose that was introduced before 1901—in other words, before the beginning of the twentieth century. The reader will notice a few roses that date from a bit later than 1901 spilling into the Field Guide section, but in each of these cases, the roses were developed before the cutoff date or are simply such true examples of their class that they are undeniably pure in their Old Rose nature.

As we enter the twenty-first century, acknowledging roses introduced before 1901 as "old" makes sense for several reasons. First, and without doubt, the span of one hundred years certainly allows for sufficient time to establish a rose as being old in horticultural terms as well as old chronologically. Secondly, it wasn't until the first year of that new century that a truly innovative and world-shattering rose was produced that would prove to be the most influential patriarch of the new century. Squarely and significantly on the cusp of the twentieth century, one of the most dynamic roses of all time came into being, one that forever changed the character of all that followed and continues to cast its sway over the family of roses today. That rose is 'Soleil d'Or.' Produced by the French hybridizer Joseph Pernet-Ducher, 'Soleil d'Or' is considered the first Modern Rose.

OLD ROSE SHAPES AND FORMS

'Austrian Copper'
SINGLE

'Henri Martin'
POMPON

'Fantin-Latour'
SHALLOW-CUPPED

'Lady Hillingdon'
TEA ROSE

'Paul Neyron'
GLOBULAR

'Souvenir de la Malmaison'
QUARTERED

'Belle de Crécy'
ROSETTE

'Crested Moss'
CUPPED

'Madame Ernst Calvat'
REFLEXED

'Tricolore de Flandre'
STRIPED

'Cardinal de Richelieu'
BUTTON-EYE

'Autumn Damask'
INFORMAL

'Hebe's Lip'
SEMI-DOUBLE

'Francis Dubreuil'
DOUBLE

Rosa multiflora carnea
GREEN EYE

'Old Blush'
FULL

a flat matte green, somewhat rough in texture, and often quite a bit paler on the reverse. Individual leaflets are usually folded slightly along the midrib. Fragrance is best described as rosy, with tones of classic attar or Damask. Blossoms range in color from pale pink to the deepest dark purple, but never anything approaching true scarlet. A large number of these French Roses were either striped or mottled, and sprinkled with a contrasting color. This color variegation is genetic in origin, and not caused by any sort of virus, as is true with tulips and camellias.

Strictly spring-flowering, Gallicas are among the most winter-hardy of all roses.

DAMASK. Nearly as old as the Gallicas, the origins of Damask Roses are just as clouded by time. It is equally probable that Crusaders brought back plants of

A tall grower, 'Alba Semi-plena' will tolerate partial shade and some drought and still be able to produce a handsome crop of flowers each spring.

this class to remind them of the exotic lands they had visited. Damasks develop into large, spreading shrubs, often 6 feet or more in height with an equal spread. The long canes arch out over the garden, frequently pulled down from the immense number and weight of the flowers produced along their length. Damask foliage is usually gray-green, roughly textured, and silvery on the reverse. The terminal leaflet is often folded along the midrib and held at a downward angle. The canes are well-supplied with large, malicious prickles. The range of flower color is limited to pale blush to white and reddish pink. Damasks are often more cherished for their fragrance, an intoxicating, rich, and deep Old Rose perfume, than just about any other trait they manifest.

At one time, Damask Roses were divided into two groups: Summer Damasks and Autumn Damasks. The two groups are nearly identical except that Autumn Damasks rebloom fully and Summer Damasks bloom only in spring or early summer. Sometimes you read that the two are the product of different parents, but in actuality, both forms consistently mutate (sport) back and forth to each other, indicating to me that nothing more is involved here than an ancient mutation that allowed for the repeat bloom of the Autumn Damasks.

The Damask Roses are extremely winter-hardy in most regions of the United States.

ALBA. No one is sure just how old this class is, but Alba Roses were illustrated in Renaissance

The charmingly diminutive pompon blooms of 'Rose de Meaux' are placed near a walk or border in order to best show off her spring crop of flowers.

paintings, and some authorities even feel that they can be discerned in illuminated medieval manuscripts. Alba is Latin for "white," and the island of Britain was named Albion by the early Roman conquerors. (Whether this appellation came from the white cliffs above the Strait of Dover or from the white roses seen in the island's interior by those Roman legionnaires has remained a mystery.)

Albas were probably produced from an accidental cross between the "Dog Rose" (*Rosa canina*) and a Damask, but no one was present to record the event. Albas are upright-growing, thorny shrubs, tending to the tall side on the whole, with blue-gray foliage and pale pink to white, impressively fragrant flowers. These tough plants will tolerate some shade and drought, and are generally free of disease and extremely winter-hardy.

Alba roses are strictly spring-flowering.

CENTIFOLIA. Possibly the result of a serendipitous cross between Damask and Alba Roses in seventeenth-century France or Holland, these Centifolias are not the same hundred-petaled roses mentioned by Roman writers in the first century, which have probably long since died out. Centifolias are commonly called "Cabbage Roses" in Europe because of their large, deeply globular, petal-packed, intensely fragrant flowers. They develop into medium-size, thorny, lax-growing shrubs with soft, pale green foliage.

Centifolias are also known as the "Rose of Provence," and there has been a great deal of confusion between this name and that of the "Rose of Provins" (the Gallica Rose).

Centifolia roses are winter-hardy in most regions of the country, and strictly spring-flowering.

MOSS. First appearing as sports (mutations) of Centifolias in the

THE MAN WHO NAMED EVERYTHING

A Swedish botanist in the eighteenth century came up with the system we use to scientifically identify all plants and animals. Carl von Linné, known today under the Latin form of his name, Linnaeus, developed the system using the sexual parts of plants for their classification. Linnaeus called his scheme the "binomial system" because it used only two names to classify everything: a generic name and a specific name. This is analogous to our first and last names, only in reverse order—*family name* followed by *individual name*.

Linnaeus grouped plants by close relationships of their reproductive or sexual organs, and gave closely related plants a generic name. In the case of roses, this generic name was *Rosa.* He also found that the reproductive organs of many other plants, including peaches, plums, boysenberries, and strawberries, among others, shared identical characteristics and were thus classified in the greater Rose family. Members of a genus that differed in some small attributes but still shared overall reproductive similarities were given different specific, or species, names. A species differs from other members of a genus only in details of geographical distribution and structure, but it shares an overall similarity of sexual organs. Binomial classification very quickly replaced the older, more cumbersome system, and we still use Linnaeus's classification strategy today, with only minor modifications for clarity and uniformity.

To these categories, modern botanists have added two subordinate sections: variety and cultivar. The term *variety* denotes a naturally occurring slight variation of a particular species. The term *cultivar* denotes an artificial hybridization (and thus a *culti*vated *var*iety), which can only be kept in cultivation by asexual propagation.

You will see Latin binomial names applied to many of our oldest OGRs, but today we recognize that these roses are cultivated forms and not true species.

---

seventeenth century, Moss Roses added a new dimension to the fragrance of OGRs. Mossing appears as feathery growth along the flower stem, known as the pedicel, and extends on up to the sepals as an extension of glandular hairs and small prickles. This green to brown mossing is soft to the touch and smells strongly of pine pitch or balsam.

Medium to large shrubs with lax, arching, thorny canes and soft gray to green foliage, Moss Roses do have a propensity to mildew, especially along the thorny stems and moss-enclosed buds, where air circulation is limited and moisture can build up.

Generally, Moss Roses are only spring-flowering, and every bit as winter-hardy as their Centifolia sisters. In the nineteenth century, hybridizers worked to combine Mosses with some of the new remontant groups, and developed repeat-blooming Moss Roses.

CHINA. The first China Roses appeared in European gardens sometime between the middle of the eighteenth and the beginning of the nineteenth centuries. Although new to Europeans, these diminutive plants had been developed over long centuries in their homeland.

Small to moderately low-growing shrubs, Chinas have long, narrow, lance-shaped, deep green foliage that covers thin, twiggy canes furnished with abundant prickles. Small flowers are produced in large, airy clusters, often held above the rest of the plant, and range in color from white to pink to the deepest true scarlet—a color unknown in European Roses before that time. The fragrance differs from that of the passionate rosy scent of European Roses, being more spicy to peppery, with a brusque, sharp quality.

Chinas are more cold-tender than their European counterparts, but do survive out-of-doors as far north as the Mid-Atlantic states, and a bit farther north along coastlines. These remontant roses are the parents of all modern repeat-blooming and miniature roses in our gardens today.

TEA. Like the China Roses, Tea Roses were developed in China and are the product of many centuries of horticultural selection and hybridization. The Tea Roses first appeared in Europe around the first decades of the nineteenth century, having been collected from the Southern regions in China. The name "Tea" may relate to their fragrance or their association with the tea trade from Asia to Europe.

Teas are large, open-growing plants that over time will build up their thin, twiggy wood to 5 or 6 feet in height. The smooth, polished wood of the canes is often a red-bronze tone when new, and is peppered with large, hooked prickles. Reddish purple new growth contrasts nicely with the shiny, deep green foliage. Flowers are

The somewhat leggy lower canes of this old Tea Rose, 'Comtesse Riza du Parc,' are masked by underplantings of lychnis and other low-growing perennials.

W*hen grown on a sturdy support, 'Reine Victoria' will spill out over the garden, dispensing her heavenly perfume to those who pass by.*

large, often produced in clusters, and nod on fragile stems. Bloom colors range from white through pink and on to yellow, with a smattering of scarlet. Often, the colors are infused and mixed in wonderful pastel combinations resembling an ice-cream parfait. Fragrance is strong and usually fruity, but with a more tart undertone than the sweet scent of European OGRs.

Teas rebloom almost continuously, but aren't very tolerant of cold winters and can only be grown outdoors in milder regions.

PORTLAND. One of the first classes to combine the Old European roses and the newly available, repeat-blooming Asian roses, the first Portland was discovered around 1800 and named for the second Duchess of Portland. Portlands are upright-growing shrubs with matte green foliage, thorny canes, and large flowers presented on short stems. Their blooms range in color from white to pink and deep crimson, while the fragrance is that of the European OGRs, sweet and rosy. These repeat-blooming roses were among the first to possess real cold-hardiness and true scarlet red flowers.

This is a small group of roses. Only a few dozen were hybridized over the course of the nineteenth century, and none thereafter, having been nearly absorbed by that time into other classes of roses.

Portlands have good winter endurance and are among the most remontant of OGRs.

NOISETTE. The honor of developing the first repeat-blooming hybrid produced by crossing a European rose with an Asian rose belongs to John Champneys, a South Carolina rice planter. Champneys produced his first roses around 1812, using the European "Musk Rose" and the newly introduced 'Old Blush,' a repeat-blooming China. Champneys shared his discovery with friends and nurserymen in the newly founded United States, including Philippe Noisette, a Frenchman working in the Charleston area. Noisette sent plants of Champneys's rose to the family nursery in Paris in care of his brother Louis, who introduced it in his catalog and renamed it the Noisette Rose.

The earliest Noisettes were large-growing, open shrubs with small flowers produced in large clusters of white to pale pink. Later on, the Noisettes were back-crossed with Tea Roses, and from that, tall-climbing forms with large nodding flower clusters were developed. Noisette Roses come in hues of white to pink to yellow and have a spicy Tea Rose fragrance.

Noisettes are, on the whole, not very cold-tolerant, surviving best in the milder regions of the country; they are also some of the most strongly repeating of all roses.

BOURBON. Bourbon Roses received their name not from some imagined whiskylike fragrance, but from the fact that the very first specimens were discovered growing on an island in the Indian Ocean named Réunion, then a French possession called the Île de Bourbon. These roses were probably the product of a chance crossing of 'Autumn Damask' and 'Old Blush,' both of which were recorded growing on the island as hedgerows in the early years of the nineteenth century. Seeds and plants were sent to France, where nurserymen quickly discovered their potential in hybridizing.

For the most part, Bourbon Roses are large, open-growing shrubs or climbers. The long canes are supplied with fairly large, deep green foliage and prickles. Flower colors range from white through deep pink, and the fragrance is generally a strong Old Rose perfume. The Bourbons are relatively winter-hardy in most regions of the country, and strongly remontant. There are a few short-growing Bourbons, probably the product of back-crossing with China Roses, which I label as Bourbon/China Roses.

*O*ne of the most popular rose classes of the Victorian age, Moss Roses display a soft, feathery growth extending right up the stem and on to the sepals.

HYBRID PERPETUAL. At first, early hybridizers were unable to produce remontant seedlings by crossing the Old European Roses with the new China and Tea Roses. It took nearly forty years to break the fertility and genetic barriers and produce the first winter-hardy remontant roses. These early French hybrids were labeled *"hybrides remontants,"* which English nurserymen somewhat misleadingly renamed Hybrid Perpetuals.

Few of the earliest of these Hybrid Perpetuals survive, but by the 1840s, a large number were appearing in catalogs, and by the end of the century, some 4,000 had been developed, named, and introduced. No other class of rose was as popular in the nineteenth century—nearly eighty new cultivars a year had to be introduced to create those numbers. The Hybrid Perpetuals are large-growing, often upright shrubs with large flowers displayed at the tips of the canes. Colors range from white through pink to deep red and purple; only yellow and orange are not represented. For the most part, the Hybrid Perpetuals are winter-hardy in nearly all regions of the country, and more or less remontant. Rebloom can be a bit weak in the summer, with a resurgence of bloom in the fall.

HYBRID TEA. Traditionally considered the very first Hybrid Tea Rose, 'La France' was introduced in 1867 by the Lyons-based firm of Guillot. It was thought to be the product of a cross between a Hybrid Perpetual and a Tea Rose. Initially classed as a Hybrid

A ROSE FOR THE AGES

One of the wonders of the rose world not to be missed is the century-old "Tombstone Rose." This double-flowered white "Lady Banks' Rose" was planted in Tombstone, Arizona, in 1885 by Mary Gee, who with her mining engineer husband had moved from England to set up house in that remote part of southeastern Arizona. The single, rooted cutting sent to her now covers an area of some 8,000 square feet, and produces an incalculable number of flowers each spring. The trunk of her cutting is somewhere around 12 feet in circumference, and is supported by a scaffolding of pipes and wire cabling.

*T*all growing Bourbon Roses like the lovely 'Mme. Pierre Oger' are best grown on supports. They put on a fine spring display of richly scented flowers, continuing the profusion right up to the first cold nip in autumn.

Perpetual, it took some years for the appellation Hybrid Tea to catch on. For most of the nineteenth century, Hybrid Teas were developed by crossing Hybrid Perpetuals with Teas, but beginning with the first decades of the twentieth century, they were more and more the product of incestuous marriages of Hybrid Tea to Hybrid Tea. Moderately tall-growing, upright shrubs, Hybrid Teas now come in all colors except blue and black. Details of growth, foliage, bloom form, color, and fragrance will differ from cultivar to cultivar, more so than in any other class of rose.

Today's Hybrid Teas have lost some of the charm of their older sisters, with the current focus on just one form of flower: the high-pointed florist's rose mentioned earlier. A Hybrid Tea is generally an upright-growing shrub, producing one large, pointed bloom at the end of each flowering stem. Hybrid Tea flowers are usually thought of as being at their most beautiful and closest to perfection between the bud stage and the half-open blossom, leaving the rest of its bloom life to indifference and disdain—a far cry from OGRs, English Roses, and other shrub roses.

POLYANTHA. The first Polyantha Rose was introduced by the Guillots of Lyons in 1875 as 'Pâquerette.' Produced from a remontant dwarf form of *Rosa multiflora,* Polyanthas were immediately pounced upon by hybridizers for use in bringing about low-growing, perpetually flowering bedding roses. Not only were they remontant, but because of their *R. multiflora* heritage, they were extremely cold-hardy.

Polyanthas are low-growing, compact shrubs that develop slowly on thin, twiggy canes. The small flowers are displayed in huge clusters atop shiny, deep green foliage. Almost any conceivable flower form and color is represented in this class, except for yellow. For the most part, Polyanthas are not overtly fragrant, but there are a few exceptions. All are wonderfully remontant.

RUGOSA. *Rosa rugosa* is native to Manchuria, northern China, Korea, and Japan, where it grows

ABSOLUTE ATTAR

The earliest rose cosmetics and perfumes were concocted by the ancient Greeks, who steeped rose petals in olive oil or other vegetable oils. In time, someone discovered that slowly heating rose petals in water would produce rose water. Rose water doesn't smell very "rosy," however, because only one of the essential oils constituting the essence of rose is capable of dissolving this way.

Later still, probably in India or Persia, someone discovered that they could produce a concentrated essence by distilling rose petals. In this process, water and petals are brought to a boil, the steam produced is collected and cooled, and the resulting oily product is called "attar of rose."

Attar is from the Persian word *atir,* for "perfumed." Although stronger than rose water, this essence is still rather ephemeral, as the heat used in producing attar affects its strength, diminishing the resulting fragrance. Nonetheless, waxy attar is often the key component in the most expensive of designer perfumes and for good reason—it takes the entire spring harvest of one acre of roses to produce one pound of attar.

Today, most perfumers use chemical solvents to produce a more concentrated rose essence. Rose petals are soaked in petroleum solvents, which remove the essential fragrances and wax from the flowers and produce a brown waxy essence called "concrete." The concrete can be further refined by dissolving it in pure alcohol, which separates the essential oils from the wax. This sticky brownish oil is called the "absolute," and is the final stage in the purification of rose fragrance. The wax retains enough scent to be used in the manufacture of lipsticks and other cosmetics.

with great abandon along the coasts. Introduced to European gardens around the beginning of the nineteenth century, Rugosas were immediately recognized for their winter-hardiness, repeat bloom, and superb fragrance. Low- to moderate-growing, extremely thorny shrubs, they will colonize large areas when planted on their own roots by sending out runners at or just below soil level. The canes are encrusted with sharp, needlelike prickles and the deep green foliage is rough and crinkled, giving this species its name (the Latin *rugosus* translates as "wrinkled").

As a group, the Rugosas demonstrate tremendous resistance to fungal infections. Unfortunately, when crossed with other roses, they fail the health test and become horrendously thorny.

Late nineteenth-century and twentieth-century hybrids have been developed in all colors, from white to pink, red, and yellow. Rugosa Roses will continue to bloom throughout the season without the need for deadheading. They follow that cycle by producing crops of brightly colored hips in addition to continuous flowers, and some hybrids will even provide fall foliage color. For the health-conscious, the hips of many Rugosas contain a high level of vitamin C.

RAMBLER AND CLIMBER. While the terms Rambler and Climber are often used synonymously, they actually describe two different styles of Climbing Roses. Ramblers descend from Asian species, such as *Rosa multiflora* and

*T*he fully petaled flowers of 'Rose de Rescht' sit right above the deep green foliage. A remontant Portland Rose, it was orginally discovered in Iran and reintroduced into gardens in the 1940s.

R. wichuraiana and others in the Synstylae group of roses. (The Synstylae are roses in which the female reproductive organs, or styles, are fused into a single column at the center of the flower.)

Ramblers are larger-growing shrubs than Climbers, with thin, ropelike canes that use their prickles to grab onto other shrubs and trees and pull themselves up and over their hosts. Ramblers produce their flowers on new growth from the last season, and for the most part are spring-blooming only.

Climbers, on the other hand, have been produced from almost every other class of rose. As roses do not produce any structure to attach themselves to other objects or plants, they are not true climbing plants, like sweet peas or wisteria, but rely on outside assistance. With some help from humans in the

P*owerfully fragrant, 'Zéphrine Drouhin' is often planted along a walkway, where her thornless charms allow safe passage while permitting her blooms to be enjoyed up close.*

form of attaching and tying the canes to a support, they will climb just beautifully, as if they'd always grown that way.

SPECIES AND THEIR CLOSE HYBRIDS.

It is thought that there are somewhere between 200 and 250 Species Roses occurring worldwide, all exclusively indigenous to the Northern Hemisphere. In botany, a species is defined as a plant that is both geographically and reproductively isolated from other members of the genus, as well as one that breeds true to seed. Roses evolved in the Northern Hemisphere all around the globe, with the greatest concentration of species native to Asia, particularly China. The family did not naturally cross the equator and expand into the tropics because their seeds require a period of dormant winter chilling before they will germinate.

Many botanists speculate that the Rose family is still in active evolution as species continue to hybridize freely with adjoining species, obfuscating the issue of which species is which. Confused? So are they. Gardeners tend to use a broader definition of what constitutes a Species Rose, and that hasn't helped either. In the eighteenth and nineteenth centuries, botanists gave species rank to almost every newly discovered and named rose, but today we have downgraded many of those roses to the rank of cultivar, recognizing that they are simply ancient garden hybrids.

Cultivars can only be produced true to form by asexual methods, that is, by cuttings or grafting—or in twenty-first-century terms, cloning. All Species Roses have five-petaled flowers. To produce flowers with more than five petals, a rose must convert its male reproductive organs (stamens) into petals. Thus, a fully double Species Rose in the wild would be greatly disadvantaged reproductively in that it would have fewer stamens and therefore less than optimum male fertility. Double forms of Species Roses occur from time to time, but they die off naturally unless helped along by human hands, most often in the form of gardeners who take cuttings or otherwise propagate them by the aforementioned asexual means.

SURVIVORS

Old Roses come in just about any imaginable combination of form, color, size, fragrance, and frequency of bloom. Although age is a key factor in dividing Old Roses from Modern Roses, as you've seen by now, there is much more to the story. Old Roses were developed with any number of flower forms, unlike our modern Hybrid Teas, which come almost exclusively in that one flower form, although admittedly in an unending range of colors. Old Roses are survivors—the weak and unhealthy are culled out with the passage of time, while

the fittest have endured and are still enjoyed in gardens around the world today.

But just the fact that they are old isn't, of itself, enough inducement to get us to plant Old Roses in our gardens. These are roses with a past, a history acquired through years of gardeners growing and cherishing them through the good and the bad. Some have been nurtured for decades by people who don't have a clue as to their names, just because they've been such good garden roses for so long.

Once upon a time, Old Roses were the hot "new" darlings of the rose world, every bit as faddish as the newest debutante growing in gardens today. Over time, natural selection takes over and the best survive. Serendipity is also a factor in this game of survival—some roses endure just because of luck. Most, though, have withstood time because they are strong, healthy

*R*ight on the cusp between Hybrid Perpetual and Hybrid Tea Roses, 'Frau Karl Druschi' is still popular after all these years.

shrubs that have few requirements beyond sun, soil, and water for healthy growth and generous bloom.

A ROSE BY ANY OTHER NAME . . . .

The rose looks fair,
fairer we it deem,
For that sweet odour
which doth in it live.

—WILLIAM SHAKESPEARE

Are Old Roses more fragrant than Modern Roses? William Paul, in his 1848 edition of *The Rose Garden,* stated that he felt the roses of his day were not as fragrant as the roses he remembered growing in his father's garden. Bearing in mind that Paul's roses are our Old Roses, his thoughts truly boggle the mind, since it's generally accepted wisdom today that Modern Roses are not as fragrant as Old Roses. While

it seems fairly clear that the percentage of fragrant to non-fragrant seedlings has remained constant through history, I'll try to answer this enigma as best as I can.

Several factors are at work here. The first is that until recently, rose hybridizers have not placed fragrance very high on their list of desirable rose traits. Color and bloom shape, winter-hardiness, and vigor have all ranked higher on their scale. The second factor is due to the way our brains store memories of fragrance. Of all our senses, smell, while not our strongest, is often the most evocative. Over five million sensing cells are reserved exclusively for smell, and our brains have a number of special ways to store our memories of fragrance. The most potent of these are emotions: anger, fear, love, melancholy, even lust. Conversely, memorized events or feelings can

The flat, quartered, dramatically perfumed blooms of 'Mme. Isaac Pereire' illustrate one of the classic Old Rose flower shapes.

actually retrieve scent memories when one's consciousness calls up a particular recollection of an event or feeling.

We evolved this trait for survival. It was vitally necessary to remember the differences in smells between wholesome and harmful foods, or between a herd of elk (the hunted) and a pride of lions (the hunters). Having gained knowledge of medicinal plants, an apothecary had to be able to tell, with the slightest whiff, which powders were used for healing and which were terribly poisonous concoctions. More nostalgically speaking, we tend to cherish roses with fragrance, and these scented roses have been protected and propagated at the expense of less scented ones.

Another factor is that the genetics of rose fragrance is more complicated than many other key traits. Fragrance seems to be carried not by a single gene but by multiple sets of genes, complicating breeding exponentially for this one desirable characteristic. Today, however, there is a trend toward placing fragrance much higher on the list of desirable traits. But where does all that fragrance come from?

Rose fragrances, in particular, are the product of some eleven chemicals that determine the messages your nose sends to your brain, from phenylethyl alcohol (orange blossom or hyacinth) to citronellol (geranium) and linalool (jonquil, lavender) to eugenol (cloves, violets). Each fragrance is a chemical compound that has a unique shape, which fits a singular type of receptor like a combination lock. When caught by your intake of breath,

these chemical keys travel up into the nostrils, finding their particular match among the cilia at the moist ceiling of your sinus cavity. Once a particular combination is keyed into the cilia, the information travels the eighth of an inch separating these mucous neurons from the olfactory bulb, which then channels the chemical information into the two major parts of the brain where similar chemical imprints have been laid—and connected to associative emotions—in the past.

These molecules are found in varying numbers and strengths, giving individual cultivars their unique perfume. The scent of a rose is an elaborate amalgam, created from a myriad of possible scent combinations of those eleven building blocks. I have been able to recognize a number of individual fragrances in the Old Roses described in this book: from citrus and pepper to Parma violets, cloves, and musk—all can be elements of what we commonly call a "rosy scent."

The best time to check for scent is early on a calm, mildly sunny or cloudy morning. Rose fragrance is carried in volatile oils and alcohols, which evaporate rapidly as the heat of the day advances. A marvelously scented rose may have exhausted its perfume by midday, but will replace those oils by the next morning.

Beyond time of day and weather, other factors can influence fragrance. Winter chilling, for one, may have something to do with one cultivar being described as extremely fragrant in one part of the country and only slightly scented

N*amed for a French hero of the Franco-Prussian War, 'Paul Neyron' is often called the "Cabbage Rose" in the United States.*

Fertilizers and the different chemical components in soils from one region to the next, however, appear to have little, if any, effect on fragrance.

Human beings are able to classify and retain thousands of pieces of scent information in our long-term memory with more accuracy than any of our other perceptions save vision, our primary stimulus. We remember what we have smelled and associate those stimuli with unforgettable events throughout our lives. I still flash back to my grandparents' beach house every time I pass a planting of star jasmine. The scent floods my mind with images of a red-tiled courtyard festooned with jasmine plants. This was where we kids had to hose off the beach sand before we could go into the house. For me, there is no stronger association to fragrance than that happy memory of long ago.

in a mild-winter zone. (A cold winter produces a deep dormancy that seems to increase the degree of fragrance produced in most roses.)

THE ROSE'S ROLE *in* HUMAN CULTURE

The rose is a cultural artifact. Being so many millions of years older than our species, roses have had a powerful effect on our evolution from the very beginning. Ancient artisans consistently employed roses in their works. They were painted on the walls of Minoan palaces and stamped on Greek coins from Rhodes. Homer wrote of the "rosy-fingered dawn." The rose was used as an allegory for both youth and death. Omar Khayyám affirms, through the lens of Edward Fitzgerald's masterful English translation of the *Rubáiyát,* "Alas, that Spring should vanish with the Rose! That Youth's sweet-scented Manuscript should close!"

For me personally, as for others, the rose acts as metaphor for the human condition. Its history is our history. The flower and humanity have co-evolved to the point that to understand the rose and where it came from is to understand a little of where we've been and where we are going. While there are those who might be heard saying things like, "Now why would a grown man spend his life studying roses?" (and as luck would have it, I have been fortunate enough to do just that), for me to be able to grow a rose upon which some Caesar pricked his finger is the ultimate soul-grounding connection—not to mention an intriguing and fun story. Our modern roses are the outpouring of a long line of development going back almost to the beginnings of civilization itself.

Writing about rose history is a little like viewing the Milky Way through a shallow-focused cam-

*O*ne of the most ancient of Gallica Roses still available today, 'Velvet Rose' was *described by John Gerard in 1597. The semi-double flowers take on more purple tones as they mature.*

era. You can make out shapes, but the farther back you go, the fuzzier the details become. There are ways, though, through the fog. Written records exist that mention the rose in ancient Sumer, and we have physical evidence that Egyptian mourners left rose wreaths behind as part of their burial rituals. During the sixth century B.C., the Greek poet Sappho named the rose Queen of Flowers. Roses have been appreciated for their fragrance and elusive beauty possibly more than any other living thing. Legends were concocted to explain everything from why white roses turned red to why rose bushes have thorns. The Greeks, who seem to have had an answer for everything in the natural world,

explained the color question by noting that a goddess pricked her finger on a rose thorn, and her dripping blood turned the white rose red.

EARLY RECORDED ROSES

The earliest roses to be grown and recorded in history were the wild roses found thriving in and around that pivotal arch known as the Fertile Crescent—the zone of arable land stretching from Mesopotamia westward through Syria and back around into Egypt, forming the cradle of Western civilization. In the West, these were the roses known to our cultural progenitors: the Sumerians, Egyptians, Greeks, and Romans.

But equally ancient roses were known to and grown by the Chinese, a people already fabricating a society with a venerable and independent tradition of agriculture and civilization. In China, however, the rose doesn't seem to have played quite as important a role as it did in the West.

The ancient Romans took the cult of the rose to pagan heights, growing and importing roses in such extravagant numbers that their excessive use was condemned —for poverty-stricken Romans, it became a choice of corn (our wheat) or roses. Nero spent a fortune on roses for his banquets, importing flowers from as far away as Egypt. The emperor Heliogabalus showered so many roses onto his guests on their banquet couches that many were actually suffocated!

Rosalia, a Roman feast celebrating the rose, was held each year on the twenty-third of May. The demand for roses so far exceeded the local supply that flowers had to be imported from the southern Italian district around the old Greek colony at Paestum, and also from Egypt. It isn't exactly clear in the surviving documents whether these roses were imported as fresh-cut flowers or as whole, own-root bushes. Cut flowers would have been a daunting problem for the time as the speed of transportation from Egypt to Rome was hardly overnight express, but it is possible some means of preservation was devised to accomplish this. No matter how the roses were shipped, they were used in such ostentatious quantities that sumptuary laws were eventually passed by the Roman Senate preventing their importation at the expense of shipping space for Egyptian grain, a much more essential purchase.

Virgil wrote in his *Georgics* of the "Twice-Bearing Roses of Paestum." It is possible that Roman gardeners piped hot water through their greenhouses to force roses into bloom more than once a year. The technology had already been developed for Roman baths, and there was plentiful cheap labor, in the form of slaves, to do the work.

A rose suspended over a Roman banqueting couch was used to indicate to the guests that conversations at supper were *sub rosa* and thus confidential, a convention maintained into the Middle Ages. Indeed, the rose's association with Roman licentiousness influenced a backlash among the early Christian fathers, and produced a condem-

*T*he single flower of fragrant Rosa banksiae normalis *looks to many more like an apple blossom than a rose. Known also as "Lady Banks' Rose," this is one of the first roses to bloom in spring.*

nation of the rose as a symbol of pagan excesses. It wasn't until the rose was conjoined with the adoration of the Virgin Mary during the high Middle Ages that our revered flower regained ecclesiastical acceptance.

THE IDENTITY PROBLEM

Historians of the rose find it impossible to give accurate names to the roses of the ancients. The descriptions that have come down to us are far too vague, other than to say that the roses described seem to fit into the earliest classes of Old Roses: Gallicas, Damasks, and possibly Albas. All that can be said for certain is that the Greeks and Romans grew and loved roses of many different breeds, shapes, and colors. The Centifolia Roses mentioned by Roman writers seem to

have died out long before our "Rose of Provence" Centifolias appeared. (The word *centifolia* was used by early writers to describe a fully petaled flower, one with at least one hundred petals.) This more recent group was developed independently by late seventeenth-century French and Dutch plantsmen, probably from natural (or open) pollination between *Rosa canina* and Damask Roses.

In the late eighth century, the newly crowned Holy Roman Emperor Charlemagne (c. 742–814) issued a decree from his capital at Aachen (Aix-la-Chapelle), in Germany, sited on today's Dutch-Belgian border, that all the cities in his empire were to forthwith and forevermore plant roses in public gardens. The Decree Concerning Towns listed more than eighty plants along with ros-

A large shrub of the single pink Gallica Rose 'Complicata' has been planted so that the single white "Musk Rose" spills over and through its greenery.

es and lilies that were thought to have medicinal value. The emperor was doubtlessly influenced by monastic apothecaries working at the Benedictine Monastery of St. Gall, which was established near Lake Constance in Switzerland. Charlemagne's influence continued through the Middle Ages, when roses were grown in every monastery garden for their use in pharmacological preparations.

The era of the Crusades was another important time for the introduction of new roses from the ancient cradle of Western civilization. Crusading knights are credited with interjecting new strains of Damask and Gallica Roses into northern European gardens. Knightly aristocrats may seem to be unlikely gardeners, but a privileged few carried their families along as they conquered and occupied Eastern principalities in the name of the Cross. Devout pilgrims plying dusty Holy Land roads may have been equally responsible for introducing exotic roses upon returning from their pious travels, as sort of "living postcards" to dazzle the folks back home.

Saladin, the Kurdish Sultan of Egypt, retook Jerusalem from the Christians in 1187, precipitating the Third Crusade. He reportedly ordered a shipment of 500 camel-loads of rosewater from Damascus, which he used to purify the Mosque of Omar after the Christian Kings of Jerusalem had converted it into a church.

During the years of the High Middle Ages, roses were grown in gardens and illustrated in manuscripts. Little factual information has been gleaned on the types of

L ike a strange Sputnik about to launch, the resemblance of the spiky hips of Rosa roxburgii *to the European horse chestnut is what give this Species Rose its common English name, "Chestnut Rose."*

roses grown, but portraits of recognizable roses illustrate the borders of illuminated prayer books. Gothic cathedral interiors were brightened by Rose Windows made of brilliant, rainbow-colored stained glass. Unlike Roman buildings, which carried the huge weight of the domes and roofs through massive stone pillars and solid walls, the architects of the new Gothic cathedrals designed their buildings so that the weight was thrust out and supported by massive piers, or buttresses, allowing for these enormous windows to light up their vaulting interiors.

This brings us to the first English Civil War, or as we know it, the Wars of the Roses, and the famous—but apocryphal!—telling of that pivotal moment. Our image of "the choosing," so indelible in our thoughts on the subject, is due purely because of a certain popular sixteenth-century playwright

THE RISE AND FALL OF THE OLD ROSE

One of the first reasonably comprehensive lists of roses we have comes from John Gerard's *Herball, or Generall Historie of Plantes,* published in 1597. Gerard was a member of the Barber-Surgeons Company and head gardener to William Cecil, created Lord Burghley by Elizabeth I. He served as head gardener at both Cecil's London garden in the Strand, and at Theobalds Park in Hertfordshire. He also gave a list of the different roses he grew in his own Holborn garden, some sixteen in all.

John Parkinson, who served as apothecary to King James I and botanist to Charles I, published his *Paradisi in Sole Paradisus Terrestris* (a pun on his name, The Park on Earth of Park-in-Sun) in 1629 and mentions some twenty-nine roses. By 1795, the list of roses grown in England had increased to around ninety in Mary Lawrance's great work, *A Collection of Roses from Nature,* the first monograph on roses. She drew and engraved the illustrations herself; the final lithographs were hand-colored by her and her family, around their family dining table, with one member painting an individual color and passing the plate on to the next in line for the next color.

The next great work was the seminal *Les Roses,* by Pierre-Joseph Redouté, published in serialized format between 1817 and 1824, three years after the death of his patron, Joséphine Bonaparte. *Les Roses* expanded the list of cultivated roses to nearly 170.

Redouté taught himself the newly invented technique of stipple engraving, which he used to reproduce his rose paintings for publication. Instead of engraving a lithographic stone, this new technique used a copper plate for printing. Each color was applied by hand to the plate and one image was produced, then the copper plate was cleaned of ink and the colors applied for the next impression, making for a long and laborious process—and a very expensive, though exquisitely beautiful, publication.

By 1848, some 1,500 different roses were listed, described, and offered for sale in William Paul's *The Rose Garden.* Paul periodically reissued his book catalog, updating the list with newly introduced cultivars and eliminating those that had fallen out of favor. The 1848 edition listed nearly 800 Alba, Centifolia, Moss, Damask, and Gallica Roses. By the tenth edition, issued in 1910, that list had fallen to below ninety roses of the same classes. In sixty years, the number of Old Roses listed in catalogs had declined by some eighty-nine percent.

Rosa centifolia bullata, by Pierre-Joseph Redouté.

Striped and mottled roses were the height of fashion in the eighteenth and nineteenth centuries. 'Variegata di Bologna' will produce a large shrub and cover itself with carnival-colored blooms.

and his Tudor patrons. Yes, the Wars of the Roses was a historical event, and yes, the two opposing sides in this English Civil War did use two different roses as their respective emblems: a red rose for Lancaster and a white rose for York. Almost all the other "facts" of the story were fabricated afterward by the Tudors and their political propagandist, William Shakespeare, who created a version of history that amplified the Tudor position in history and at the same time solidified our perceptions of that time.

Shakespeare, the dramatic writer, needed to create situations out of raw historical facts that presented him with opportunities to write great drama. One such construct was the scene in *Henry VI, Part One* where the two antagonizing factions of the Wars of the Roses meet in the Temple Garden.

Each camp selects a uniquely colored rose to signal their fealty. Shakespeare thus gives us an image that—without historical foundation—remains to this day in our popular mythic consciousness.

The early cultivars of Old Roses that we can definitely put names to start appearing more and more consistently in the paintings of the early Renaissance. Among the earliest roses to materialize in artistic works of this period are crisp white blooms that could well be the first Albas ever illustrated. White roses were used as a symbol of chastity and purity, and often accompanied portraits of the Virgin Mary. Which Alba cultivars were being depicted is difficult to identify, but either 'Alba Maxima' or 'Alba Semiplena' seem good possibilities. Roses very much like these two are illustrated in manuscripts as growing on wooden trellises or lattice-

R osa soulieana *is one of those huge Species Roses happily relegated to the back of the border. They're put to their best use, though, when planted as a security hedge. This will go a long way towards discouraging unwanted guests on your property.*

work fences hemming in pleasure gardens. Such gardens always had a grassy area and a fountain with benches placed under rosy bowers designed for dallying.

By the late Renaissance in northern Europe, Dutch and Flemish painters had discovered the beauty and variety of roses being developed in their own countries. Painters were illustrating this new horticultural bounty almost as soon as new plants were off-loaded from the East Indies trading ships. Flemish artists specialized in providing the newly emerging burgher middle class with ever larger canvases, illustrating the luxuriant variety of horticultural treasures filtering in from newly discovered realms of the fabled spice-rich East, and reflecting the increased wealth of colonial domination.

Paintings of this period combine a ridiculously diverse selection of flowers and plants, many of which would never be seen togeth-

er naturally, or flowering at the same time; but the goal was to construct gloriously painted bouquets of living color. Master artists sketched flowers and constructed books of illustrations from which their sophisticated patrons could make selections for their tastes and decor. If a well-heeled patron craved a yellow "Rose of Provence" (a color that didn't exist), it was no problem to substitute a color here or there to match. Just as a rising entrepreneur today must drive the latest luxury car to demonstrate social position, a Dutch burgher would commission an extravagant still-life for his parlor, combining the newest and rarest flora available: striped tulips, orchids, exotic fruits, and roses.

Right about this time, books and pamphlets printed with movable type were becoming commonly available, not to mention affordable, and one of the more popular subjects was the "Herbal," a monograph of sorts for those wishing to enhance their health and daily vigor. But wild inaccuracies commonly found their way into these "learned" treatises. John Gerard copied his text from a German writer, then greatly embellished the work with fantastic stories of new uses for the plants. One of Gerard's most far-fetched stories told of how he personally created yellow roses. He stated as absolute fact that to get a yellow rose to bloom, all one needed to do was to graft a pink rose onto a "broom" (our cytisus plant), and the yellow, sweet pea–like flowers would impart their color to the rose. Gerard swore that this procedure would produce yellow roses, though the two plants are not related and a graft between these disparate plant families would have no chance of surviving.

The astrologer-physician Nicholas Culpeper (1616–54) prescribed a dry conserve made from hips of *Rosa canina* for cases of "fainting, swooning, weakness, and trembling of the heart." He also recommended this conserve of "sugar of rose" to fortify a weak stomach and promote digestion, and act as a general prophylactic "in time of infection." Herbals proved popular not only as sources of medicinal information for those not able to afford a doctor, but also as indispensable founts of information for gardeners.

The first Botanical Garden, established at Padua, Italy in 1545, was developed by the medical faculty specifically for growing plants used in the pharmacopeia of the day. Doctors needed pharmaceutical plants for their patients as there were no corner drugstores. And they needed to know how to properly identify and grow important and often poisonous medicinal herbs.

The Chelsea Physic Garden in London was founded in 1673 by the Society of Apothecaries and became an important repository of medicinal plants as well as an information bank for methods of cultivation. It later became the center for growing and studying newly introduced horticultural wealth, including roses, arriving in Europe from an expanding web of commercial and colonial empires.

After the death of Queen Anne in 1714, Britain's Parliament elected to invite the Hanoverian George I to be king of the newly created United Kingdom over the other contender for the crown, his Stuart cousin James, the Old Pretender. The Jacobite party (Stuart supporters) in Scotland took up the Alba, or White Rose, as the insignia

*O*ften a planting of the striped 'Rosa Mundi' will revert back to its parent, the solid-colored 'Apothecary's Rose.'

of their clandestine efforts to re-establish Stuart rule in place of the Hanoverian kings. James's son Charles, the Young Pretender, also had supporters who wore the white rose as a symbol of their loyalty to the Stuart dynasty. The Jacobite cause never engendered substantial support in Britain and the rebels were eventually vanquished.

Roses may or may not have traveled with the very first European colonists to the New World, but it is clear that early on, Spanish mission fathers made a point of bringing along the old Roman 'Autumn Damask,' which they called the "Rose of Castile," for both medicinal and liturgical use on their ecclesiastical enterprises. The "Rose of Castile" eventually made its way into mission gardens as remote as the Alta California frontier.

Early English colonists escaping religious persecution and the Civil War back home attempted to bring with them every necessity of life to help them create a safe environment in the New England wilderness where they were homesteading. Along with a cherished copy of Gerard's *Herball,* they brought cuttings and seeds of important medicinal plants and herbs they would need in caring for the sick and injured. Cuttings or rooted starts of the Gallica Rose 'Officinalis' were surely tucked away in the personal possessions of a number of "goodwives."

JOSÉPHINE'S LEGACY

The world of roses got its modern jump start with the patronage of Joséphine Bonaparte. She established a world-renowned collection at her home, Château Malmaison, on the outskirts of Paris, which she and Napoléon had purchased in 1799 as a tranquil retreat away from the commotion of the capital. Joséphine decided to

Possibly a hybrid between a Gallica and the "Frankfurt Rose," 'Empress Joséphine' brings back nostalgic memories of the gardens at Château Malmaison and Joséphine's collection of over 260 rose cultivars and species.

assemble and display every species of rose she could lay her hands on. Napoléon gave instructions to the French Navy that when they boarded and searched ships at sea, crews were to look for and confiscate any plants or seeds of roses they might come across. Joséphine spent so much money creating her garden and decorating the house that Napoléon had to step in and cover her substantial debts. In just one year she spent some £2,600 with the English nursery of Kennedy and Lee—while her husband was at war with Britain. At the height of its continental naval blockade, the British Admiralty granted a safe-conduct pass to the Kennedy and Lee firm to deliver an order of the new China Roses to Joséphine at Malmaison.

Joséphine's massive collection of roses at Malmaison was instrumental in establishing the popularity of the rose in nineteenth-century gardens. She hired the flower painter of all flower painters, Pierre-Joseph Redouté, to create an enduring record of the roses in her collection. Redouté had survived the French Revolution intact, at least physically. He had been court painter to Queen Marie-Antoinette, although unlike that ill-fated lady, he managed to keep his head and become the new Empress's court flower painter. Redouté's great rose work wasn't published until a few years after Joséphine's death, but his three-volume *Les Roses,* which was issued between 1817 and 1824, is considered one of the most beautiful and important books ever published. Complete with a commentary by renowned botanist Claude-

Named for the cockade Napoléon wore in his hat, 'Crested Moss' is unique among the Moss Roses in having its mossing only on the sepals.

Antoine Thory, *Les Roses* became the standard by which all future rose books and illustrations would be measured. Many of the 170 roses Redouté illustrated are still growing and thriving in our gardens. His portrait of 'Blush Noisette' is one of the all-time masterpieces of botanical illustration. After the fall of Napoléon, Redouté was retained as court flower painter by the new Bourbon king, Louis-Philippe, in 1830. Redouté died in 1840 at the age of eighty-one, while painting a lily.

Empress Joséphine's other great legacy was that she set the standard for rose growing in Western society at that time. Her gardeners spread out all over France after her death, and established gardens and rose nurseries that still inspire us in indirect ways today. It became de rigueur for the Empire's nouveau riche to follow Joséphine's lead,

Often discovered growing in abandoned or derelict farmyards and homesites, Tea and China Roses will survive and thrive, frequently living for a hundred years or more.

and once it was clear roses were the thing, people scrambled over themselves to join in the frenzied competition to see who could amass the largest collection. Joséphine's influence was swiftly felt across the English Channel as well. Even while at war with Napoléon, the English were determined to keep up with trends and social fashions and thus made a concerted effort to collect roses for the garden just like their continental cousins. Thus, the Empress influenced a whole generation of French and British gardeners and nurserymen.

Closer to home, many of the men who worked and received their early training at the Château Malmaison went on to become rose hybridizers and established the modern French rose-breeding industry. During Joséphine's own short residence at Malmaison, her gardener Dupont was able to amass some 260 rose species and cultivars for her. Dupont passed on Joséphine's legacy to Alexandre Hardy, who took over the Luxembourg Garden from him and raised many roses of note, 'Mme. Hardy' and 'Safrano' among them. Later, Hardy took on a young apprentice by the name of Jacques-Julien Margottin, who worked for him at the Luxembourg Garden for some years before moving on to found his own rose nursery. Born in the same year that Redouté published *Les Roses,* Margottin died in 1892 but managed, through his son Jules, to hand Joséphine's torch to the future, igniting a new generation and a new century of rose lovers.

No other individual in history has come close to the sway that Joséphine wielded over our culture's love of the rose family. When I am asked by visitors to my garden, "Why all the French names?" I don't have to look too far for the answer: "Joséphine!"

THE ROSE IN AMERICA

Across the "Pond," Thomas Jefferson was very active in importing seeds and plants that he hoped would improve the lives and diet of his fellow citizens in the newly founded United States of America. Along with the best new varieties of European fruits, Jefferson also ordered ornamental plants and seeds for his personal garden at Monticello. In November of 1791, Jefferson recorded in his Garden Book that he had ordered sixteen plants of eight cultivars for the garden, among them Moss, China, Musk, White, Centifolia, and 'Rosa Mundi' Roses. Jefferson ordered his fruit trees and roses from the firm headed by William Prince in Flushing, New York, and requested that Prince ship the plants by sea to his agent in Richmond, Virginia.

William Prince's firm was one of the largest nurseries in the United States at that time, supplying plants of nearly seven hundred different roses to the new republic. Prince was among the first to grow plants of the newly developed Noisettes sent by the hybridizer John Champneys, of Charleston, South Carolina.

New York City was the home of another early American production, 'Harison's Yellow,' developed right in the heart of Manhattan by George F. Harison, a local attorney. Harison maintained a farm on that island, and documentation shows that his rose started appearing in nursery catalogs around 1830, just in time for the first push into the newly opening West. There was hardly a pioneer mother who didn't include a rooted piece of 'Harison's Yellow' with the treasures she brought for her family's new home out West. Even today, one can almost follow the immigrant trails across the country to Texas, California, and Oregon by simply mapping plantings of 'Harison's Yellow.'

Between 1850, the year California was admitted to statehood, and 1900, records show that nearly 4,000 different cultivars of roses were offered for sale in the young state. Many new French hybrids were listed for sale in California within months of their French introduction. The sea voyage from Europe or New York to San Francisco took approximately six months, so apparently, as soon as a new cultivar was put on the market, in many cases it was loaded aboard a ship heading for the Golden West.

THE AGE OF EXPLORATION

The eighteenth and nineteenth centuries were a time of great exploration as Europeans traveled to all corners of the globe, unearthing heretofore unknown horticultural treasures to enrich their lives and gardens. While most of the new commercial elite were more interested in acquiring spices and gold, new plants began to filter into the new international econ-

*T*he deeply cupped flowers of 'Hermosa' demonstrate an affinity to the larger-flowered Bourbon Roses.

omy. Maize, tomatoes, potatoes, peppers, tobacco, sugar, and chocolate imported from the New World, plus orchids, roses, tea, coffee, and spices imported from Asia and Africa anchored the new colonial economies.

Europeans found China to be one of the greatest sources of new garden plants. To this day, China is known as the Mother of Gardens in honor of her opulent horticultural legacy. Asia (and China specifically) appears to have been the home of the greatest number of Species Roses, with more than a third of them native to this center of rose evolution.

In China, Europeans were confined to a handful of official trading cities, mostly in the south, and even in these cities they were prevented from leaving specific assigned areas, or zones, by Chinese officials. These "factories," as they were known, comprised ware-

houses and wharves where European and Chinese merchants traded in luxury goods, spices, silks, porcelain, and tea. The Portuguese and Dutch traders usually paid for their imports in spices collected from their Asian colonial empires, but the Chinese demanded that the British pay in specie, specifically gold or silver coin. This chasm between the British and Chinese in the matter of payment was to have lasting consequences.

The British crown dispatched a commercial mission to the Chinese emperor in Beijing in 1792, headed by Lord Macartney. Macartney was charged by his government with establishing trading relations with the Chinese that would be more favorable to the British. Unfortunately, Chinese authorities remained adamant in their demands for payment solely in specie, refusing British manufactured goods for their silks and tea.

Although a diplomatic failure, Macartney's mission did bring back a rose, *Rosa bracteata,* named the "Macartney Rose" in his honor. Discovered growing in the coastal region of China by Macartney's secretary, Sir George Staunton, *R. bracteata* soon made its way to the newly founded United States, where Thomas Jefferson planted it at Monticello in 1799. In the warm growing conditions of the South, it rapidly became a pest, spreading by rhizome and colonizing huge areas of prime agricultural land. Lord Macartney was awarded a signet ring by King George III with an intaglio design of his rose carved into the stone as a reward for his efforts on behalf of the British Crown.

Back in southern China, bored European merchants with time on their hands waiting for the next ship to arrive were not allowed out of their factory compounds. Tedious days and weeks of inactivity were interspersed with brief periods of intense duties inventorying and loading ships with the exotic products of the East. Looking about for amusements to occupy themselves in this strange and fascinating land, they discovered that a hot, humid South China day could be filled exploring local garden nurseries close enough at hand for Chinese authorities to allow access.

For some merchants, an afternoon exploring for new plants to send home was a way to break the tedium of a dangerous and risky post. The first China and Tea Roses shipped to Europe were probably discovered growing in local nurseries operated by native Chinese. At some point around the middle to late eighteenth century, the first repeat-blooming China Roses found their way to Europe.

Whether as living plants or seeds, a few of these roses survived the long trip by sea and began appearing in northern European gardens. It is estimated that only one in a thousand plants survived the voyage. One solution was to off-load and grow the precious living cargo for a time in gardens especially founded for the purpose at various ports-of-call along the returning trade routes. After they regained strength and health, it was possible to repropagate fragile plants for the continuing voyage home to Europe.

Tea Roses made their appearance just after the beginning of the new century. At first these roses were considered simple horticultural novelties, too tender to grow outdoors in the cold northern European climes. But within a short time, gardeners discovered that many were hardy enough to survive outside, particularly in areas like the south of France, and with protection they could even be grown outside greenhouses in the southern English shires as well.

These new roses didn't cease blooming in midsummer but continued on and on into autumn, right up to the first frost. This reblooming trait was completely new to nurserymen who immediately attempted to spread this desirable feature to their Western roses. But Gregor Mendel (1822–84), an Augustinian monk and founder of the science of genetics, didn't publish the rules of inheritance until

*A*n old cherry tree provides support for a climbing rose to scamper up and over, where it can then spill out into the spring garden, providing vibrant color in all directions.

1866, and even then he was largely ignored, so hybridizers were completely unaware that the roses they were crossing were incompatible and that the one trait they were hoping for—remontancy—was recessive and would not appear in first generation (f_1) seedlings. What was produced were very large, vigorous shrubs that grew and grew. But no matter what these gardeners did to and for them, the new roses bloomed only in spring. These shrubs were given the appellation "hybrid," which in those times denoted sterility. Hybrid China Roses demonstrated what we now know as "hybrid vigor"; that is, because the two-parent lineages were so dissimilar, they produced extremely vigorous but only once-blooming offspring. In fact, the seedlings produced were unable to reproduce sexually. It took nearly forty years for hybridizers to overcome this sterility barrier and yield an utterly new class of roses, the Hybrid Perpetuals.

First introduced in France as 'Mme. Ferdinand Jamin,' this Hybrid Perpetual was renamed 'American Beauty' for the U.S. market, and thus entered into history under that very famous title.

No one recorded where Tea Roses were first collected, or how they got their name. For years, rose scholars have speculated that the first Tea Roses to arrive in Europe must have smelled like fresh, unprocessed tea, but this is an unlikely hypothesis as no one since has been able to recognize any trace of tea fragrance in the group. An alternative theory on the naming of Tea Roses has to do with the European trading companies active in the Far East at the time.

The English, French, and Dutch East India Companies were most active in importing tea to fill the growing demand for this new consumer craze. The British quickly became a nation of tea drinkers in the early years of the eighteenth century, and the importing of tea to fulfill the demand was one of the engines driving commerce at that time. Quality grades of tea were produced only in China, and the Chinese jealously safeguarded their monopoly. In England tea was precious, costing as much as £1 for a pound of high-quality product. Some historians feel that inasmuch as the commerce from Asia was assigned to the tea fleets, this might be the origin for the name of the Tea Rose. Additionally, the shipping of cuttings or live plants bundled up with tea may explain the tea fragrance that was mentioned so prominently.

There is another theory that has recently impressed scholars. European traders were sequestered in the treaty ports; the main seaport at that time was Canton, a city on the South China Sea now called Guangzhou. As it happens, there existed a celebrated garden district

A few Hybrid Perpetual Roses, like 'Marchioness of Lorne,' have a propensity for size and will appreciate some sort of garden structure to support their long, arching canes.

right at the European edge of Guangzhou, and in this one particular neighborhood was concentrated the local nursery trade. Europeans with time on their hands were welcomed, and there are many records of how they would stroll through the quarter delighting in the color and fragrance of the environs. The main nursery of the precinct was known as the *Fa-Te* Nursery. Sundry English plant collectors as late as the 1850s record buying plants from *Fa-Te* to be sent back home. It isn't much of a leap of linguistic legerdemain for a rose from *Fa-Te* to be transposed into spoken English as *tea*.

The British East India Company controlled the lucrative China and Asia trade at the same time they were consolidating their colonial hold on India. The subcontinent was a huge market for

THE MAN WHO WOULD
BE ROSE KING

Born in 1858 in the heart of French rose country, Joseph Pernet started his career in the rose industry as an apprentice to his father, Jean, at the age of twelve, working in the fields and greenhouses. A tough taskmaster with a heart of gold, Joseph Pernet was a wonderful mentor to all his apprentices. As he set his personal standards so high, he expected no less from family and employees alike. He must have been a difficult man to work for, but those who did so adored him.

Pernet was also a man who held integrity in the highest esteem. Late in his life, one of his roses won a major prize at a British rose competition, yet he refused the prize of £1,000 as to accept would have required him to rename the rose from its French dedication to that of the sponsor of the English prize. A compromise was finally reached, with the rose retaining its French name in France (that being 'Mme. Edouard Herriot'), while in the United Kingdom it was to be known as 'The Daily Mail Rose.'

Pernet's working life was spent in the rose fields around Lyons, first for his father and later for several other rose growers and hybridizers who taught him his trade. When he began his career, the Tea Rose ruled the rose world. But not too long afterward, the first tentative steps were made at creating the class that would, in time, come to be known as Hybrid Tea. The very first Hybrid Tea, 'La France,' was produced by a rival hybridizer from Lyons, Jean-Baptiste Guillot, in 1867. At first, this novel rose was classed as a Hybrid Perpetual, and it was a number of years before the French officially recognized the formation of a new category. As one might expect, it took even longer for the Royal National Rose Society in England to accept this designation.

Pernet began working for the widow Ducher, and later married her daughter Marie in 1882. He eventually showed his great respect for the Ducher family and their place in rose history by hyphenating his own name to Pernet-Ducher. Joseph and Marie produced two sons, Claudius and Georges. In one of the most tragic stories imaginable, Pernet lost both his boys on the grisly, blood-soaked battlefields of the First World War. Years later, the still grieving father dedicated two of his roses to his sons: 'Souvenier de Claudius Pernet' in 1920, and 'Souvenier de Georges Pernet' in 1921.

Pernet-Ducher began his dogged pursuit of winter-hardy, repeat-flowering yellow roses as early as the 1880s. Over the years, he attempted to combine the canary yellow of *Rosa foetida* with the strong reblooming traits of a number of Hybrid Perpetuals. For years he persisted with this project, never giving up, producing one cross after another, and struggling with *R. foetida*'s low fertility rate to produce a rose with the desired characteristics. The problem was that *R. foetida* has always produced only about seven percent viable pollen, thus creating a laborious and daunting task in hybridizing long before DNA or gene splicing were known.

In time, Pernet-Ducher decided to focus on the double form of *R. foetida*, known as 'Persian Yellow,' but even this rose presented obstacles. It's not clear how many generations were produced, but it is speculated that using the pollen of 'Persian Yellow,' he succeeded in producing seed from the old Hybrid Perpetual 'Antoine Ducher.'

This first generation, or "f_1 hybrid," as it is called by geneticists, would not have been remontant, as the repeat-blooming trait is carried on a recessive gene. However, quite possibly as an accidental cross produced in the field, a second generation, or "f_2 seedling," resulted, which did happen to transmit the required doubling of the recessive gene, thus producing a remontant hybrid. Pernet-Ducher took notice of this seedling in his growing fields only through its serendipitous discovery by a visitor.

Pernet-Ducher immediately began propagating his fortuitous seedling and eventually introduced it in the fall of 1900, naming it "Golden Sun"—what we know as 'Soleil d'Or.' This seminal rose established a group that for a time was categorized as "Pernetiana," in honor of the hybridizer. But very soon, it was recognized that these new yellow cultivars were Hybrid Teas, and they were subsequently combined with that class.

'Soleil d'Or' was quickly incorporated into every available rose, siring such prodigious spawn that today, it would be nearly impossible to find a contemporary rose that doesn't trace its ancestry back to this founder. No other single rose has influenced our perception of what a rose is as has this progenitor. 'Soleil d'Or' is the catalyst upon which subsequent hybrids were founded.

Joseph Pernet-Ducher is thus, in my estimation, the creator of Modern Roses, and I believe that his seminal production, 'Soleil d'Or,' should be recognized as the first truly twentieth-century rose.

While many historians and rosarians will persist in acknowledging 'La France' as the first Modern Rose, for me its place in history remains simply that of the first Hybrid Tea—as such, it still finds a noble place in the history of roses. But I find it quite fitting that at the beginning of a new millennium and new century, we recognize the contributions of the past century's most influential rose, 'Soleil d'Or.' No other has so branded its form into our gardens; no other has so contributed its genes and imprinted its character on more than 100 years of roses.

Photo: Courtesy of the American Rose Society, Modern Roses II, *1940.*

*O*ld Roses like this early Noisette 'Fellenberg' are frequently found growing amid the bracken fern and weeds of historic cemeteries throughout North America, often planted more than a century ago in memory of a departed loved one.

British manufactured goods, but at that time, India produced few crops that could pay for those goods. What the British needed was a crop to grow in India that would be accepted in China to compensate for all those expensive items the Chinese forced them to purchase with their precious and limited stock of gold and silver. Then some "resourceful" bureaucrat in the British East India Company came up with the idea of growing and processing opium in India, which would be used not for the domestic or home market, but to sell exclusively to the Chinese! This "cash crop," with a ready market in China, would be used to pay for the luxury goods and would help balance British trade deficits.

The Chinese government prohibited the importation of opium from British possessions in India, and authorities seized and destroyed nearly 20,000 chests of opium stored in Canton warehouses. Fighting erupted, and the Chinese demanded that the British turn over persons thought to have killed Chinese citizens. The British refused, precipitating the first of the Opium Wars between Britain and China in 1839. That war was concluded in 1842 by the Treaty of Nanking, in which the Chinese acceded to all demands and ceded the island of Hong Kong to the British. The original territory of Hong Kong was enlarged by later wars and treaties over the years, until in 1898, the Chinese signed an agreement granting Britain a 99-year lease (which expired in 1997).

After the first Opium War, the British cast about looking for a new crop to replace opium to pay for Chinese imports. Robert Fortune, a Scottish gardener, was sent to China by the Horticultural Society of London (later renamed the Royal Horticultural Society). He arrived in Hong Kong in 1843 and proceeded to visit Canton nurseries looking for plants to introduce to English gardeners. Fortune made several trips to China, and beginning in 1848, he made three extensive collecting forays through the Chinese countryside looking for prime cultivars of *Camellia sinensis,* the tea plant, which Chinese authorities had been understandably reluctant to part with.

Fortune's commission from his government was to find the best plants of tea for growing in the Indian colonies, so he concealed his European identity and traveled about the country masquerading as a native. One of the first industrial spies, he was successful in obtaining premium tea cultivars for Indian plantations, and his collections were used to inaugurate the Indian tea industry. When you consider that in 1839 alone, the British imported 200 tons of Chinese tea, the savings to Britain were well worth the effort and expense.

While Fortune was traveling about the Chinese hinterland spying out tea, he kept a sharp eye for appealing flora and later introduced several roses from these trips. 'Fortune's Double Yellow' and 'Fortune's Five-Coloured Rose'

were just two of his discoveries during this time. He is said to have introduced some 120 new species into European gardens, making him one of the most important plant collectors of the age. Fortune may have been an early 007, and he certainly had an eye for a great garden plant.

REPEAT-BLOOMING HYBRIDS

The middle years of the nineteenth century were taken up with the development of Hybrid Perpetuals. The French first back-crossed the few fertile cultivars of Hybrid China Roses, which themselves were the product of Old European Roses such as Gallicas and Damasks and the newly introduced China Roses. Sometime in the 1830s, the first of a class of hardy, repeat-blooming hybrids were introduced in France. For lack of a better name, they were labeled *hybrides remontants,* which was

A bushy Noisette, 'Mary Washington' was first discovered growing in the Mount Vernon garden around 1891.

Introduced in 1861, 'General Washington' continues an American trend of naming roses for presidents and first ladies.

adapted to the English tongue as Hybrid Perpetual.

Over the next sixty years, the Hybrid Perpetual class reigned over the rose world, and during that time some 4,000 cultivars were introduced. Unfortunately, many were just not distinct enough or healthy enough to survive, so we are left with a mere handful today.

It wasn't until the 1870s that English gentleman farmer Henry Bennett decided to apply some of the wealth of experience he had gained breeding horses and cattle to developing new roses. His first seedlings were disappointing, so he decided to travel to France and observe what the French were doing. He was shocked to discover that they were not taking advantage of any of the modern methods of scientific hybridization developed since Mendel had published his findings on genetics and inheritance. Bennett knew full well the importance of keeping adequate records for breeding. He returned home and in 1879 began introducing what he entitled his *Pedigree Hybrids of the Tea Rose,* later shortened to *Hybrid Tea,* which the French translated as *Hybrides de Thé.*

Old Roses reveal to us where we have come from and suggest myriad paths we can explore in our search for the perfect rose. To many growers and hybridizers of Modern Roses, our love affair with the old is but self-indulgent nostalgia. When asked to answer such indictments, I point to the growing popularity of the new shrub roses, such as David Austin's English Roses and the French Romanticas and Generosas, from Meilland and Guillot respectively. A larger and more diverse gardening audience is being created for all types of roses by these new-style shrubs masquerading in their "old-fashionedness."

Popularity is fleeting, and notoriety isn't in itself enough to protect and promote our grandes dames. Old Roses are survivors, enduring disease, climate, insects—and that most deadly of all fates, falling out of style—to point us the way to incorporating roses into the twenty-first century landscape. Hybridizers worldwide are struggling to create winter-hardy, disease-free roses, when all they, and we, need do is look about us to discover there are hundreds of spectacular answers to the mystery available to all in the form of Old Roses.

ROSE GROWING MADE EASY

Ask your average person his or her ideas about growing roses, and you'll more than likely get this type of response: "Oh, they're so beautiful, but I can't bother with growing roses—they're just too demanding." The consensus has long been that roses are a mystery, and that to have them thriving in your garden beds means you have a particularly refined shade of green thumb. The challenges, the pests, the diseases—all are far too overwhelming to make the effort worthwhile. But *nothing* could be further from the truth!

WHAT ROSES NEED

In reality, roses are rather undemanding when compared with many other plant families. Growing healthy roses is simple and easy, as long as you take into consideration the four basic needs of all roses: sun, soil, water, and informed selection. Although all four needs are important, the most fundamental is sun.

SUN. Roses are sun-loving plants—the more sun, the happier they are. All roses grow best with at least six to eight hours of direct sun daily. A few roses will tolerate less, but with only four to six hours of sun a day, there is more potential for disease, and also decreased flower production—often as low as fifty percent of normal bloom. Less than optimal sun accounts for weaker, more spindly growth, and leaves the plant open to attacks from pests and diseases. Just as we're able to shrug off infection or disease more easily and quickly when we take care of our bodies with ample rest and proper diet, the same holds true for roses.

Green plants rely on the energy provided by sunlight to convert water absorbed from the soil, and carbon dioxide absorbed from the atmosphere, into the sugars and starches from which all carbon-based life, both animal and vegetable, is made. The solar panels we

Even though it is once-blooming, Ramblers like 'Alexandre Girault' put on a tremendous spring display when allowed to spill out over a wall or through a tree.

call leaves convert the sun's energy into stable, storable chemical power-packs that can be called upon at a later time to fuel life on the molecular level. Almost all life on earth is supported by chlorophyll, the component of plants that we see as green pigment. Chlorophyll is a biochemical food processor, using sunlight to combine and convert every six molecules of water (H_2O) and every six molecules of carbon dioxide (CO_2) into their own vital sugars ($C_6H_{12}O_6$), leaving a waste product of six molecules of free oxygen (O_2) and water vapor, which are dispelled into the atmosphere. The processed sugar material is further converted to carbohydrate starches and stored in the plant's cells for later retrieval. This operation continues day in and day out, fueled by the inexhaustible supply of sunlight, and then yields the harvest we prize: leaves, vegetables, fruits, and of course, flowers.

SOIL. If sunlight is the engine that runs the factory, soil is the foundation and reservoir that provides the raw elements for the factory's operation. Soil is a complex amalgam of weathered rock, decomposed organic matter, and living organisms. Soil provides the anchoring medium for the roots, but soil also acts as a huge sponge, absorbing and distributing water so that a plant's root system can access this vital liquid at regular intervals. A sort of symbiosis occurs between soil and plants. Plants protect and preserve the soil they live in by helping to minimize erosion and by eventually becoming part of the biomass that enriches that very same spot of earth. Likewise, soil provides essential materials needed for life in the form of minerals and nutrients, which are dissolved in the water and then absorbed by the root systems.

Roses are not too finicky about the soil they grow in, just as long as it is well-drained and not too acid or alkaline. Roses will thrive if the soil drains well, whether it's predominantly clay or sandy loam. Heavy clay soils will need amending with homemade compost or commercial planting mix. The organic humus in these products will help to improve the tilth of the soil so that very fine clay particles form larger clumps that will allow water and air to move more freely through the soil. Conversely, loam with a high ratio of sand will also need amending with compost or planter's mix to help retain more water and nutrients. Just about any soil will profit from mixing 50 percent compost into the planting soil at planting time.

WATER. Roses require a steady supply of water for optimal growth and flower production. In most regions of the country, natural rain can meet their needs, but in times of drought, or in drier regions, it will be necessary to supplement with regular, periodic irrigation. The garden needs 1 to 2 inches of water per week to keep roses happy and blooming. That amounts to about a thirty-minute run of the hose or sprinkler per week. It's always best to water early in the day so that if rose foliage gets wet, it has

a chance to dry before evening, thereby lessening the chance of promoting fungal diseases. A little more on the needy side, remontant roses demand a steadier supply of moisture to help ensure continuous production of flowers, so bear that in mind when selecting reblooming additions to your garden.

SELECTION. Making informed choices in the purchase and placement of your garden shrubs is vital for growing healthy, happy, long-lived roses.

Before you buy, do some research to see if the rose you are thinking of growing will thrive in your area. Is your choice more winter- or summer-hardy? Will it be subject to diseases and pests specific to your growing zone? This is where you start doing some homework. Check with local public rose gardens, ask your nurseryman for

A reasonably winter-hardy Rambler introduced in 1906, 'Tausendschön' lines up to its English common name, "Thousand Beauties."

advice, and check out rose gardens in your community to see what their owners' experiences have been with the cultivars you are contemplating. Unless you're willing to put extra time and effort into a particularly rare or special rose, why purchase a cultivar that will require special attention, or one that isn't well adapted to your growing region? There are so many good (as in "easy") roses to choose from, there's no reason to fight Mother Nature.

As savvy gardeners search out ways to simplify and reduce their dependence on costly and dangerous chemicals, they are discovering the tremendous staying power of roses that have survived pests, disease, neglect, and the "falling-out-of-fashion" legacy, and have

LENGTHENING THE LIFE OF CUT OLD ROSES

The first order of business when using living plants and flowers for cut arrangements is to know when and how to cut. Roses, like most flowers, need to be cut early in the day when they are still turgid and at their freshest. Take a bucket or container of water with you so that you can place the cut flowers into water as soon as they are removed from the shrub. Before adding each stem to your bouquet, make a fresh diagonal

cut, under the water, ¼ to ½ inch or so up the stem from the original cut. Re-cutting each stem underwater allows the rose to take up water into the fresh cut without the interference of the bubble of air you would get by cutting out of the bucket, which would block the passage of water to the flower.

Next, place the freshly recut stem into hot (not boiling) tap water. Water as hot as will flow from the tap will condition the blooms for longer vase life. Then prep your bouquet by adding a food source and preservative to the hot water. A floral preservative purchased from a florist or garden shop is adequate, although I prefer to use two or three ounces of regular (not sugar-free) lemon-lime soda pop for the artificial preservative. The sugar in the soda will feed the living flower, and the citric acid will kill harmful bacteria, which can block the water-transferring cells in the stem. Non-sugared diet sodas will not work because it is the sugars that feed the blossom.

Change your vase water daily, re-cutting the stems under fresh water each time. Following these procedures can increase the vase life of cut roses from two or three days up to ten or twelve days or more.

persisted despite the vicissitudes of time.

Gardeners in the coldest zones of the country are continually disappointed at the low survival rate of our newest commercial cultivars. Many of these roses simply will not survive the harsh winter conditions of many regions without expensive or time-consuming protective measures. This begs the question, Why not plant roses that will require little or no special care? Many of the Old Garden Roses descend from species that are native to the northern parts of Europe, Asia, and North America and have little difficulty wintering over.

At the other end of the spectrum, gardeners in warm to subtropical regions find it difficult to get many Modern Roses to survive more than a year or two because of a lack of any winter to speak of. Many gardeners in the deep South must treat their favorite Hybrid Teas like annuals, replacing them every year or so. But China and Tea Roses were developed in a region of southern China with nearly similar growing conditions to those in our South. A quick glance around historic estates and homesteads throughout the Gulf States provides us with bountiful examples of Old Roses that can survive these unique growing conditions. China and Tea Roses and their descendants, the Noisettes, endure for decades when planted as own-root shrubs in hot, humid zones. Gardeners in the North can but envy their Southern counterparts the perfection and fruity fragrances of these roses unless they choose to grow them in a greenhouse environment.

*N*ative originally to China, Multifloria Roses like this single-flowered form are large climbers and need external support to put on the best display.

For those of us who garden in the hot but arid Southwest, hardiness is more a matter of whether the rose will survive heat, not cold. Many roses that would not have a problem enduring the coldest northern winters simply refuse to grow in our arid desert soils. Here, we select for specific cultivars that will tolerate, and indeed thrive in, our unique growing conditions.

PURCHASING ROSES

Just fifteen years ago, one would've been hard pressed to find a dozen nurseries in the country carrying more than a handful of the selections listed in this book. But the market for Old Roses in the United States is growing each year, with an abundance of small nurseries offering an ever-increasing supply of unusual cultivars for sale in their catalogs. Market awareness has even penetrated the average local garden center, with more and more

*T*he classically inspired "Temple of Love" sits at the head of the Rose Garden at The Huntington Botanical Gardens in San Marino, California, in a wash of white 'French Lace' and peachy apricot 'Tamora' roses.

offering selections of the choicest Old Roses. Even the gargantuan mail-order retailers are offering a few Old Roses in their glossy color catalogs.

When shopping for Old Roses, the gardener will come across two basic types of plants: own-root and grafted. As with all roses, Old Roses are propagated asexually, either by grafting or as cuttings. Most Modern Roses are regularly propagated by grafting a bud of the selected cultivar onto a prepared rootstock. This is the fastest and most economical way to produce large quantities of plants for sale. The grafted plants used commercially are two-year-old, field-grown, bare-root shrubs that most of us are used to purchasing through our local nursery. Grafted cultivars usually have a garden life of about fifteen to twenty years.

The second method of propagation utilizes the rose's own inherent abilities to produce root systems. Flowering stems are harvested, separated, placed in special growing habitats, and encouraged to form roots. These own-root shrubs take a little longer to grow to the same size as a grafted rose, but will catch up within a season or two and have an open-ended lifespan. It's not hard to find own-root roses living beyond the century mark.

Among Old Rose aficionados, you'll find own-root purists and graft devoteés. Over the years, the majority have come to favor own-root plants, but in truth, both propagation methods have their good points and drawbacks.

Proponents of own-root roses point to the fact that their roses are more likely to be winter-hardy, as most of the rootstocks used for grafted plants can be tender in some of the colder regions of the country. Own-root aficionados also like to point out that their plants are less likely to harbor harmful plant viruses. But this is only true if the parent stock from which the cuttings were harvested was free of such viruses. Grafted plants can be equally free if the parent cultivar and rootstocks are clean.

As far as I'm concerned, whether to purchase own-root or grafted roses is more a matter of personal choice and need at the time. Since grafted plants are already two years old when you purchase them, they will be larger at planting and take less time for the shrub to reach mature size. Own-root plants will be significantly smaller on receipt and will take at least a season or two to reach maturity. On the other hand, suppliers of own-root plants tend to offer a more comprehensive selection in their catalogs. Over the years, I have found it really makes little difference which method of propagation you choose, as long as the selections you plant are well-adapted to your region.

PLANTING AND TRANSPLANTING

Planting an Old Rose is no different from planting any other rose. Just follow these simple steps. Prepare a planting hole approximately 2 feet long, wide, and deep.

Mix the soil you have removed from the hole with organic compost or bagged planter's mix at a 50-50 rate to provide an optimum, long-term home for your roses.

Because clay soils are heavy and retain more water, they have very little space for air. Mixing in organic compost is important as it allows for better drainage and increases porous space for air and water, both of which are vital to the health and growth of most plants. Sandy soils, on the other hand, have plenty of space for air but drain off water too rapidly, requiring more frequent irrigation. Adding compost helps sandy soils act more like a sponge, retaining that much-needed moisture around the roots of your roses.

Fill the hole with water. If the water drains off in an hour or two, the soil won't become saturated, preventing root growth. If it takes longer to drain, say half the day or overnight, then you will need to improve your drainage situation. It may be necessary to dig deeper to break through an impermeable soil layer. In some extreme cases, it may even be necessary to install a drainage system or build raised beds (above ground level) for your roses.

In colder regions, plant roses so that the crown, or bud union (the point of grafting), is 2 to 3 inches below ground. This protects the tender growth point from freezing and dying. Many Old Roses are rock-hardy to cold, but their rootstocks might not be as robust, so it's best to protect them by planting them deep to allow for some insulation from the coldest weather.

In milder regions, it's best to

plant grafted and own-root roses with their crown or bud union right at soil level. You will sometimes read recommendations to plant the bud union 2 to 3 inches above ground level, but I have found this produces a weaker plant that rocks about in the wind. I have also learned that planting the shrub with the bud union just at soil level allows for a more symmetrically-shaped plant, in that a shrub planted in this manner produces new canes from all sides instead of only from the side receiving the most sun.

When planting own-root Old Roses, remember that many will produce long runners and form offshoots across your garden. Gallica Roses are especially prone to spreading out and taking over beds, but many other groups of Old Roses share this tendency to spread out as well. If this proves to be a problem, it might be best to try to plant grafted instead of own-root shrubs. But if you don't object to having your roses run about the garden, or if you can only find own-root plants of your selections, be ready to use your shovel to dig up runners. One advantage with this, however, is that you can pot up those runners and give them to friends—a great way to make contacts with other rosarians.

When planting Old Roses, learn what the mature size of the shrub will be, and provide enough space for that ultimate growth. Crowding roses too close together encourages disease and pests and will make it much more difficult to maintain your garden without constant monitoring. Since you don't want to have to dig up and replant

roses placed too close together, do the homework and save yourself that extra toil.

It is usually recommended that you move large rose plants only when they are dormant, or at pruning time, but you can move your mature shrub successfully at any time, even in the hottest summer, as long as you remove *all* its leaves first. Defoliating the bush will put it into temporary dormancy without causing harm. It will also prevent shock to the plant. After removing the leaves, dig up as large a ball of roots as you can handle, and prune the plant back to balance the roots to the top. Actually, I have been successful at moving large climbing roses using this method without shortening the canes at all. But remember, leave just *one leaf* on the bush and you will have problems. You must strip the rose completely before digging it up.

COMPANION PLANTING

In the last decade or so, much has changed in rose gardens around the world. Look at professional and home gardens today, and you will see all kinds of plants mixed into rose gardens as well as the reverse—roses integrated into border gardens or terraced plots. The use of companion plants can run from something as simple as growing an annual ground cover like alyssum to keep the rose roots cool to something as complicated as growing an English perennial border filled with roses and interspersed with dozens of exotic annual and perennial plant species.

You might have read that roses don't like to have anything planted

Exclamation points of spiky foxglove and yucca lift the eye and give a vertical effect to a mixed border planted with 'Shower of Gold,' a Rambler from 1910.

around their roots, but in fact, roses thrive in mixed plantings. As gardeners rediscover the beauty of a rose garden planted with more than roses and dirt, an exciting challenge comes in selecting colors, foliage textures, and plant shapes that harmonize and complement one another. A healthy mixed border of roses and companion plants will also deter weeds, thus eliminating the backbreaking task of hand-weeding the beds.

Let your imagination be your guide. Learn about the more exotic annuals and tempting perennials on the market; find out if they'll work in your climate zone, and then in your particular garden setup. Try color combinations that

please you even if no one else seems impressed.

Experiment—you can always move a plant to a new site if it doesn't work in that particular spot. Add tall, spiky plants such as delphinium, lily, foxglove, lupin, veronica, iris, and salvia as exclamation points. Mix in exotic grasses and plants with grasslike foliage, such as daylilies, agapanthus, kniphofia, and dianthus, to cover up the bare lower stems of certain roses. Use the soft gray leaves of lamb's ears or silver-leaved dusty miller to accent a dark corner. Plant low-growing borders of thyme, basil, oregano, and chives—just don't use any chemicals if you plan to harvest and use the herbs.

A mixed planting of annuals and perennials extends the flowering season of a bed of once-blooming roses, providing color and fragrance well into the summer.

Plants such as marigolds and herbs such as chives are often mentioned as having properties that are repellent to aphids and other bugs. So far they've not been effective for me, but it is entirely possible they may work for others—and they are attractive and certainly do no harm. The chives can be harvested for your next baked potato as long as you don't use insecticides, but then, if you're using plants to deter bugs, you're probably not using insecticides anyway.

Many gardens can benefit from some thought to variations in height. Layering ground covers with low-growing plants, and sitting shorter roses in front of taller or supported roses in the back of a bed, can add new excitement to your space, lifting the eye and giving new depth and magnitude

to an otherwise rather two-dimensional space.

To help prevent and eliminate weeds, plant a ground cover of lemon-scented thyme. Not only will the thyme spread out, covering the soil, but the fragrant, citrusy foliage will perfume the garden as you move about the beds, dead-heading and grooming. Annual plants such as alyssum will self-seed, creating a natural growing mulch, preventing weeds, and keeping the roots of the roses cool and moist for longer periods between waterings.

The colorful flowers and foliage of companion plants will extend the flowering season of a bed of once-blooming Old Roses, stretching the display on into the summer, and with luck, even into fall. Nothing inspires the eye and senses as does a well-conceived bedding of roses and companion plants. The pastels, pinks, and blues of spring blend into the hotter reds, oranges, purples, and yellows of summer, contrasting with your roses and extending the beauty of color and fragrance well past rose season.

MULCHING AND WEEDING

All roses will benefit from a generous layer of organic compost spread 2 to 3 inches deep over the roots and bed. A mulch will help conserve precious moisture in the soil during dry spells as well act as a deterrent against weeds.

I personally prefer an organic compost over an inorganic mulch because as the organic amendments break down, they contribute humus and natural acids to the soil, helping to replenish lost nutrients. That's not to say that inorganic mulches, such as lava rock or scoria, arc not useful. They need not be replaced as frequently as the organic mulches, which must be replenished yearly. But I like the rich, organic look of a black humusy mulch. You will impress both your gardening and non-gardening friends with your horticultural skills and wonderfully dark soil when you have a deep layer of black compost spread over the garden.

It is very easy to make your own garden compost mulch. If you aren't doing this already, you should make a point of adding it to your garden regimen. Simply find an unused corner of your yard and begin making a processing mound. If you want to make a little investment, there are many types of compost bins available at garden centers and in most gardening mail-order catalogs. When you've set up your spot or bin, begin saving things you've been discarding—like grass clippings from the lawn, leaves and small twigs from the trees, kitchen scraps like banana peels and citrus rinds, pet fur, and any other organic detritus—and pile it into your mound. Add a handful of garden fertilizer, preferably one with at least 10 percent nitrogen, and add water.

It's then important to do two things. Regularly check your compost to ensure that it's moist but not dripping wet, and turn the pile with a pitchfork or other implement once or twice per week. In around four to six weeks, you'll have a regular supply of usable compost with which to make your

garden plants very happy. Grass clippings are high in nitrogen and can be spread around the garden uncomposted, but I prefer to mix my grass clippings into the compost pile, reducing their biomass and breaking them down before spreading them over the beds.

Don't worry about flies or smell. A well-maintained compost mound will generate enough heat to kill any pests and weed seeds while breaking down into a rich, loamy, usable compost. Some types of insects will inhabit the outer reaches of the pile and will aid in the decomposition. Once this processing plant gets started, a natural oven develops at about 160° Fahrenheit, which fuels the breakdown of the various components.

The best part of composting is that while you're creating a ready supply of soil amendment for your gardening needs, you're also manufacturing a natural recycling center in your own yard, which will reduce the amount of waste you'll have to cart to the curb each week. If every home used a compost pile, just think how significantly we'd be able to decrease the tonnage of waste matter being dumped into landfills every day. It's the wave of the future as well as a legacy of the past.

If you aren't disposed to creating your own compost, there are proprietary products on the market for you. In many regions you can even order compost in bulk, by the truckload. Region to region, organic mulches such as pine needles, rice hulls, cocoa hulls and commercial mushroom composts are readily available for a price.

I am often asked about using

steer manure for either feeding the garden or mulching. As a low-nitrogen mulch or top dressing, steer manure is fine as long as it has been well composted by the supplier, but it's essential that as much sodium as possible has been removed. Feed cattle are given a lot of salt to encourage water retention, creating more and juicier meat, and thus a higher price. That salt can be concentrated in the manure and if you garden in a region, as I do, where sodium buildup in the soil is a problem, steer manure is not recommended.

Other animal manures can be useful alternatives; just make sure that you get as much information about the chemical makeup as you can. For example, you'd want to apply chicken manure very sparingly as it is very hot, having a high nitrogen content, and can burn easily. Many people with access to horse manure swear by it, noting the weed-free nature of the product and its beneficial effect on their roses.

If you define a weed, as some folks do, as any plant that grows where it isn't wanted, then just about anything can be considered a weed. Weeds drink up precious moisture and nutrients from the garden, and can be a host to undesirable pests and diseases. Most fungal pests such as rust, mildew, and blackspot require a secondary host, often a weedy patch near the garden, in which to complete their life cycle. Eliminating these weeds will go a long way in preventing the spread of funguses in your garden.

Weeds can be prevented by using that 2- to 3-inch mulch I mentioned, with either the organic or inorganic compost. Currently, there are also woven, fabriclike products that allow air and water to move into the soil but prevent soil-based weed seeds from germinating. These garden fabrics have the added benefit over black plastic that they last longer and are much more aesthetically pleasing to the eye. Simply cut the fabric to fit the bed, secure it to the ground, and cover with mulch.

There are numerous chemical products that will kill existing weeds or act to prevent specific weed seeds from germinating. I try to avoid these unless absolutely necessary—many chemical herbicides can be exceedingly toxic to roses. If you must, though, use such products with care, following all label instructions and taking care to keep any chemicals off yourself and desirable plants. Chemical pre-emergent weed controls may have their place in a well-thought-out garden management plan, but their use must be timed and understood well in advance of your need for them. Caution must also be exercised with many of the current contact weed killers on the market. Many of them are extremely toxic to roses and their use in or even *near* the rose garden should be carefully monitored.

PRUNING

For the most part, pruning is the same for all classes of roses. A few of the Old Roses, however, have specific requirements that differ from their more modern cousins.

All once-blooming roses are pruned soon after they finish flowering in early summer. This is the best time to prune them, removing

'*Park Wilhelmshöhe,' a modern Gallica introduced in 1987, continues the long tradition of this beautiful and cold-hardy class of Old Roses.*

about one-third to one-half of the year's growth. Tip back flowering shoots to four or six bud eyes, and remove any dieback.

Damask Roses are the most likely to suffer dieback when their foundation canes are pruned. Avoid cutting into such a major cane on these roses. If you need to prune a Damask, prune the cane back to its base, either at a juncture with another cane or down to the bud union itself.

The remontant Old Roses may be pruned just as you would Hybrid Teas and Floribundas. Pruning time will differ from region to region, with the best time usually being after the last frost, just before or at the point when new growth starts. In my mild winter climate, I start pruning in early January and finish no later than mid February. In many regions of the country, you may be pruning in May. Check to see when local gardens and retail nurseries offer pruning demonstrations to find out the appropriate time to commence pruning.

I prefer being rather light with the pruners. I believe it is unnecessary to prune more than one-third to one-half of the last year's growth. A plant that grows to 8 feet in height and is cut back to 2 feet at pruning time will spend most of its energy growing back to its previous size of 8 feet and thus will not produce nearly as many flowers. The rule of thumb usually tossed about is that a moderate pruning will produce more but slightly smaller flowers, while a hard pruning will produce fewer but larger flowers.

Remember that pruning roses need not be a religious experience—it's simply a necessary step in the care of these plants, nothing more. A few basic rules and facts will guide you through this less-than-mysterious process. Use sharp, scissor-action pruners; in other words, pruners having blades that cross edges to cut. I don't recommend the blade-and-anvil type pruners as they tend to crush the stem as they cut and often damage growth buds, causing dieback.

Make certain you keep your pruners clean, sharp, and well-oiled. A pair of long-handled loppers will give you more leverage for cutting larger canes, and as your roses mature, you'll probably want to get a small, folding pruner's saw. This great little tool will work on any canes that have become too large even for loppers, and they'll allow you to work in tight spaces where maneuvering loppers would be cumbersome or even impossible.

I start by pulling any dead leaves and detritus from around the base of the bush, so that I can see the whole plant and determine where things stand. I then remove deadwood, making a point of giving some clearance to the central hub of the bush. Use hand pruners for small branches, and the loppers or saw for the thicker canes.

Next, I remove any canes that cross through the center of the shrub or that rub against one another. This is vital, both to open

up the center of the plant to air and light, and to remove any potential source of infection produced by the canes' rubbing away their protective outer sheaths. Some large shrubs tend to be more dome-shaped, and thus it would not be possible to open them up as you would a more compact shrub.

Finally, I prune back all growth to about one-third (or in some cases one-half) of the total growth. Prune to just above a bud-eye facing in the desired direction for that cane. The bud-eye is the point just above where a leaf joined the stem. At that junction, you should be able to see a small, lighter-colored growth (bud-eye) from which the new shoot will emanate. You'll normally want to prune to outward-growing buds as you generally want the new cane to grow away from the center of the plant. Remember, the direction in which the bud-eye faces is the direction in which the cane will grow. On some larger or older canes it may not be possible to see a bud-eye. In that case simply prune where you think might be best, check back after new growth has begun, and prune back to just above that actively growing shoot. The trick is to eliminate all dead stubs at the tips of branches or new canes, as these invariably lead to dieback.

I leave as many healthy, vigorous growing canes as I feel the shrub can support, remembering that I will need sufficient room to be able to work around the roses for weeding and deadheading through the coming months. To help the shrub renew itself, you can remove one old cane (over three years old) for each new cane produced. The optimum flowering life of a rose cane is around three years, so replacing old canes with new helps rejuvenate the shrub, promoting new growth and better flower production.

Once you have finished pruning, remove any leaves remaining on the shrubs. You'll find that there are few leaves left at this point, but their removal will spur the bush to go fully dormant. Rake up all the detritus from under the roses and clean up the beds. As noted, this material is a potential source of infection, and you can put it into your compost pile because the heat generated will kill off most any problem agents.

In regions where stem borers are active, you will want to seal all cuts larger than the diameter of a pencil. Stem borers are small insects that deposit their eggs on the ends of newly cut canes; their larvae then bore down into the pith, killing the cane in which they reside. You'll see stem borer activity as small holes at the ends of freshly cut canes. Sealing canes with either white glue or a non-toxic compound formulated for roses will prevent infestation. I find that Elmer's glue does the trick, and its opening is just right for dotting the tips of cut canes. Don't use tar or petroleum-based products to seal rose canes as this will also cause dieback. Water-based white glue works just fine, and it evens dries clear.

After pruning, cleaning up, and sealing the canes, you may want to use a dormant spray to help control any over-wintering pests, either bugs or fungus. Nurseries sell dormant sprays in one of two forms: either lime-sulphur, known as "Bordeaux spray," or oil-and-copper, often simply called "dormant spray." Either will do the job sufficiently. Dormant sprays should be applied twice within the two weeks immediately following the completion of your pruning. These sprays help to lessen any subsequent reinfestation of pests or disease. This is not to say you won't see bugs or fungal problems in spring, but they should be less prominent and not start quite so early.

FERTILIZING

Feeding Old Roses isn't much different from feeding any other rose. Before deciding on a fertilizing regimen, it's important to do a simple soil test, which will define your garden's needs. Basic do-it-yourself test kits can be bought at a nursery, or you can pay a service

Cascading out of tall trees, the exquisite creamy white flowers of 'Mme. Alfred Carrière' reflect the late afternoon glow like a festive display of Chinese lanterns.

a fee to test the soil for you.

Nitrogen (the symbol N on the Periodic Table), phosphorus (P), and potassium (K) are the three macro-elements all plants need in relatively large amounts in order to maintain healthy growth. By law, fertilizer packages must list these three ingredients as their percentage of product weight. As an example, a 100-pound bag with a listed NPK of 10-10-10 would contain 10 pounds each of nitrogen, phosphorus, and potassium. The other 70 pounds in the bag comprise filler and inert ingredients.

Nitrogen is listed first because plants tend to use more of this element, which encourages growth and green foliage. Roses demand a great deal of nitrogen, and most rose foods contain at least 10 percent nitrogen by weight. As it makes for very happy roses, I look for a product with a bit more nitrogen, say around 15 percent or so. It's well worth spending a few minutes reading fertilizer labels at the garden center to find a product that meets your plants' needs.

Once-blooming Old Roses aren't as demanding as are remontant roses with their fertilizing needs. Usually a good feeding in early spring, just before bloom, will be enough for them. Remontant roses will appreciate regular feedings between bloom cycles to help flower production along. I recommend two feedings of a dry fertilizer, the first just before bloom and the second in midsummer. I supplement the dry fertilizer with a liquid or spray-on fertilizer between applications of the dry type, usually at six-week intervals.

Personally, I prefer timed-release fertilizers as these products continually feed your roses over three to four months, releasing their nutrients at a slow, predetermined rate governed by temperature and moisture. When using timed-release products, just be sure that they are well-incorporated into the soil or covered by mulch so that they will be able to react with your watering and the natural chemical makeup of your soil.

Many gardeners prefer to use organic fertilizers over chemical, and the two camps have vociferous proponents. Organic fertilizers last longer, in part because it takes longer for subterranean organisms to break them down into their useful components. Consequently, it takes longer before your roses can absorb their nutrients. Chemical fertilizers, on the other hand, break down much more rapidly but they have a tendency to burn more easily and can also be harmful to those same soil organisms. A well-planned feeding regimen is the key: take your pick or make the most of both, using earlier deposits of organic amendments and carefully incremented applications of chemical products.

I'm frequently asked what to do when yellow leaves appear on rose bushes. Often the cause of yellowing leaves is not a lack of nitrogen but of iron. Iron is a key ingredient of chlorophyll, the component that makes leaves green. Heavy clay or alkaline soils bind up the available iron and prevent it from being absorbed by the roots. This condition, called chlorosis, can be corrected by the application of a chelated iron product.

Most soils in nature contain enough iron, but occasionally the iron is not "digestible." An application of chelated iron will correct the situation.

I have emphasized the need for a soil test because I have long been aware that we Americans apply far too much nitrogen in our gardens. True, roses do need healthy doses of this ingredient for good growth, but too much will promote soft, succulent growth that is extremely prone to attacks by fungal diseases and insects. The real challenge is finding that all-important balance between too much and not enough. That's where your best judgment and day-to-day experience in your own garden will come in handy. I'm often able to get my garden through an entire season with just one or two applications of timed-release fertilizer, and the roses continue to thrive and bloom.

TRAINING

Many Old Roses, although not true climbers, can end up growing a bit large for our smaller modern gardens, particularly in more temperate zones. This is where research comes in handy: know how large the cultivars you are considering will grow *before* purchasing and planting them. If, however, you have your heart set on a rose you can't possibly live without, there are a number of things you can do to help it fit into your garden space.

Pruning will help control a shrub to a certain extent, but as I mentioned, an inappropriately large shrub will still grow too large before it blooms, no matter how hard you've pruned it. Training that rose shrub is a much simpler

alternative, and one that will make you and your roses very happy in the end. A shrub trained onto or over a structure is one way of taking advantage of a rose's natural habit without resorting to drastic pruning, and you'll be enchanted by the lovely seasonal cascade of color and fragrance.

A large Old Rose bush can sometimes grow to 8 feet tall by 8 feet in width—which means it's covering some 64 square feet of ground in your garden. That same shrub can be maintained at a more desirable size of 4 feet, or a total of 16 square feet, by a simple technique called self-pegging. To self-peg, all you need are a pair of gloves, pruners, some plastic tie tape (otherwise known as green garden tape), and occasionally, a second pair of gloved hands to help you out with the larger canes.

Prune the shrub as you normally would in spring, removing dead canes and thinning out excess growth, but leave a number of tall canes unpruned. Bend one of the long arching canes back on itself, tying it with the garden tape onto itself or another branch of the same shrub. Continue working around the shrub, bending and tying, until all the long canes are tied in this manner.

Self-pegging takes advantage of the rose's natural instinct to bloom all along the arched canes. If allowed to grow vertically, a cane will produce one or two clusters of flowers at the tip of the cane only. By arching the cane so that the growing tip is *below* the level of the rest of the cane, you trap the hormones the plant produces in the growing tip, which normally prevent flowers from forming lower down on the cane. The hormones are trapped in the tip by nothing more than gravity, and thus every bud-eye along the self-pegged stem will break and form a flowering shoot. Instead of one cluster of three flowers at the tip, a self-pegged cane will give you twenty to thirty flowering shoots. It's well worth the effort.

Arches, catenaries, trellises, and pergolas are commonly utilized in classic garden designs to give a sense of depth and height to a garden. Climbing roses can then be trained up and over these structures to provide a shady walk or garden entrance.

Simple structures for training roses can be built out of concrete reinforcement bars, otherwise known as rebar. Rebar comes in a number of thicknesses, and your local building supply store will cut it to the lengths you need. I construct arches out of rebar, anchoring the ends in short lengths of galvanized pipe. As the roses grow, they mask the structural components, filling in the space with lush vegetation. You can build a substantial arch using two or three pieces of rebar, tying them together with garden tape or wire. I also find that building tepees or tripods out of three lengths of rebar, wiring the top together, and training tall growing Old Roses around the structure is a great way to control their size and produce maximum bloom while creating a unique look in the bed. One of the nice things about rebar is that it will eventually rust to a nice patina, which will blend into the garden so that it becomes even less visible.

DEADHEADING

Deadheading is the simple act of removing spent blooms to tidy up the bush and encourage more bloom. Remontant roses will not form new flowers once hips and seed are formed.

Deadheading also allows gardeners to spend some time examining each rose bush up close, to see if any problems or infections are manifesting themselves. When deadheading, remember: caution and complete attention to the work at hand are key. Be aware of where your hands are at all times. If you are right-handed, hold your pruners in that hand, and with your left hand grasp the dead flower, making sure you clearly see where it is before making any cuts. More than one fingertip has been lost or nearly so because its owner forgot how sharp a good pair of pruners can be.

Roses have compound foliage, meaning that the complete leaf comprises multiple leaflets. Nearest the tips of a cane, you'll find mostly three-leaflet foliage. Look a little farther down the stem to be deadheaded for the first or second five-leaflet compound leaf, and cut just above an outward facing set. Some roses will have seven or more leaflets to a complete set; you can prune to these sets as well. Unlike seasonal pruning, you will want to leave at least two sets of leaves at the base of the flowering shoot to provide energy for more flower production. Additionally, you'll be pruning to outward-growing buds, which will help to properly shape the shrub and discourage inward, or cane-crossing, growth.

*O*ne of the longest flowering of the Old Roses, Rosa multiflora 'Carnea' often continues blooming from late spring well into midsummer—as it is doing in this picture along the Huntington Rose Garden's Arbor Walk.

Many rose gardeners deadhead every day, choosing to use the time for observing how their garden is doing and plucking the occasional weed. For many, including myself, this is one of the most pleasant and calming garden chores. Whether you have five or five hundred roses, take the time to enjoy and commune with your flowers. You'll be surprised by how good for the soul this really is.

COLD-HARDINESS

The once-blooming Old Roses—the Gallicas, Damasks, Albas, Rugosas, and of course, most Species Roses—will survive most winters with practically no need for special attention. This is one of the great advantages of the Old Roses over many Modern Roses, which can be quite tender, demanding more substantial attention with regard to their winter survival.

Tea, China, and Noisette Roses are just not suitable for the colder regions. In these areas, plant the smaller shrubs in pots and move them indoors during the coldest months, either into an insulated garage or basement or within the protection of a greenhouse or solar-

Deadheading climbers, like this wonderful 'Crépuscule,' will keep the tall shrubs from forming hips as well as help to extend the bloom and fragrance almost year-round.

ium. In marginal regions, it may be best to mound up tender shrubs with straw or dried leaves, weighting this down with branches of pine or something similar.

The simplest method of cold-protection for roses is to once again plant only those cultivars that you see growing in your community, or those listed as hardy for your climate zone in your favorite catalog. That's the one, foolproof method of ensuring winter survival of your precious plants.

Gardeners in the warmer regions and the dry Southwest are becoming aware of another consideration: the question of whether the roses that interest them are heat-tolerant. Southwestern winters are not cold enough to present a concern, but the summers certainly are very hot. In these areas, it's best to consider how heat-tolerant a cultivar is before planting, or find some way to keep the bushes cool during the height of summer.

INSECT CONTROL

Bugs are a fact of gardening, plain and simple. Plant a beautiful, healthy bedful of your favorite greenery, and something with six legs is going to find it and eat it. Roses are no exception, but like all plants, they have evolved to survive and coexist with creatures that would use them as their latest picnic. So is it really necessary to "nuke" our gardens on a regular basis in order to keep the wee beasties away from our roses? For many gardeners today, the answer is an emphatic and resounding no.

I stopped using insecticides, except in the rarest and most dire of situations, some years back. The idea was to reestablish something of a natural balance in the garden. It was clear that every time we sprayed some poisonous concoction for one pest or infection, we had an explosion of something else that needed an even more toxic solution. After a few years of using the least toxic interventions, I was not surprised to see predatory insects reestablishing themselves in my rose beds, along with a healthy bird population. It became more and more clear that if I were to just let nature run its course, my roses would still be there in the morning. In fact, they'd be ever so much healthier than if I struggled and fought with nature every step of the way.

I use water to knock off aphids and spider mites. What could be easier than that? Only on the rare occasions when that is not enough and the little guys threaten to decimate the entire area do I resort to soap compounds, which usually do the trick without the use of harsh toxins. I turn to toxic chemicals only as a last-ditch effort, and in truth, I haven't used one now for at least five years. Even then, I'm very strict, limiting their use to specific plants—*never* using them as a general garden prophylactic. What kills a bad bug will harm a good one as well, and may even kill some other beneficial animals or at least scare them out of my garden altogether.

No natural system will be bug free, so you'll have to learn to live with your garden's residents. It's really just a matter of learning to trust the natural way of things: if pests arrive, solutions won't be far behind in most circumstances. So how many aphids can you tolerate before making a mad dash for a toxic chemical? The answer lies with you and your ability to teach yourself an environmentally friendly way of looking at your garden.

First, it will be necessary for you to make some basic decisions about how you plan to use the garden, as well as at what level of tolerance you will be able to maintain a happy medium. Only then will you be ready to begin switching from a chemically dependent gardening regimen to the new strategy, free of chemical addiction.

The first bugs on everybody's list are aphids. *Aphids* is always spelled in the plural for a reason—they're all born female, and pregnant. Aphids, or as the English call them, greenfly, are tiny, soft-shelled insects with sucking mouth parts. They insert their hypodermic-like proboscis into the cellular structure of a rose stem and feed on the sugars produced by the leaves. A large infestation (and they are all large) will weaken the plant as the aphids continue to sap its strength.

Hose off aphids with a strong stream of water. For this you don't need a special hose attachment,

*C*herished for its fragrance and thornless canes, 'Zèphrine Drouhin' will even tolerate some shade and continue its bloom throughout the rose season.

just use your thumb to direct a strong stream of water onto the infested canes and stems. You'd be surprised how many you'll knock off. Then crush or rub off by hand the few that remain. It will be necessary to repeat the water method regularly to get control of this persistent pest.

Aphids are often farmed for their sugar secretions by garden ants. If you see ants moving aphids about, you can be sure that you'll soon have more than one bush with the beasties on them. A simple alternative is to minimize the ant problem: use ant stakes to bring the farmers under control. In my hot, dry region, aphids are only a problem in the cooler spring weather. By the time we heat up in June or July, aphids are no longer a threat.

Spider mites, very small arachnid relatives of our common spiders, are a major pest for some regions. The mites prefer to live on the underside of rose leaves, sapping their strength and destroying foliage all at once. You can identify a spider mite infestation by taking a plain piece of white paper out into the garden. Shake several leaves over the paper in direct sunlight and see if any small, dustlike particles fall off and move about. If they do, you have spider mites.

Here again, water is the best control. With a showerhead-type water wand on the end of your hose, use a strong spray of water to rinse off the underside of infested rose leaves. Repeat every other day for seven to ten days, or until you don't see any more spider mites. If you have a major infestation of this pest and want to resort to a

chemical approach, check with your local nurseryman or county agricultural agent for their recommendations.

Thrips are another of those always-in-the-plural pests. These very small insects live inside the flower buds and open blooms of roses. Thrips are particularly attracted to white and pale-colored flowers. Damage from thrips will show up as brown streaks and tips on freshly opened rose petals.

Since thrips reside inside buds, the only chemical remedies are systemic insecticides. These insecticides are absorbed by either the foliage or the root system, and make the entire plant toxic to whatever is eating it. For many, this is an unacceptably toxic remedy.

You can use one of the less toxic insecticides, like a pyrethrum-based solution, and spray it above the roses on a warm, windless morning. Thrips mate on the wing above the flowers they infest. On calm mornings, spraying the air above will lower the population to acceptable levels.

I am fortunate that we have not experienced Japanese beetles in my area of the country. These large, colorful beetles do major damage to roses in many parts of the U.S. and have, until recently, defied most measures to control them. Pheromone-baited traps will attract and kill male beetles, but as procreation is such a powerful driving force in nature, you may just be putting out a call for every male Japanese beetle within miles. So you'll have to make certain you have plenty of traps before you begin laying them out. Milky spore, or *Bacillus popilliae,* kills beetle larvae in the soil, and will provide some relief from this pest when used over your entire garden—and possibly the neighbors' gardens as well.

Let's face it. From time to time, we're all going to be bothered by any number of pests, from deer to bugs to snails, looking for a free meal—but they're only doing what comes as naturally to them as our own needs to eat and propagate. Learning to expand our limitations, and tempering our need for absolute perfection in the garden, may someday be a matter of life or death for more than just what we consider pests. But no system is perfect; sometimes, it may be necessary to employ some kind of artificial deterrent to save a prized rosebed. Please be circumspect, though, and go for the least toxic alternatives first. And in each case, check with your local nurseryman or county agricultural agent for advice.

Not all rose pests have six legs. For many of our slightly more rural gardeners, deer can be a major problem. Roses are to deer what ice cream is to us—irresistible. The only surefire solution to deer predation on your prize roses is a 12- to 16-foot-high fence. Many products are manufactured and marketed as deer repellents, and some work for a while, but once the deer become familiar with the product, they learn to avoid it. It stops working and the deer are back foraging on your roses. The best advice I have heard, after the high fence idea, is to keep changing repellents so that the deer don't become familiar with any one product.

DISEASE CONTROL

I can't think of any subject that turns off more people from growing roses than the concept of disease control. Ask just about anyone and you will hear that roses are difficult plants that require copious amounts of toxic sprays to keep mildew and other infections at bay.

It is true that many roses will be affected by problems over the course of a year, but if you learn about your home region, or climate zone, you'll find there are good, healthy roses that will grow with robust fervor and thrive easily with little intervention.

One does read from time to time that Old Roses are the perfect garden choice because they are so disease-free. My personal experience is that, although many Old Roses are easy to grow and relatively resistant to disease problems, there are many that are not so carefree. Old Roses *are* survivors, overcoming problems and enduring over decades and centuries, but to say that they are *never* affected by garden problems is simply not true.

My approach to disease control is quite straightforward and is identical to that for pest control. I can live with a certain amount of disease. I prefer to emphasize good horticultural practices. A well-grown, healthy rose shrub will be much more likely to shrug off a problem on its own and continue flowering with little to no interference from me. Attention to proper planting, spacing, fertilizing, irrigation, and selection will produce plants that are more naturally resistant to disease. I recommend that you rinse off rose foliage from

The pink-flowered 'Marie Louise' and the white 'Albéric Barbier' intermingle over and through a rustic fence, overpowering garden visitors with their magnificent joint display of bloom and fragrance.

time to time to clean off any pollution and dirt, making certain your bushes have a chance to dry completely before nightfall. This will go a long way in keeping your roses healthy and strong enough to fight off infestations.

When speaking of rose diseases, the big three we all seem to face are powdery mildew (mildew for short), blackspot, and rust. All three are caused by fungi and spread through the air by wind. And all have rather specific climatic and environmental needs before they become a problem infestation. Knowing what triggers these diseases will help you develop a control strategy.

The disease you hear most about is mildew. Mildew manifests itself as a white, powdery growth on the surface of the foliage and stems of roses. It is more of a problem in the early spring when conditions are prime for its rapid

growth. In the South and Midwest, where humidity is the order of the summertime day, mildew seems an ongoing assailant. Daytime temperatures need to be warm but not too hot, and nighttime conditions need to be cool and moist. In my Southwestern garden, mildew is a problem in spring right up to the onset of our hot weather around the Fourth of July, and then is not a problem again until the days and evenings start to cool around mid autumn.

Mildew saps the strength from the plants and disfigures flowers, but it is not deadly. Cleansing rose foliage with water is a good place to start the cure. This action will help to rinse off dirt and pollution, which make a haven for mildew; and as long as it is done early enough so that the foliage has a chance to dry before nightfall, it will go a long way toward keeping your plants healthy. But when conditions are ripe and you have planted susceptible cultivars, mildew will make a home in your roses.

Blackspot is a more serious threat to your roses than mildew. Blackspot manifests itself as dark, round blotches on the foliage. Though small at first, these blotches will expand and join up, eventually killing the infected foliage. A heavy infestation will defoliate the bush and eventually weaken or even kill the shrub. Blackspot is most acute in hot, humid weather. Regions of the country with summer rain and warm, humid weather are most likely to have severe problems with blackspot.

The first line of defense against blackspot is to plant blackspot-resistant roses. This will require some research on your part, and even some experimentation to identify the healthiest cultivars for your particular needs and region of the country, but it is all well worth the trouble.

Rust manifests itself as reddish pustules on the underside of rose foliage. These pustules will, in the most serious infestations, turn black. Rust is usually a problem in cool, moist weather, and is also attracted to certain rose cultivars that seem to have no resistance to it whatsoever. In the dry West, rust is a problem mostly in the fall when the day temperatures are still warm and the evenings have cooled, and there is some natural moisture in the air.

To control rust, it is important to plant only rust-resistant cultivars. Once rust has attacked, try picking off infected foliage and discarding the leaves in the compost pile. As with all fungal diseases, it is best to keep the foliage dry. Water the garden early in the day so that the foliage has a chance to dry off before evening.

BIOCOMPATIBLE FUNGICIDES

The latest in disease control for rose problems is the development of new biocompatible fungicides. Biocompatible means that the product is essentially non-toxic and breaks down into its component parts quickly and naturally in the environment. Biocompatible products take advantage of a weakness in the life cycle of the pathogen to defeat it and allow us to have a clean and healthy garden.

Several products contain formulations that include potassium bicarbonate. This potassium salt is combined with a wetting agent and horticultural oil that not only prevents mildew, rust, and blackspot,

A genteel, repeat-flowering Moss Rose, 'Deuil de Paul Fontaine' is susceptible to infestations of powdery mildew and will need some attention to prevent the problem.

but eradicates existing infestations. Currently available fungicides will not eradicate existing problems, but only prevent problems from occurring when used regularly before they spring up.

Some gardeners are formulating their own biocompatable fungicide from household items. For each gallon of spray, they mix in one tablespoon each of baking soda, white vinegar, and horticultural oil. If you don't have horticultural oil, you can use canola oil as it will mix with the water. This formulation should not be used when the daytime temperature will exceed 80° Fahrenheit because the oil will burn the foliage. Although not as effective as the potassium-based products, the baking soda remedy will give good control for mildew, blackspot, and rust.

Neem oil, an extract from an Indian tree, has been on the market a few years and seems to give some control for mildew. Neem oil is less toxic than aspirin and has been used for centuries in India to combat insects as well as this fungal problem. Several products that contain neem oil are offered for the home-garden market and are worth consideration if you decide to use a chemical deterrent.

I give a new bush three years to develop before I decide if it's worth retaining. One of the hardest lessons new gardeners have to learn is how to be merciless when it comes to an unhealthy cultivar. If a rose doesn't flower sufficiently or is simply too prone to disease, I prune it with the shovel. Out it goes so that I can then plant a shrub I know, or at least hope, will not have those problems. Like most of us, I have limited space that I want to fill with the best plants and flowers I can. Harden your hearts and follow my example, and you will be much happier gardeners.

For many gardeners today, toxic chemicals are simply not an option—they elect to live with a certain level of problems and maintain their gardens with as low a level of chemical intervention as possible. New products are appearing on the market that focus on less- or non-toxic solutions to disease control. The level of intervention you choose is up to you. Inform yourself as to the choices and alternatives available, and formulate a program with which you are comfortable. Don't depend on the experts to tell you what to do. Remember, it's your garden—and you're the one who'll be living with it.

A KEY *to* *the* FIELD GUIDE

Photographs of all cultivars and species in the Field Guide were taken during the spring and early summer in the gardens of The Huntington Library, Art Collections, and Botanical Gardens, located in San Marino, California; Descanso Gardens, located in La Cañada-Flintridge, California; Heirloom Old Garden Roses, located in St. Paul, Oregon; Heritage Roses of Tanglewood Farms, located in Fort Bragg, California; and Vintage Gardens, located in Sebastopol, California.

Rose species and cultivars are listed alphabetically. The **CULTIVAR NAME** appears as the title, followed by the **CLASS** and **YEAR OF INTRODUCTION** (the year the cultivar was first offered for sale).

HYBRIDIZER lists the name of the person who produced the cultivar.

SUITABILITY indicates just how easy or difficult a cultivar is to grow.

AVAILABILITY lists the best information known regarding consumer access. **WIDE** indicates a rose that should be easy to find, even to finding it at a local garden center; **MAIL-ORDER** cultivars are those listed in a variety of catalogs; and **LIMITED MAIL-ORDER** denotes a rose available through catalogs listed in Appendix A.

STATURE & HABIT indicates the size to which a particular cultivar will grow in both **WARM** and **COOL CLIMATES**.

FRAGRANCE describes the flower's scent.

USES gives a few of the primary applications for each cultivar.

PARENTAGE is listed where that information is available. The female (or seed) parent is always listed first and the male (or pollen) parent is listed second.

DISEASES indicates problems you will most likely face in caring for that cultivar, as it is known to be especially susceptible to those listed.

HARDINESS lists a cultivar's tolerance of both **HOT-** and **COLD-CLIMATE** extremes.

BLOOM lists whether a cultivar flowers only once, in **SPRING,** or is **REMONTANT,** meaning that it blooms repeatedly throughout the season, and sometimes into fall.

ALBA SEMI-PLENA

[*Alba, Ancient*]

Even during the 1820s, easily the pinnacle of their popularity, the Alba rose group never quite attained greatness—there just weren't enough of them to go around, and their color range was limited. Over time, though, they won rose lovers' hearts with their fantastic fragrance and superior garden virtues. Today, they retain pride of place in the Old Rose garden.

'Alba Semi-plena' is a particular delight, having charms to tame the heart of the most rabid rosaphobe. It is also a survivor under adverse conditions. Even shade is no obstacle for this cultivar—I've seen it flowering under an entire canopy of conifers in the Pacific Northwest. Diseases simply roll off the soft gray-green foliage, and the tall canes can create a terrific security barrier.

Semi-plena is a lanky shrub that can reach heights of 6 feet or more while retaining a diameter of around 3 feet; if left to its own roots, it can turn into a lovely, fountainlike thicket of 7 feet or more around. The blue-green canes are endowed with large, sharply curved reddish prickles, and the foliage creates a charming counterpoint to contrasting and deeper greens of other garden life.

Flowers are produced in large clusters from short, somewhat pointed buds that terminate with long, extremely ornamental sepals that slowly peel back, revealing pure white, semi-double blooms with a mass of golden stamens at their centers. Blossoms are powerfully fragrant with effervescent rose and champagne aromas, and the fall crop of scarlet hips effectively extends the interest of this shrub well into winter.

This cultivar is one of the oldest forms of the white rose. It is sometimes listed as a Species Rose and given the Latin designation *Rosa alba semi-plena.* It will sometimes sport to a double form, 'Alba Maxima,' the "Great Double White" that is also called the "Jacobite Rose" from its association with Bonnie Prince Charlie.

HYBRIDIZER: unknown

SUITABILITY: all levels

AVAILABILITY: mail-order

STATURE & HABIT: warm climate, 6' × 5'; cool climate, 7' × 5'

FRAGRANCE: rose attar and champagne

USES: hedge, shade, border, cutting, perfume

PARENTAGE: sport of 'Alba Maxima,' to which it sometimes reverts

DISEASES: clean

HARDINESS: hot climate, good; cold climate, excellent

BLOOM: spring

Alba Semi-plena

ALBÉRIC BARBIER

[*Rambler, 1900*]

Whenever first introduced, the Wichuraiana rambler hybrids created quite a stir; they were among the most cold-tolerant, hardiest climbing roses produced to that point. 'Albéric Barbier' is a true rambler in that its heritage gives it physical characteristics that allow it to spread and rise vertically all on its own, using thin, supple, ropelike canes to scramble over walls or trellises. One often finds this cultivar spilling out of an ancient fruit tree or peeking over the wall of some nearly forgotten secret garden.

Growing out to at least 12 feet wide, this cultivar has been known to reach heights of over 25 feet. The cablelike canes are almost free of prickles but are replete with polished, disease-free, bottle green, lance-shaped foliage. Buttery flowers are produced in small clusters at the end of the garlanded canes. Elegantly pointed buds of bright yellow open to informally shaped flat flowers, which range from a soft yellow on outer petals to more lemony tones in their centers. Blooms breathe a soft fragrance of green apples and fruit as they fade off to pure white with age. The leathery foliage is impervious to most diseases, although from time to time, I have noticed a mild case of blackspot. Most books state that Albéric will produce a second flush of bloom later in the year, but I have to say that in my warm climate, it is strictly a once-blooming rose.

Whether *R. wichuraiana* or *R. luciae* was used in the hybridization of this cultivar is of little importance other than for historical interest, but some think that a *R. luciae* parentage might explain the small amount of repeat-bloom that Albéric presents under certain circumstances.

This rose is named for one of the brothers who hybridized it and managed the family rose firm in Orléans.

HYBRIDIZER: Barbier Brothers, Orléans, France
SUITABILITY: all levels
AVAILABILITY: wide
STATURE & HABIT: warm climate, 20' × 10'; cool climate, 20' × 20'
FRAGRANCE: apples and fruit

USES: climber, trained into trees, partial shade
PARENTAGE: *Rosa wichuraiana* × 'Shirley Hibberd'
DISEASES: blackspot, mildew
HARDINESS: hot climate, good; cold climate, excellent
BLOOM: spring

Albéric Barbier

ALISTER STELLA GRAY

[*Noisette, 1894*]

Sometimes listed as "Golden Rambler," this cultivar is one of the finest of the yellow-flowered climbing Old Roses. It also happens to be one of the first I ever grew. I planted two bushes to cover an entrance arch to a small patio, and Alister proceeded to create a charming and inviting ambiance, never failing to fill whatever niche I've put him in. Although the individual flowers are small, the size of the clusters and bright color make this Tea-Noisette an outstanding addition to the garden.

'Alister Stella Gray' can be defined either as a tall shrub or a low climber, as he will reach 6 to 8 feet in height. The vigorous vertical canes remain more or less upright until they reach their full height, at which time the weight pulls them over, creating a graceful arch. The canes are amply protected by large, sharp prickles. The oval-shaped foliage is shadowy green and stays reasonably free of pests. Flowers are produced in large clusters of dark yellow buds that first open to egg-yolk orange-yellow flowers with darker centers. The sanguine bronze of the new growth makes a nice foil for the generously produced blooms. As the lightly scented flowers age, they lose their dark centers and fade to a soft lemony-yellow, then to a weathered ivory. Repeat bloom is somewhat sporadic as the season progresses, but fall bloom is usually quite good and the clusters of buds produced are even larger than the spring flush. The scent has a base of that earthy, traditional Tea Rose bouquet and then, to my nose, adds a combination of pepper and ginger spice to a fruity undertone. No Noisette Rose is reliably cold-hardy, but Alister is often recommended for marginal regions.

Alister was introduced to the rose world by the English firm of William Paul, and was named for the hybridizer's father.

HYBRIDIZER: Alexander Hill Gray, Bath, England
SUITABILITY: all levels
AVAILABILITY: wide
STATURE & HABIT: warm climate, 15' × 10'; cool climate, 10' × 6'
FRAGRANCE: earthy Tea Rose with pepper

USES: climber, pillar, trained into trees
PARENTAGE: unknown
DISEASES: clean
HARDINESS: hot climate, good; cold climate, tender
BLOOM: remontant

Alister Stella Gray

AMÉLIA

[*Alba, 1823*]

Although thousands of Old Roses are still in existence today, a great many extremely beautiful and useful cultivars remain ignored by or unknown to even the most sophisticated gardeners. Limited availability can often be a factor, as is the case for this charming cultivar. Don't let her dainty feminine blossoms fool you. Like her Alba sisters, 'Amélia' is a survivor, even tolerating an amount of shade that would keep other roses from blooming altogether. Given optimal conditions of sun and water, 'Amélia' will repay your care with armloads of deliciously scented blooms; but even barring the ideal, this winter-hardy beauty will stand up to the challenge and impart her share of joy.

'Amélia' will not grow quite as large as some of the other Albas, reaching a mature height of only around 4 feet, and a spread of 3 feet. Fir green foliage, which is slightly folded along the midrib, covers the grass-green canes. Flowers are produced in small clusters and open to semi-double, bright, clear pink blooms with a boss of bright golden stamens at their centers. This cultivar also has really good disease resistance. The sweet scent 'Amélia' sighs, though historically described as Tea-like, for me retains a slight spicy effervescence along with that rosy odor.

Plant 'Amélia' where her smaller size and gracefully arching branches will spill out over the garden walk. She will come alive when placed where spikes of wild blue indigo or the bell-shaped flowers of campanula are allowed to grow around her base.

'Amélia' is an excellent rose for the novice. Undemanding in her care and easy to excel with, she will repay even the most perfunctory gardener with a heavenly scented garden.

HYBRIDIZER: Jean-Pierre Vibert, Angers, France
SUITABILITY: all levels
AVAILABILITY: limited mail-order
STATURE & HABIT: warm climate, 5' × 4'; cool climate, 4' × 3'
FRAGRANCE: Tea and spice

USES: border, low hedge, hips, cutting, poor soil, shade
PARENTAGE: unknown
DISEASES: clean
HARDINESS: hot climate, good; cold climate, excellent
BLOOM: spring

Amélia

APOTHECARY'S ROSE

[*Gallica, 1310*]

The truly ancient 'Apothecary's Rose' masquerades under a plethora of synonyms. *Rosa gallica officinalis,* just plain "Officinalis," *R. rubra,* and "Red Rose of Lancaster" are merely the tip of the iceberg as names go. The Latin name *officinalis* was given because this cultivar was heavily utilized for its many medicinal properties. It was also grown in huge quantities in the Provins region (southeast of Paris) for its petals, which were dried, combined with sugar, and made into a conserve.

A typical Gallica, 'Apothecary's Rose' grows around 3 or 4 feet in height and about as wide, although much wider if planted as an own-root shrub. The thin canes carry typical Gallica-like thorns, small and hairlike, mixed with thin but sharp prickles along their entire length right up to the flowers. The soft green foliage is hardly bothered by pest or disease. Flowers are produced on short stems in small clusters at the end of the canes. Buds are textured red, opening to semi-double, loosely petaled flowers in a shade between deep pink and red-purple, with a mass of bright yellow stamens at their centers. The fragrance is sharp and sweet. The nicely compact shrub covers itself with flowers for a number of weeks each spring.

This is one of those Gallica cultivars that seem reluctant to bloom at its best throughout the warmer regions of the country (including my garden), while its striped sport, 'Rosa Mundi,' for some unknown reason has no problem in that respect. In the upper Midwest, however, 'Apothecary's Rose' is very hardy and blooms magnificently, although tending to have problems with mildew during the dog days of summer. In the Pacific Northwest, the shrub is cold- and drought-tolerant, and quite fragrant.

'Apothecary's Rose' is thought to be the rose that Count Thibaut IV (1201–53) brought back from the Seventh Crusade in 1250 and planted at his château in Provins. If it is true that old "Thibaut le Chansonnier" introduced this cultivar into European gardens, then we all should be singing his praises well into the new millennium!

HYBRIDIZER: unknown
SUITABILITY: all levels
AVAILABILITY: wide
STATURE & HABIT: warm climate, 4' × 4'; cool climate, 4' × 4'
FRAGRANCE: sharp sweetness, rose attar

USES: border, container, low hedge, hips, cutting, poor soil, potpourri
PARENTAGE: unknown
DISEASES: mildew
HARDINESS: hot climate, poor; cold climate, good
BLOOM: spring

Apothecary's Rose

AUSTRIAN COPPER

[*Species Hybrid, 1590*]

Early botanists gave this garden rose species rank, and named it *Rosa foetida bicolor.* Its place as a true species is in doubt today, however, because of the low rate of male fertility.

A large, loose-growing shrub, 'Austrian Copper' will grow as tall as 8 feet on its own roots and colonize quite a large area by pushing out runners just below soil level. Canes are ochre-colored with scattered, straight, sharp brown prickles. The seven- to nine-leaflet, compound foliage is a medium shade of green and unfortunately quite prone to blackspot. Flowers are produced in small batches of peaked buds that at first are yellow with streaks of coppery red. As the five-petaled flowers open, the upper sides of the petals take on a shade of bright crimson-orange with the underside retaining a brilliant lemon hue. There is a handsome boss of yellow stamens at the center of these single flowers. The fragrance is sometimes listed as fetid or smelling of rotting meat, but to my senses it is more spicy and fruity with a hint of musk. Occasionally a branch or two will sport back to its parent form, the brilliant canary of 'Austrian Briar.'

'Austrian Copper' is often encountered growing on abandoned homesteads throughout the country. Blackspot aside, this is a tough rose, enduring poor soils, drought, and lack of care, and coming back each spring with shockingly bright flowers.

'Austrian Copper' was probably introduced into European gardens in the 15th century from Turkey through Austria. The Kingdom of Austria was in a perpetual state of war with the Grand Turk through the 15th and 16th centuries, and a number of interesting garden plants, including the tulip, made their way into European life from that contact. Another possible source of introduction may have been through the Moors of Spain into the low country of Holland, but there is less historical evidence for this.

HYBRIDIZER: unknown
SUITABILITY: all levels
AVAILABILITY: wide
STATURE & HABIT: warm
   climate, 5' × 5';
   cool climate, 8' × 6'
FRAGRANCE: sometimes fetid,
   usually spicy and fruity with
   musk

USES: border, partial shade,
   poor soil, cutting
PARENTAGE: sport of 'Austrian
   Briar'
DISEASES: blackspot
HARDINESS: hot climate, good;
   cold climate, excellent
BLOOM: spring

Austrian Copper

AUTUMN DAMASK

[*Damask, Ancient*]

I am often asked, "What is the oldest rose in the garden?" and I think I'd have to answer 'Autumn Damask,' a rose known to the Greek colonists of Italy and listed by Virgil around 30 B.C. as the "Twice-Flowering Rose of Paestum." Paestum was a former Greek colony in southern Italy, which by the time of Virgil was known throughout the empire for the production of cut rose flowers for the Roman market. Quite possibly, Roman rose gardeners (known as rosarians) adapted a heating technique used in the public baths to warm their greenhouses and thus force roses into bloom throughout the year.

'Autumn Damask' is an open, somewhat sprawling bush growing 5 to 8 feet tall as well as wide. The corbeau green canes are covered with red prickles that are curved and vary in size from tiny bristles to quite formidable saber-thorns. The slate green foliage is oval, with the terminal leaflet folded along the midrib and pointed downward. Buds, first showing red and later opening to clear pink double flowers, are produced in medium-size bunches. The petals are so crammed in the flowers that they look like they have been crushed. The strong, sweet, Damask Rose fragrance is fresh and lively, permeating the air. Although listed as remontant, this ancient cultivar will bloom heavily in spring and produce a scattering of flowers throughout the summer, with a final fall flush mostly in the warmer regions of the country.

The French call this rose "Quatre Saisons," or the "Four Seasons Rose"; it's also known by *Rosa damascena semperflorens, Rosa bifera,* and the "Rose of Castille." The parentage of this cultivar is lost to time, but one often reads that 'Autumn Damask' and the once-blooming 'Summer Damask' are from different breeding lines, although the fact that the repeat-blooming 'Autumn Damask' often sports to 'Summer Damask' is apparently ignored by these experts. In fact, the two forms are identical in every way except for their flowering season.

HYBRIDIZER: unknown
SUITABILITY: intermediate
AVAILABILITY: wide
STATURE & HABIT: warm
   climate, 8' × 6';
   cool climate, 5' × 5'
FRAGRANCE: strong Damask

USES: rear of border, hedge,
   pegging, poor soil, cutting
PARENTAGE: unknown
DISEASES: clean
HARDINESS: hot climate, very
   good; cold climate, moderate
BLOOM: intermittent

Autumn Damask

BARON GIROD DE L'AIN

[*Hybrid Perpetual, 1897*]

'Baron Girod de l'Ain' is a sport of the red Hybrid Perpetual Rose 'Eugène Fürst,' which was hybridized by the Belgium firm of Soupert et Notting in 1875. Still grown extensively by lovers of OGRs for his unique flowers, this Baron deserves a central focus in the modern garden.

A vigorous shrub, the Baron produces small clusters of flower at the ends of its upright-growing 4- to 5-foot emerald canes. His prickles are small and ruby-toned. Flowers first open to deeply cupped, brilliant crimson blooms, which are delicately edged with white. It's as if each individual petal is highlighted with a chalk marker so that only the slightest tip of the petal is coated. One writer described this effect as looking like a Flemish carnation. As the fragrant cups continue to open, the outer guard petals reflex back, forming a petticoat effect. The bush repeats its flowering cycle, and the cucumber green foliage remains reasonably free of disease. The fragrance is solidly reminiscent of fine soap.

The Baron's white-tipped blossoms are almost unique among all roses for their display. Strong-growing, healthy red roses are few, and this one's vigor as a garden shrub is why I strongly recommend him. Place the Baron where his crimson red flowers will contrast with a white ground cover of snow-in-summer or the soft gray-green foliage of artemisia 'Silver King.' To get the best out of this fine old cultivar, give the Baron a deep mulching with your finest homemade garden compost or thoroughly rotted manure.

Ain is a department of France, in the east-central region near the Swiss border.

HYBRIDIZER: Reverchon
SUITABILITY: intermediate
AVAILABILITY: wide
STATURE & HABIT: warm
climate, 5' × 5';
cool climate, 4' × 4'
FRAGRANCE: solidly of fine
soaps

USES: border, container,
cutting
PARENTAGE: sport of 'Eugène
Fürst'
DISEASES: mildew, rust
HARDINESS: hot climate, very
good; cold climate, good
BLOOM: remontant

Baron Girod
de l'Ain

BARONNE PRÉVOST

[*Hybrid Perpetual, 1842*]

I n the 19th century, Hybrid Perpetual Roses were king. As many as 4,000 cultivars were introduced between the 1830s and the turn of the century! This presents the lover of OGRs with quite a variety from which to select. The earliest hybrids are far and away superior, and 'Baronne Prévost' is one of the best and most dependable cultivars of the whole class. This rose is often brought to me for identification, having outlived its original gardener and surviving down through the years as a beloved but unknown garden plant.

A vigorous, lofty cultivar, 'Baronne Prévost' will reach 5 or 6 feet with almost an equal spread. The viridian canes are covered with a multitude of red to ochre prickles that extend on out to the flower stalk. The deep green foliage can be bothered with blackspot and mildew from time to time, so be prepared in regions where those problems exist. Flowers are produced right above the foliage, somewhat like a Portland Rose, individually or in small arrays. Long, ornamental sepals peel back to reveal bright vermilion buds that open to clear rosy pink, wonderfully grape-scented double flowers. The fragrance is actually complex—somewhat like a tall bearded iris's version of a grape-juice smell. The repeat of this early Hybrid Perpetual is dependable and regular. Because a number of diseases can present themselves as problems, site the plant so that it receives the most sun and air circulation.

In some regions of the country, such as the Pacific Northwest, the Baronne will be a bit leggy; self-pegging will help keep the shrub under control, as well as increase the amount of bloom produced. It is equally cold-hardy and drought-tolerant in most regions of the country.

The hybridizer, Desprez, named this cultivar for the sister of a friend who was known as a breeder of dahlias. Desprez later sold the Baronne to Pierre Cochet for around 100 francs.

HYBRIDIZER: Desprez, Yèbles, France

SUITABILITY: all levels

AVAILABILITY: wide

STATURE & HABIT: warm climate, 6' × 6'; cool climate, 5' × 4'

FRAGRANCE: fruity, like grape juice

USES: border, hedge, pegging, cutting

PARENTAGE: unknown

DISEASES: blackspot, mildew

HARDINESS: hot climate, good; cold climate, very good

BLOOM: remontant

Baronne Prévost

BELLA DONNA

[*Damask, Before 1848*]

William Paul was the first nurseryman to list this cultivar, which he did in his book *The Rose Garden* in 1848. He gave 'Bella Donna' a very simple description, and that is about all that is known of its origins. Given a chance in the garden, this rose will please even the most jaded rose grower as it requires little but the basics that all roses need: sun, soil, and water.

Moderate-size, almost thornless thin green canes terminate in small clusters of dark, ruddy buds with lovely foliate sepals. The foliage is a pleasing deep matte green with reasonable disease resistance. Blooms are deep pink to lilac pink, very double and flat, with a charming nutmeg and spice essence mixed into the base of Damask Rose attar. Flowers are darker at the center, fading to light pink at the edges, and quartered. The shrub is somewhat lax and arching, so self-pegging is recommended. Like all Damask Roses, 'Bella Donna' resents hard pruning—cutting into the older, larger canes will often result in severe dieback. The best way to prevent dieback is to prune roses from this group lightly in summer, right after flowering has finished, and when it is necessary to prune into a larger cane, remove the entire cane back to the bud union. It will be necessary to give Damask Roses only a light cleanup when you do your spring pruning.

Although only once-flowering, 'Bella Donna' puts all her energy into an awe-inspiring production in spring, literally covering herself with such a bounty of blooms that the canes are pulled over from the substantial weight of the display! Many gardeners shy away from planting once-blooming OGRs, but their magnificent production of flower and fragrance more than pays for their space in the garden.

Little known in this country and absent from British catalogs, 'Bella Donna' is truly a garden gem.

HYBRIDIZER: unknown
SUITABILITY: all levels
AVAILABILITY: limited mail-order
STATURE & HABIT: warm climate, 4' × 4'; cool climate, 3' × 4'
FRAGRANCE: rose attar with nutmeg and spices

USES: border, hedge, pegging, cutting
PARENTAGE: unknown
DISEASES: clean
HARDINESS: hot climate, good; cold climate, very good
BLOOM: spring

Bella Donna

BELLE DE CRÉCY

[Gallica, 1829]

Until the 1840s, Gallica Roses ruled the world of garden roses, far outnumbering all the other classes combined. Easily raised by nurserymen from seed, large numbers of new cultivars were offered for sale by Dutch and French nurseries.

'Belle de Crécy' is unique and one of the most loved of the Gallicas. She is a real stunner when at her best in full spring bloom, but easily overlooked in the border when out of season. A low, mound-forming shrub, this cultivar will reach 4 feet in height and as much across. The thin, parrot green canes will sprawl without some kind of support. The seven-leaflet foliage is darker green, lighter on the reverse, and rather flat in tone; leaves are long and oval in shape. Small pale red prickles, mixed in shape and size, extend all along the canes. Spherical buds open to tones of pink and white. Blossoms display shades of cherry pink often marked and flecked with lighter pink, and as they age, they take on purple and lavender-gray hues with a button-eye gracing the center of each bloom. At full bloom, all the stages of these unbelievably sumptuous flowers are displayed at once. The scent is strong of pepper and fine soap, adding a pleasing kick to the rosy bouquet of your garden.

Plant this beauty with white flowers as a background—no point in being subtle. Mulch well with homemade compost or rotted manure, and water to ensure strong flower production. Prune after flowering to encourage new growth for next year's flowering. Expect some mildew, but not enough to be a major concern.

Crécy is thought to be named for the Château de Crécy near Dreux, France, which was one of Mme. de Pompadour's numerous homes. *Crécy* is also the French word for "carrot," a vegetable first grown as a cultivated crop near a town of that name.

HYBRIDIZER: Roeser, Crécy-en-Brie, France; introduced by Alexandre Hardy, Paris, France

SUITABILITY: all levels

AVAILABILITY: wide

STATURE & HABIT: warm climate, 4' × 4' ; cool climate, 4' × 3'

FRAGRANCE: pepper and rose

USES: border, low hedge, cutting

PARENTAGE: unknown

DISEASES: mildew

HARDINESS: hot climate, good; cold climate, good

BLOOM: spring

Belle de Crécy

BELLE ISIS

[*Gallica, 1845*]

Not quite a typical Gallica, 'Belle Isis' is thought by some to show influences from a Centifolia parent. The shrub is shorter and more floppy than is the norm for Gallicas, and she is also one of the few pale pink French Roses. 'Belle Isis' is one of the OGRs David Austin used in developing his new class of English Roses. His 'Constance Spry' is a daughter of this Belle, and through Constance, Austin produced a great many of his later introductions.

Reaching 3 or 4 feet in height, the lean canes of this rose are weighed over by an exuberance of flowers. Canes are a pale jade green, covered with blushing, hairlike thorns in a mixture of sizes and shapes. The foliage has an absinthe hue, and the serrated leaflets remain small. Buds are produced in small bundles of three to five; the sepals are quite ornate with their leafy fingers girding up the round, rosy buds. Flowers open pale pink, deeper at the centers, and fading to nearly white at the edges of the shallow-cupped blooms; at full flower, they display a pronounced button-eye at their centers. The shrub is reasonably free from pests.

'Belle Isis' emits a light, sweet, almost musky scent very reminiscent of myrrh. Myrrh is the dried, aromatic gum rendered from a woody, stunted-looking tree native to the Arabian Peninsula. Noted in many early writings, it was valued above some precious gems and metals for its ability to dissipate other, less agreeable aromas. Some years ago, a colleague brought back a sample of myrrh she had collected from the wild on a trip to Oman. I was astounded by the similarities to my 'Belle Isis,' although to my nose, the scent of true myrrh is more earthy with heavy undertones of pine.

Isis was the Egyptian goddess of fertility, the wife *and* sister to Osiris.

HYBRIDIZER: Parmentier, Enghein, Belgium
SUITABILITY: all levels
AVAILABILITY: wide
STATURE & HABIT: warm climate, 4' × 4'; cool climate, 4' × 3'
FRAGRANCE: myrrh

USES: border, poor soil, container, cutting
PARENTAGE: unknown
DISEASES: mildew
HARDINESS: hot climate, good; cold climate, good
BLOOM: spring

Belle Isis

BELLE OF PORTUGAL

[*Climber, 1900*]

I n warm and mild regions of the country, one can hardly miss this cultivar scrambling over walls and covering entire houses. In some areas, 'Belle of Portugal' (also listed as 'Belle Portugaise') is so commonplace that she is fondly known as the "Portuguese Hussy."

This is a naturally massive rose, often reaching heights of 20 feet or more. The new growth is a light grassy green, edged with red. The lance-shaped foliage is large and medium green, and the new prickles are small and light red. Large, hooked gray prickles are scattered over the mature canes, buttressing ruby red, elegantly pointed Tea Rose-shaped buds. Flowers are produced individually and in small clusters. They open to large, loose, nodding soft pink to salmon pink flowers. Flower stems are long, and a deep brown color; they're perfect for cutting. As flowers age, the petal form becomes even more loose and informal. Large, pear-shaped soft green hips finish off the picture in fall. The wafting aroma is like an essence of warm sweetbread—very unusual. The scent is often likened to that of a Tea Rose—sharp, spicy, and pervasive. The foliage will suffer occasionally from mildew, but it really isn't something to worry about. Belle is strictly a once-blooming rose, but if she is pruned right after her first bloom in spring, you can entice her into a second crop of flowers right away.

In most parts of the country, 'Belle of Portugal' is considered rather tender, although I have seen her climbing to the third floor and covering a barn in the cool foothills of the California Sierra Nevada. An early California plantsman, Dr. Franchesci-Fenzi, is thought to have imported the first plants of this cultivar into the United States, growing them in his garden in Santa Barbara not long after their introduction in Lisbon.

HYBRIDIZER: Henri Cayeux, Lisbon, Portugal

SUITABILITY: intermediate

AVAILABILITY: mail-order

STATURE & HABIT: warm climate, 20' × 10'; cool climate, 15' × 10'

FRAGRANCE: rosy with hints of warm sweetbread

USES: climber, partial shade, cutting, trained into trees

PARENTAGE: *R. gigantea* × 'Reine Marie Henriette'

DISEASES: mildew

HARDINESS: hot climate, excellent; cold climate, tender

BLOOM: spring

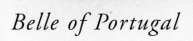

Belle of Portugal

BIZARRE TRIOMPHANT

[Gallica, Before 1790]

For much of the life of this very old cultivar, there was no name for it. In the 1950s, it was listed as 'Charles de Mills,' which is still the most common appellation used in catalogs. Who Charles de Mills was or where the name came from is a complete mystery to rose scholars. Current research indicates that this cultivar first appeared in French catalogs around 1790 under the designation 'Bizarre Triomphant.' Mrs. Catherine Frances Gore, in her *Rose Fancier's Manual* of 1838, also lists several other synonyms: "Rose Ardoisé" (slate-colored rose), "Violette Bronzée," and "Rose Bleue."

'Bizarre Triomphant' is a low-growing, compact shrub, 3 or 4 feet tall and wide. The short, gaunt canes are almost completely devoid of prickles. The wrinkled foliage is deep chalk green, paler on the backside. The petiole, or leaf stalk, is distinctively red in the region of the narrow, leaflike stipules. Exceedingly plump round buds, deep red to black, have a sawed-off look as they start to open. Flowers are fully petaled and quartered, often with a green eye at the center; their color ranges from deep crimson red to purple, with shades of slate purple as the blooms age. The scent, unfortunately, is rather slight of rose, although the foliage is reasonably free of disease; like all the French Roses, this cultivar is extremely winter-hardy.

Although this shrub does exceptionally well in cold regions, you may not see a single flower for two or three years in warmer climes. 'Bizarre Triomphant' is a rose that appreciates—and almost requires—high culture. Mulch is vital to its well-being, so you'll need to provide thoroughly rotted organic compost, and feed and water regularly for the best blossom production. With that care, it is quite hardy and rather carefree. When selecting stock, remember that Gallicas will colonize a large area of the garden if planted as an own-root shrub.

Whether you prefer to call this cultivar 'Bizarre Triomphant' or 'Charles de Mills,' it is a delightful rose well worth its soil.

HYBRIDIZER: unknown
SUITABILITY: all levels
AVAILABILITY: wide
STATURE & HABIT: warm
    climate, 3' × 3';
    cool climate, 4' × 4'
FRAGRANCE: slight rose

USES: border, hedge, cutting
PARENTAGE: unknown
DISEASES: clean
HARDINESS: hot climate, fair;
    cold climate, excellent
BLOOM: spring

Bizarre
Triomphant

BLANC DOUBLE DE COUBERT

[*Hybrid Rugosa, 1892*]

Whether you grow 'Blanc Double de Coubert' for its handsome, disease-resistant foliage or its overpowering fragrance, for the almost continuous crop of blossoms or the fall display of huge oval ruby hips, you will not be disappointed. This Hybrid Rugosa is descended from extremely hardy wild roses that originated in northern Japan, Korea, and Manchuria, where they still colonize large areas along the seashore.

On average, Blanc makes a compact, shrubby mound from 3 to 5 feet tall and almost as wide. The dark green foliage is nicely rugose, with seven to nine compound leaflets, and never bothered by disease. Flowers are produced in small, tight bundles, and the individual buds are longer than wide with lovely, ornamental sepals that extend above the dense buds. Half-open flowers are urn-shaped and often have a blush tint to the white. The open, semi-double blooms are pure milk white, and extremely fragrant of a rose meadow essence. Short inner petals, or petaloids, often curl inward to form a button-eye. Like all Rugosa Roses, this one comes fully armored with strong green prickles right out to the flowering stems.

'Blanc Double de Coubert' will grow and thrive under some extreme conditions—it will even tolerate some shade and thrive in gardens that receive salt spray from the ocean. Additionally, it is rather impartial as to the soil in which it grows. Blanc will continue producing its strongly scented blooms while providing a bumper crop of tomato-red hips. All in all, this is one tough customer.

HYBRIDIZER: Cochet-Cochet, Grisy-Suisnes, France
SUITABILITY: all levels
AVAILABILITY: wide
STATURE & HABIT: warm climate, 2½ ' × 3'; cool climate, 5' × 4'
FRAGRANCE: strong rosy meadow scent

USES: border, hedge, container, shade, cutting, hips
PARENTAGE: *R. rugosa* × 'Sombreuil'
DISEASES: clean
HARDINESS: hot climate, good; cold climate, excellent
BLOOM: remontant

Blanc Double de Coubert

BLANCHEFLEUR

[*Centifolia, 1835*]

This cultivar is sometimes listed as a Damask, but most now place her among the Centifolia (or Cabbage) Roses. A late development among European roses, these Centifolias have no direct connection to the roses that the earlier Roman writers called Centifolia.

'Blanchefleur' is moderately tall and erect, growing to 5 or 6 feet in height and just a bit less in spread. The long, thin canes are masked with small scarlet prickles and soft, deep lime foliage; new growth is celadon green, lighter on the reverse. Flowers are produced in small clusters of vermilion pink buds that open to soft cream-colored blooms tinted with blush pink. They are fully petaled, with a bright green button-eye, and have a shallow, cuplike form. The honey-sweet fragrance is enticing. Foliage can be troubled by mildew from time to time, and the spindly canes can vault over, bending from the full weight of all the flowers along the canes.

Like so many other types of roses, the French like to appropriate this class, calling them "Provence Roses," but it is now thought that the class probably originated in the Netherlands in the 16th or 17th centuries from open-pollinated garden crosses. Bees were still the hybridizers of the day!

'Blanchefleur' and her Centifolia sisters are often overlooked because of their once-blooming habit, but they are hardy in the colder regions and very free with their flowers and fragrance. Place this cultivar at the center of a low border of perennials and grasses, where the curving, flower-laden canes and lovely fragrance can best be appreciated.

HYBRIDIZER: Jean-Pierre
  Vibert, Angers, France
SUITABILITY: all levels
AVAILABILITY: limited mail-
  order
STATURE & HABIT: warm
  climate, 5' × 4';
  cool climate, 6' × 5'
FRAGRANCE: sweet, honeylike

USES: border, hedge, shade
PARENTAGE: unknown
DISEASES: mildew
HARDINESS: hot climate, good;
  cold climate, good
BLOOM: spring

Blanchefleur

BLUSH MOSS

[*Moss, Before 1844*]

This mild-mannered cultivar is seldom grown today. Her gaudier and newer sisters seem to dominate most gardens, but the soft, simple elegance of 'Blush Moss' should not be overlooked. Moss Roses were the roses of the Victorian era—grown in gardens, and pictured on china, fabrics, and wallpaper, they were everywhere. Victorian ladies sipped China tea from cups decorated with Moss Roses and wore hats with huge artificial Moss Roses. If any rose could be said to define an era, then the Mosses were *the* Victorian Rose.

'Blush Moss' is a fairly vigorous shrub, growing to around 4 feet tall and about as wide. The thin canes are fortified with small, hairlike bristles and cardinal red, straight prickles with matte green, elliptical foliage. The small bristlelike growth extends right on out to the flowering stems and covers the calyx and sepals with feathery, lush green growth. The moss-covered sepals pull back to reveal just a hint of pink at first, and later open fully to an abundance of soft blush, passionately fragrant, cupped flowers. The branching canes will, in fact, arch over from the full weight of all the flowers produced. The center petals are of a slightly deeper pink with the outer petals fading off to the palest rose.

Select a site with maximum sun exposure and good air circulation to lessen this cultivar's propensity to mildew, and use sufficient compost or manure to enrich the planting hole.

The soft, velvety growth on the peduncle and sepal is what gives the class its name. This mossy growth is lightly scented with pine-pitch that comes away on your fingers when touched. The flower fragrance is hard to describe, but it reminds me of cool, crisp green apples. 'Blush Moss' can be a wonderful addition of textures, even if she seems to blush in deference to her garden charms.

HYBRIDIZER: Jean-Pierre
  Vibert, Angers, France
SUITABILITY: all levels
AVAILABILITY: limited mail-
  order
STATURE & HABIT: warm
  climate, 4' × 4';
  cool climate, 3' × 3'
FRAGRANCE: cool green apples
  and pine

USES: border, container,
  cutting
PARENTAGE: unknown
DISEASES: mildew
HARDINESS: hot climate, very
  good; cold climate, excellent
BLOOM: remontant

Blush Moss

BLUSH NOISETTE

[*Noisette, 1817*]

This cultivar is a contender for the crown as the very first remontant rose, a trait produced by crossing a once-flowering Old European Rose with a remontant China Rose. It is an American production, created by a rice grower from South Carolina. Around 1800, John Champneys developed 'Blush Noisette' from what is now thought to have been an open-pollinated cross between 'Musk Rose' and the recently introduced (into the United States) 'Old Blush' or "Parsons' Pink China."

'Blush Noisette' is a moderate to tall shrub of 6 feet or more in height and at least that wide. When pruned hard, it makes a nice free-standing bush from 4 to 5 feet tall. New growth is light green, edged with ruby tones, and quite vigorous. Canes are clear emerald green, protected with large, hooked prickles. The shiny, deep jade mature foliage is gracefully lance-shaped, and has very good disease resistance. Small oval buds are produced in huge clusters of up to thirty buds per cluster, and at first are deep pink to red, opening to small blush pink blooms that fade to a bright, clear lilac-pink and finally to almost white as they age. The vigorous canes can be trained as a low climber or pillar rose. The aroma reminds me of both apple blossoms and the crisp, fresh fruit themselves, with spicy, peppery undertones. Spring bloom is produced in smaller clusters, with the fall bloom held in huge tresses of fifty to seventy-five blooms. In cool, wet weather, individual buds may ball, so some protection from mildew may be necessary, especially early in the season. This cultivar flowers from new growth, and needs a much harder pruning than does a shrub that only blooms from old wood.

Although originated by John Champneys, the Noisette class was named for the brothers Noisette, Phillip and Louis. Phillip lived in the United States and sent plants, cuttings, and seeds of Champneys's early productions to Louis, a nurseryman in Paris.

HYBRIDIZER: Louis Noisette, Paris, France
SUITABILITY: all levels
AVAILABILITY: wide
STATURE & HABIT: warm climate, 6' × 8'; cool climate, 7' × 4'
FRAGRANCE: spices, pepper

USES: climber, pegging, partial shade, cutting
PARENTAGE: seedling of 'Champneys' Pink Cluster'
DISEASES: mildew
HARDINESS: hot climate, good; cold climate, tender
BLOOM: remontant

Blush Noisette

CARDINAL DE RICHELIEU

[*Gallica, 1840*]

Deep crimson-purple roses were almost always given ecclesiastical names in the 18th and 19th centuries. 'Cardinal de Richelieu' is classed among the Gallicas but is of hybrid origins, probably with a China Rose as one of his parents. While still once-blooming, this China parent passed on glossy and quite un-Gallica foliage, as well as a fondness for abundant bloom even in the mildest climate zones.

Tall for a Gallica Rose, the Cardinal can reach 5 or 6 feet; the smooth and shiny bottle green foliage is rather atypical for a Gallica. Almost thornless canes are topped by rotund vermilion buds that open to velvety, fragrant blossoms. The color of the flowers can range from pink to red to deep purple, often displaying highlights of lighter shades and even white. The center petals form a dome of lavender-pink tones, and the outer petals reflex in hues of the deepest wine-rich purple with white bases. As the flower ages, all the petals reflex back, and finish in the deepest grape purple colors imaginable. Many Gallica Roses demand a good measure of winter cold to produce a respectable crop of spring bloom, but not so this one. The Cardinal will confer heaps of floral bouquets regardless of the region. For me, the peppery tinge added to the grassy rose scent never gets very strong, but in the Pacific Northwest, this is considered among the most fragrant of roses. The foliage can suffer from a bit of mildew, but on the whole is quite healthy.

Armand-Jean du Plessis, Duc de Richelieu (1585–1642), prelate and statesman, was the powerful chief minister to Louis XIII.

HYBRIDIZER: Jean Laffay, Bellevue-Meudon, France
SUITABILITY: all levels
AVAILABILITY: wide
STATURE & HABIT: warm climate, 6' × 5'; cool climate, 4' × 3'
FRAGRANCE: rose and pepper
USES: border, hedge, pegging, container, cutting
PARENTAGE: unknown
DISEASES: clean
HARDINESS: hot climate, excellent; cold climate, very good
BLOOM: spring

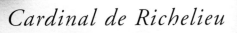

Cardinal de Richelieu

CATHERINE MERMET

[*Tea, 1869*]

One complaint often heard from rose growers is that Tea Roses have weak flower stems, and that the flowers consequently hang their heads. Not so 'Catherine Mermet.' Bolt upright, she displays her flowers on strong, straight stems for all to see and love. If one were to come across Catherine planted among her modern cousins, the Hybrid Teas, one would think her just one of the girls.

This cultivar forms a bushy shrub of 5 feet. The new growth is cordovan, maturing to shiny forest green foliage, which admittedly can have problems with mildew. The new canes are dark sienna red with a scattering of large, hooked red prickles. Flowers are produced individually or in small clusters of three. The buds are long and elegantly pointed, cameo-colored with deeper pink tones to the edges of the petals. The voluptuous flowers open to high-centered blooms of soft lilac-pink with just a hint of yellow at their base; the color will be a bit more intense when she is grown in hotter zones. Fully open flowers will have a rather unkempt, shaggy shape, and the large blossoms suffer in rainy climates, but flowers last well when cut for bouquets. Catherine emits a lovely, almost hygienically clean Tea Rose scent mixed with a bit of spice and fruit.

This is a rose that will appreciate high culture; in marginal areas, site her where she will receive the most warmth. Prune rather lightly, no more than a third of her growth each year. Remember that Tea Roses produce their flowers on rather small wood compared with the Hybrid Teas, and so need to build up their growth slowly over a number of years. Regular deadheading will also encourage this cultivar to bloom more frequently throughout the season.

'Catherine Mermet' was produced by the French firm of Guillot, which has been operated by the same family since 1828.

HYBRIDIZER: Jean-Baptiste Guillot (Fils), Lyons, France

SUITABILITY: all levels

AVAILABILITY: mail-order

STATURE & HABIT: warm climate, 5' × 3'; cool climate, 4' × 3'

FRAGRANCE: clean Tea Rose, a touch of spice and fruit

USES: border, container, cutting

PARENTAGE: unknown

DISEASES: mildew

HARDINESS: hot climate, good; cold climate, tender

BLOOM: remontant

Catherine
Mermet

CÉCILE BRÜNNER

[*Polyantha, 1881*]

I doubt that the widow Ducher, so many years ago, had any idea just what impact her new Polyantha Rose would have on the garden world, but the renaissance of Old Garden Roses today is due in part to the strong following 'Cécile Brünner' has commanded for well over 100 years. Also known as "Mignon" and the "Sweetheart Rose," she is loved for her charming garden ways, her spicy fragrance, and the perfection of her individual blossoms.

Not just another low-growing, compact Polyantha, 'Cécile Brünner' is easily kept to around 3 feet, but if left on her own she will in time reach a substantial 6 feet in height with an equal spread. Polished brownish green canes are defended with intermittent but immense bronze, hooked prickles scattered along the branched stems. The three- to seven-leaflet compound leaves are normally clean, small, oval, and deep olive green; and the foliage is only occasionally bothered by mildew. Flowers are produced in enormous, airy, open corymbs that extend well above the rest of the bush. Bright pink buds are pointed in the classic manner of a miniature Hybrid Tea Rose, opening to fully double, miniature rosettes of exquisite shape and perfume. The pink of the bloom is underlaid with a tinge of yellow, and the beautiful leafy sepals fold back and frame the opening flower. Cécile's gorgeous rebloom is continuous and generous throughout the season, and her wafting fragrance is peppery with a sweet, spicy undertone.

There are several forms of Cécile in the trade, the most common being 'Climbing Cécile Brünner,' which is identical to the bush form in all but size. It will easily reach 20 feet or more in height and width.

This sweetheart was named for the young daughter of Ulrich Brünner, a grower of roses from Lausanne. Her first name rhymes with Lucille.

HYBRIDIZER: Veuve Ducher, Lyons, France
SUITABILITY: all levels
AVAILABILITY: wide
STATURE & HABIT: warm climate, 3' × 3'; cool climate, 2' × 2'
FRAGRANCE: pepper and spice

USES: hedge, cutting, container
PARENTAGE: Polyantha × 'Mme. de Tartas'
DISEASES: clean
HARDINESS: hot climate, good; cold climate, good
BLOOM: remontant

Cécile Brünner

CELESTIAL

[*Alba, 1759*]

'Celestial' or "Céleste," or as Redouté painted it, *R. damascena* 'Aurora,' is one of the most delectable of Old Garden Roses—an embodiment of ephemeral and ageless beauty. It is thought to have originated in Holland, and was by no means common even in Redouté's time.

The tall, shaggy-growing shrub will reach 6 feet in height with an equal spread. New canes are absinthine and well defended with large, ruby red prickles, both hooked and straight. The seven-leaflet, compound foliage is gray-green of an unusually flat tone, sometimes described as lead green. Buds are exquisitely formed, long and tapered, and of a uniform soft pink tint. As the buds unfurl, the petals spool out, creating a tube. Fully open, the blossoms are semi-double, exhibiting a homogeneously clear, clean pink with a darker tint only at their centers. And as the inner petaloids mature, they reveal a fine boss of saffron stamens. The fragrance is of a celestially sweet attar. Although treasured for her delicate bloom, this is a durable rose that should not be pruned too hard, probably by one-third at the most, after she finishes flowering in midsummer.

Alba Roses are cold-hardy, drought resistant, and shade tolerant, so take advantage of these qualities when siting her in your garden. Do give her room, though, to allow the arching, blossom-laden branches to flourish.

In a time of consumer cynicism, convincing a rose grower that a rose is truly "heavenly" can present some challenges. Plant this one; you will be convinced. No other OGR quite evokes her aristocratic charms.

HYBRIDIZER: unknown
SUITABILITY: all levels
AVAILABILITY: wide
STATURE & HABIT: warm climate, 6' × 6'; cool climate, 6' × 4'
FRAGRANCE: very strong, sweet rose attar

USES: border, hedge, partial shade, cutting
PARENTAGE: unknown
DISEASES: clean
HARDINESS: hot climate, good; cold climate, good
BLOOM: spring

Celestial

CELSIANA

[*Damask, 1732*]

'Celsiana' is the archetypal Damask Rose, admired from one end of the country to the other. In Pennsylvania, she is listed as having one of the longest blooming cycles of any Old Rose. She's also known for her pleasing fragrance and her resistance to all diseases but blackspot. In the Pacific Northwest, 'Celsiana' is listed as one of the most drought- and cold-hardy of all OGRs, again possessing a pleasing fragrance with clean, disease-free foliage. What more could one ask from a simple Old Garden Rose?

Not tall for a Damask, this cultivar will reach around 6 feet in height and about as wide. The gray-green foliage is lighter on the reverse, and the long emerald canes are clothed with thorns that range from hairlike, glandular bristles to long, straight red prickles. Her bloom is produced in large clusters of terminally placed buds, which at first are pink to ruby. As the buds unveil, the petals take on shades of soft, silky carnation pink, which fade as the bloom ages to shell tones, ending up almost white. All this is set off by a mass of golden yellow stamens at the center of the flower. The fragrance is strong Damask, sweet and redolent of rose perfume.

'Celsiana' has one of the longest blooming periods of any OGR, often extending her lovely flowers on into midsummer. The weight of the blooms will, in fact, cause the long canes to arch over. Damask Roses are notorious for resenting hard pruning, so it's best to prune this cultivar just after the bloom is finished in early summer. You might plant a wide drift of repeat-blooming, tall bearded irises in shades of yellow and apricot in front of 'Celsiana,' where their tall, grass green, lance-shaped foliage will cover the bare lower canes of the rose.

Not a very old cultivar as Damasks go, 'Celsiana' was named in honor of Jacques-Martin Cels, a horticultural author who first distributed this cultivar to French gardens.

HYBRIDIZER: unknown

SUITABILITY: all levels

AVAILABILITY: wide

STATURE & HABIT: warm climate, 6' × 6'; cool climate, 5' × 4'

FRAGRANCE: strong and sweet Damask Rose perfume

USES: border, hedge, pegging, cutting

PARENTAGE: unknown

DISEASES: clean

HARDINESS: hot climate, good; cold climate, very good

BLOOM: spring

Celsiana

CHESTNUT ROSE

[Species Hybrid, 1814]

Introduced to Europe from Guangzhou, China (previously known as Canton), around 1820, the 'Chestnut Rose' acquired its name from the resemblance of its buds and hips to those of the European horse chestnut. Both are covered with spikes and also resemble a burr. This double-flowered form is no longer listed as a species but is today recognized as a garden hybrid of the true species, *Rosa roxburghii plena*. "Chinquapin Rose" and "Burr Rose" are also names this interesting hybrid has acquired through its garden history.

A vigorous grower, 'Chestnut Rose' can reach upwards of 8 feet. The tanned brown canes are almost unique among roses in that the bark peels off in long ropes, giving this cultivar just one more reason to be included in your collection. The clean, disease-free foliage is a deep hunter green, and individual leaves are composed of from seven to fifteen tiny, compound leaflets, giving the overall plant a pleasingly fernlike look. Placed right below each leaf node are paired, straight red prickles, long and pinlike, often pointing aloft from the canes.

Before opening, the green buds are covered over with sharp, triangular spikes. An unusual feature of the bud is alternating smooth and spiky sepals: one smooth, the next quilled, and so on. Hips mature to large, prickly, highly ornamental orange-red fruit in the fall, extending its appeal late into the year. Of note, however, is that 'Chestnut Rose' is more cold-tender than the single species form. Fragrance is listed as slight—for me that means next to no scent at all.

John Lindley, the English botanist who first described the 'Chestnut Rose' in 1820, had only a Chinese painting of the rose upon which to base his description. The flowers are truly remontant and much less ephemeral than the single-flowered species, so it should be no surprise that the double form predated the single-flowered form in its introduction to European garden cultivation by almost a century.

HYBRIDIZER: unknown
SUITABILITY: all levels
AVAILABILITY: mail-order
STATURE & HABIT: warm
   climate, 6' × 6';
   cool climate, 6' × 5'
FRAGRANCE: slight rosy attar to
   none in warmer climate

USES: border, shade, poor soil,
   bark, hips, fall foliage
PARENTAGE: double-flower form
   of species
DISEASES: clean
HARDINESS: hot climate, good;
   cold climate, tender
BLOOM: remontant

Chestnut Rose

COMMON MOSS

[*Moss, 1696*]

Moss Roses first appeared in France and Holland near the end of the 17th century as sports of Centifolia Roses. Also known as *Rosa centifolia muscosa,* "Old Pink Moss," and "Old Moss," 'Common Moss' was the first of this unusual group. It was unique at the time for its display of soft, velvety growth resembling some woodland mosses. Extending up the flower stem and out onto the sepals of the calyx, the feathery, barklike moss gives off the aroma of pine sap.

This first Moss Rose is an open-growing shrub to 5 feet and a bit wider. The bright, absinthe green canes are outfitted with small reddish prickles that continue right up the flowering stems past the bracts, becoming soft and mosslike on the peduncle and calyx. The holly green, ovoid foliage is somewhat rumpled and dentate along the margins. Upon first opening, clusters of buds are a deep primrose to red, and open completely to very double, shallow-cupped flowers with a small button-eye. The blooms are a uniform shade of bright carnation pink, lighter at the margins and with deeper tones at the base of the petals. The fragrance is strong of Old Rose, and is very sweet.

As with the other Moss Roses, the foliage of this cultivar is susceptible to mildew, as are the buds and flower stems. It's a good idea to take early preventive measures before the problem strikes. But these are charming roses, and the new biocompatible fungicides are wonderfully effective—and safe for both you and the environment. If you give this shrub plenty of room, its pendulous canes can truly display a profusion of bloom. Not crowding will also allow for adequate light and air circulation around the plant, thus eliminating mildew's optimal growing conditions.

Train 'Common Moss' by self-pegging to maximize flower production, and you'll find that with all those garlands of bloom filling the air, there is nothing common about this beauty.

HYBRIDIZER: unknown
SUITABILITY: all levels
AVAILABILITY: wide
STATURE & HABIT: warm climate, 5' × 5'; cool climate, 4' × 4'
FRAGRANCE: strong and sweet of Old Rose

USES: border, cutting
PARENTAGE: sport of Centifolia Rose
DISEASES: mildew
HARDINESS: hot climate, good; cold climate, good
BLOOM: spring

Common Moss

COMTE DE CHAMBORD

[*Portland, 1860*]

'Comte de Chambord' is an impeccable Portland cultivar that is intensely scented with a divine Old Rose fragrance. My experience is that this rose tends to grow rather upright on strong, stiff canes to 4 feet or a bit more. The flowers are held, typically for a Portland, right at the tips of the canes amid a nest of foliage.

Corpulent, erect green canes are covered with a multitude of sharp, curved red prickles. Foliage is shiny emerald green, and quite disease resistant. Flowers are produced in small, tight clusters that sit right above the foliage, which frames the opening flowers like a tussie-mussie. The blooms are at first globular, with peachblossom to lilac tones, opening to a familiar cupped-and-quartered formation. The Comte reblooms almost continuously, sharing his ravishing Damask redolence with his lucky gardener on warm, still mornings. A deep, organic mulch and attention to water will encourage this rose to bloom throughout the season.

Give this treasure of an Old Rose a chance to settle into your garden. It may take three years or so, but the wait is worth it. Blackspot may be a problem in the upper Midwest, so take that into consideration. Site the shrub to the front of the border, where his naturally upright habit of growth among mixed perennials will create an unequaled garden composition. Plant tall oriental lilies around this rose in shades of white and magenta so that their summer flowering will complement one another. A border of savory opal basil would be fantastic skirting the lower canes and, if you refrain from toxic chemicals, will provide your table with delicious pesto all summer long.

HYBRIDIZER: Robert & Moreau, Angers, France
SUITABILITY: all levels
AVAILABILITY: wide
STATURE & HABIT: warm climate, 5' × 3'; cool climate, 3' × 2'
FRAGRANCE: wonderfully strong Damask Rose

USES: border, container, cutting
PARENTAGE: 'Baronne Prévost' × Portland Rose
DISEASES: clean
HARDINESS: hot climate, good; cold climate, good
BLOOM: remontant

Comte de Chambord

COMTESSE DE MURINAIS

[*Moss, 1843*]

Moss Roses are divided into two groups: the true Mosses, derived from Centifolia Roses, which exhibit soft green moss; and the Damask Mosses, with bristly brown hairlike structures. 'Comtesse de Murinais' is one of the Damask-derived Moss Roses. "White Moss," as she is sometimes known, is a high, gangly shrub that, when given the best of care, will require some sort of artificial support for her canes. Like others of her family, the mossy growth of this cultivar is strongly scented with an incense of pine pitch.

The Comtesse will easily reach 6 feet in height and width, sometimes more. Canes are lime-colored, aging to a red-brown, and the plentiful prickles become mossy as they extend up the flower stem onto the ovary and sepals. The foliage is an absinthe green, and like all Moss cultivars will need some thought to mildew prevention, either by placement or by use of one of the biocompatible fungicides. The flowers are produced in large clusters of deep amaranth buds that are covered with bristly, fragrant brownish green moss. As the flowers open, they reveal pale pink petals and age to platinum tones with a pronounced button-eye; the blooms are often quartered at their centers. The shrub is doubly fragrant with the scent of the moss and the lovely perfume of the flowers.

As noted, 'Comtesse de Murinais' will display her bouquets of blossoms to their fullest if helped a bit by a set of supports, such as a tripod or trellis. Curve the long, limber canes over and wrap them around the structure, and this rose will produce flowers at each node along her canes. Self-pegging will achieve the same results.

The historical Comtesse de Murinais would surely be proud of her namesake's beauty, fragrance, and endurance.

HYBRIDIZER: Jean-Pierre Vibert, Angers, France
SUITABILITY: all levels
AVAILABILITY: mail-order
STATURE & HABIT: warm climate, 6' × 6'; cool climate, 6' × 4'
FRAGRANCE: strong of mossy musk and fresh rose

USES: border, hedge, cutting
PARENTAGE: unknown
DISEASES: mildew
HARDINESS: hot climate, good; cold climate, very good
BLOOM: spring

Comtesse de
Murinais

COMTESSE DU CAYLA

[*China, 1902*]

This Comtesse is a true Old Rose in every aspect but two: although hybridized long beforehand, her date of introduction just misses our official cutoff for OGRs; and as far as color is concerned, her flowers are among the most strikingly modern-looking of all Old Roses. Somewhat tall-growing, 'Comtesse du Cayla' has rather large flowers for a China—a characteristic she probably acquired from a Tea Rose parent. This cultivar will build up on old wood to an eventual 4 or 5 feet. It is best to prune only lightly as she, like all Chinas, prefers to bloom on surprisingly small twigs.

New growth is mulberry-colored, and the canes are a livid brown with scattered, hooked prickles of the same color. Foliage is small, shiny, verdant green, and typically China Rose-like. Small sprays of bright red-and-gold buds open to semi-double flowers—a captivating blend of coral and scarlet with hints of yellow and orange. The petals age to salmon orange and carry an entire panoply of fragrance. The zesty aroma begins with a strong tobacco tar odor, then fades a bit with age, leaving the redolence of Tea Rose right to the end. The brilliant coloring of the bloom creates quite a contrast with the almost plum tones of the new growth.

In 'Comtesse du Cayla,' we have a rose that bisects two classes as shamelessly as it does two eras. Officially it stands strong as a China, but in all honesty it could just as easily be classified as a Tea, even as it straddles the line between the Victorian and the Modern Rose archetypes.

HYBRIDIZER: Pierre Guillot, Lyons, France

SUITABILITY: all levels

AVAILABILITY: mail-order

STATURE & HABIT: warm climate, 4' × 4'; cool climate, 3' × 3'

FRAGRANCE: complex, tobacco tar aging to Tea Rose

USES: border, container, cutting

PARENTAGE: unknown

DISEASES: mildew

HARDINESS: hot climate, very good; cold climate, tender

BLOOM: remontant

Comtesse du Cayla

CRÉPUSCULE

[*Noisette, 1904*]

Although almost unknown in the trade, 'Crépuscule' is well worth growing. Given a warm climate in which to flourish, this elegant, delicately flowered Noisette will embellish your garden with its glowing blossoms. I first saw this charmer growing on a fence in New Zealand, and upon returning to the United States, I was able to acquire a plant for my garden. It took some time to find the right spot, but once I realized it was a climber, I placed the shrub in a bower shading a quiet bench. We've both been quite happy ever since.

A short climber or pillar rose, 'Crépuscule' will eventually reach 8 to 12 feet, arching out to 5 or 6 feet in width, sometimes more. New growth is coppery on almost thornless, polished, chalk green canes. Foliage is very clean and pointed, remaining small and aging to a light green as the canes turn brown with age. Small, pointed lemon yellow buds are produced in arrays of threes and fours. The buds offer their surprise when they open to perfectly Tea-shaped, high-centered flowers ranging from yellow-orange to reddish apricot in color, with a feathering of golden yellow at the base of the petals. Every blossom exhales a captivating scent that is best described as having an earthy air, with undertones of lemon and spice and a finish of pepper. The individual blooms are small, only 1½ inches across, and reflex back to reveal a somewhat informal arrangement of petals. The small, round, shiny green hips should be removed regularly to encourage repeat bloom, although the hips will mature to dark reddish brown in the fall if left on the plant.

This is not a cold-hardy cultivar, so when growing it at the lower extremes of the temperate range, plant it in the most protected site in your garden. A warm south- or west-facing wall should suffice. Try under-planting this brightly colored cultivar with grape purple penstemon, or for an even more startling effect, place a bed of deep maroon chocolate cosmos underneath.

'Crépuscule' means "twilight" in French.

HYBRIDIZER: Francis Dubreuil, Lyons, France

SUITABILITY: all levels

AVAILABILITY: wide

STATURE & HABIT: warm climate, 12' × 8'; cool climate, 12' × 5'

FRAGRANCE: earthy, with hints of lemon, spice, and pepper

USES: climber, pillar, trained into trees

PARENTAGE: unknown

DISEASES: clean

HARDINESS: hot climate, very good; cold climate, tender

BLOOM: remontant

Crépuscule

CRESTED MOSS

[*Moss, 1827*]

Most authorities classify 'Crested Moss' among the Centifolias, and there are sufficient precedents for doing so, but for simplicity's sake, I am going to place this cultivar among the Moss lineage. This is yet another beautiful flower that's sometimes had its charms hidden by a plethora of confusing names: *Rosa centifolia cristata,* "Cristata," "Chapeau de Napoléon," "Napoléon's Hat." I particularly love the old name "Chapeau de Napoléon." It's so viscerally evocative—Napoléon astride a horse, wearing his tricorn hat, overlooking the battlefield at Austerlitz, surrounded by the *vieille garde.*

This rose will grow to around 6 feet tall and about the same across, but unless it is given a support structure, it presents a rather floppy sight as the long, thorny canes are quite lax. Ragged somber green foliage clothes the Nile green canes, which are amply fortified with tawny prickles of mixed sizes and shapes. The outstanding feature is the buds: the mossy growth on this unusual cultivar is limited to the tips and edges of the sepals, but it makes up for that with featherlike protuberances so extended and crested that the sepals appear to be much enlarged, enveloping the buds with tiny wings as they first open.

Flowers are produced in small clusters and open to an enchanting clear pink, shaded somewhat darker in the center, and deeply cupped. The fragrance wafting through the air from the blooms is rather strong and grassy, mixed with rose attar and ginger. Foliage can be bothered from time to time with mildew, but is otherwise clean.

Vibert, who introduced this cultivar, claimed to have discovered it growing on the wall of a convent near Fribourg, Switzerland, around 1820.

HYBRIDIZER: Jean-Pierre
  Vibert, Angers, France
SUITABILITY: all levels
AVAILABILITY: wide
STATURE & HABIT: warm
  climate, 6' × 6';
  cool climate, 5' × 4'
FRAGRANCE: grass, attar, ginger

USES: border, pegging, cutting
PARENTAGE: unknown
DISEASES: mildew
HARDINESS: hot climate, good;
  cold climate, very good
BLOOM: spring

Crested Moss

DR. HUEY

[*Climber, 1914*]

'D r. Huey' is included here because it is one of the roses most frequently encountered for identification. The good Doctor was, and still is, used extensively by the U.S. nursery industry as understock—that is, the plant base upon which other rose cultivars are grafted. In spring, his deep ruby flowers can be seen in old gardens and cemeteries all over the country, and every one of these plants is the remnant of some newer, now-long-forgotten rose cultivar that died, leaving only the root stock to continue and flourish. Each spring I am asked to identify a deep maroon Old Rose by numerous growers, and more times than I can count, it ends up being 'Dr. Huey.'

Although you often see it cut to grow as a standard shrub, this is actually a Climbing Rose with canes that can bend out 10 to 12 feet or so. One drawback is that the shiny deep green foliage is exceedingly prone to mildew. The stipules exhibit signs of influence from *Rosa multiflora,* with long, hairlike combs clasping the edges of the leaf stems. The wood is green with few prickles, and the Pompeiian red, semi-double blooms are formed in clusters and open rather flat, displaying white at their base and yellow stamens in the center. The Doctor's fragrance is slight at best, having a weak, acrid tinge, and his flowers will show themselves only in spring. In addition, 'Dr. Huey' is not reliably hardy in the coldest climates of the country.

The hybridizer of 'Dr. Huey,' Captain Thomas, used the OGR 'Grüss an Teplitz' as his pollen parent for this rose. Grüss is descended from the crimson Bourbon Rose 'Gloire des Rosomanes,' our "Ragged Robin," itself a very popular understock. So 'Dr. Huey' does boast a respectable OGR pedigree all on his own.

'Dr. Huey' was named for a well-known Philadelphia rose amateur of the day.

HYBRIDIZER: George C. Thomas Jr., Beverly Hills, California

SUITABILITY: all levels

AVAILABILITY: limited mail-order

STATURE & HABIT: warm climate, 12' × 10'; cool climate, 12' × 8'

FRAGRANCE: slight

USES: climber, hedge

PARENTAGE: 'Ethel' × 'Grüss an Teplitz'

DISEASES: mildew

HARDINESS: hot climate, very good; cold climate, tender

BLOOM: spring

Dr. Huey

DUCHESSE DE BRABANT

[*Tea, 1857*]

'Duchesse de Brabant' was not the first name given to this cultivar. "Comtesse de Labarathe" and "Comtesse Ouwaroff" appear, by the records, to be older, but this popular Tea Rose has been known and grown as 'Duchesse de Brabant' for so long now, both in the trade and in gardens around the world, that 'Duchesse de Brabant' she is and most likely will remain.

Like all Tea Roses, 'Duchesse de Brabant' will take some time to build up growth to her mature stature of around 5 feet or so. Typically for a Tea, growth is small and twiggy, and the elliptical, lustrous absinthe green foliage can be bothered by mildew and blackspot. Canes are dark green to red with scattered hooked, ruddy prickles. Buds are luxurious, produced in small clusters, pointed, and a soft clear carnation. The double, cupped flowers open to clear bright pink to peachy pink, with just a hint of yellow at the base of the petals. The fragrance of the Duchesse in flower is a light combination of apricot mixed with a touch of allspice and rose attar—very delicate and captivating. Flower production is almost continuous, and the freshly opened blooms have a distinct tulip look to them.

The Duchesse is not dependably cold-hardy, and in hot, humid weather blackspot and mildew can be a major problem. For the most part, however, this is a durable rose that will survive most problems and come back strong.

While collecting this rose, I have noticed that there is a wide range in variation of petal count from plant to plant. The double form has long been sold in this country as 'Duchesse de Brabant,' but the form available in other countries is often much less double.

Brabant is now the province of Belgium centered on Brussels, but the old duchy of Brabant included much of what is now Belgium and southern Holland.

HYBRIDIZER: H. B. Bernède, Bordeaux, France

SUITABILITY: intermediate

AVAILABILITY: wide

STATURE & HABIT: warm climate, 5' × 4'; cool climate, 3' × 3'

FRAGRANCE: apricots, with allspice and rose attar

USES: border, cutting, container

PARENTAGE: unknown

DISEASES: mildew, blackspot

HARDINESS: hot climate, very good; cold climate, tender

BLOOM: remontant

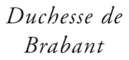

Duchesse de Brabant

DUCHESS OF PORTLAND

[Portland, Circa 1800]

So little is known about this mysterious lady in red. Where did she come from (Italy? France?), and who were her parents ('Autumn Damask'? 'Apothecary's Rose'? 'Slater's Crimson China'?)? What is clear, though, is that she has been around for a long time.

A stocky, dense shrub, the Duchess will grow to around 3 feet high by about the same across. Canes are grass green with a scattering of puce-green prickles. The oval emerald foliage is jagged and relatively free of problems. Deep crimson buds are produced in clusters, and open with single to semi-double flowers having a prominent ring of flaxen stamens at their centers. The scent is characterized as strong Damask, but I find it redolent of just-ripening fruit, like that of earthy pears, mixed with a sweet Old Rose perfume. Flowers are produced through the season, but spring and fall bloom are the most spectacular. As the Duchess does not self-clean, regular deadheading is required to help keep her flowering.

Plant several bushes of this cultivar together, closer than usual (18 to 24 inches on center), to create a perpetually flowering low hedge. The only pruning needed other than to remove old and dead canes would be to use a pair of shears to round off the hedge each spring. This Duchess will appreciate a high degree of care. A deep mulching with organic compost or well-decomposed manure, supplemental feedings with a balanced fertilizer, and regular deep irrigations during dry spells will make her very happy.

It is thought that the particular Duchess this rose is named for was Margaret Bentinck, the second Duchess of Portland. Most likely the shrub was discovered by her in her own garden, or named for her around 1782.

HYBRIDIZER: unknown
SUITABILITY: all levels
AVAILABILITY: wide
STATURE & HABIT: warm climate, 3' × 3'; cool climate 3' × 2'
FRAGRANCE: pear with Old Rose perfume

USES: border, hedge, container, cutting
PARENTAGE: unknown; possibly *R. gallica* × 'Autumn Damask'
DISEASES: mildew, rust
HARDINESS: hot climate, very good; cold climate, good
BLOOM: remontant

Duchess of Portland

EMPRESS JOSÉPHINE

[*Species Hybrid, 1824*]

"Imperatrice Joséphine," as she is known in France, was already an Old Rose when Redouté painted a portrait of her for Joséphine. Probably an old garden form of the Frankfurt Rose (*Rosa × francofurtana*), this cultivar displays influences of both a Gallica Rose and the "Cinnamon Rose" (*Rosa majalis*), but her ancestry is lost in time. Joséphine set the gardening standard for the Empire as a collector of roses and other exotic flowering plants, and her collection at Malmaison was immortalized by Redouté's watercolor portraits in *Les Roses.* Her taste for roses created a trend among the notables at her court to see who could create the most impressive rose gardens.

'Empress Joséphine' grows as a compact shrub, reaching 5 feet in both height and width. The thin, almost wiry green canes are easily bent over from the weight of the flowers when she is in bloom, and are clothed with a light scattering of prickles. The oval foliage is grass green and somewhat crinkled along the veins. The underside of the leaf is covered with tomentose (short and hairlike) gray growth. Squat, peaked buds are produced in clusters and open to barely double, bright India pink flowers, frequently with deeper rosy pink tones throughout, and displaying bright yellow stamens at their centers. The scent is heavy and pervasive of sweet Old Rose attar and potpourri. One of the outstanding features of this cultivar is the large, turban-shaped hips. These fruits are lightly dusted with hairs and turn bright carmine red, generating a spectacular explosion of fall color.

If you want to savor a crop of these hips, refrain from deadheading the Empress. Give her a light cleanup after bloom and thin out the bush, removing dead growth in spring; then leave her be. A low, shrubby plant, she is best placed along a portion of your border where her scent and brightly colored blooms can be reached and appreciated.

HYBRIDIZER: unknown
SUITABILITY: all levels
AVAILABILITY: wide
STATURE & HABIT: warm
   climate, 5½' × 5';
   cool climate, 4' × 3'
FRAGRANCE: sweet attar,
   potpourri

USES: border, hedge, cutting
PARENTAGE: unknown
DISEASES: clean
HARDINESS: hot climate, good;
   cold climate, very good
BLOOM: spring

Empress Joséphine

ENFANT DE FRANCE

[Hybrid Perpetual, 1860]

Although once again an imperial monarchy, France was at its pinnacle as a producer of roses by the mid nineteenth century. French nurserymen had taken Joséphine's lead and expanded rose breeding beyond anything that had come before. The Hybrid Perpetuals were entirely their invention and revolutionized rose growing, and this "Child of France" still proclaims its proud heritage with dignity.

'Enfant de France' is perfect for the contemporary garden, where its compact, upright habit fits our spaces and fills the air with its Old Rose perfume. The shrub attains heights of 4 feet or so by 3 or 4 feet in width, maintaining a nice, neat appearance. Burnt umber canes are covered with numerous red prickles and ovoid, wrinkled, lettuce green foliage. The pink spherical buds are produced either individually or in small clusters. Flowers open to shallow-cupped, somewhat informally shaped, clear shell pink blooms, often with a button-eye at their centers. The flowers have a fragrance of fine soap mixed with pepper and attar, and the bloom repeats well throughout the season. Somewhat subject to mildew, the foliage is reasonably resistant to most other problems.

This cultivar could be placed just as logically among the Portland class, as it shares a number of traits with that group as well. The large shallow-cupped, flat flowers sit right atop the deep grassy foliage, but the height of this cultivar is primarily what places it within the Hybrid Perpetual group.

Some question still exists in the minds of a number of Old Rose historians whether this foundling may or may not be the rose introduced under this name. In the 19th century, records were not all that exact, and often nurserymen reused good commercial names to sell their new productions. But whatever its lineage, this rose is well deserving of a place in your garden.

HYBRIDIZER: Lartay, Bordeaux, France

SUITABILITY: all levels

AVAILABILITY: mail-order

STATURE & HABIT: warm climate, 4' × 4'; cool climate, 3' × 2'

FRAGRANCE: strong Old Rose

USES: border, container, cutting

PARENTAGE: unknown

DISEASES: mildew

HARDINESS: hot climate, good; cold climate, good

BLOOM: remontant

Enfant de France

EUGÈNE DE BEAUHARNAIS

[*Bourbon/China, 1838*]

"Prince Eugène," as he is sometimes called, is a true garden standout. The deep crimson purple blooms and sweet perfume are intoxicating enough, but add to this an almost ceaseless flowering cycle and the simplicity of an undemanding shrub.

'Eugène de Beauharnais' is a compact but upright bush, which will attain a height of 3 feet or so and about the same width. New growth is edged in purple, and the lance-shaped mature foliage is rich emerald green with an amaranthine cast to the underside of the leaflets. Canes are meadow green with a sprinkling of ruddy-hued, curved scimitar prickles. Flowers are borne in snug clusters, with the foliage growing right up to the base of the blooms. They open a deep, rich carmine and darken in the sun to imperial purple, very double, cupped and fragrant blossoms. The repeat bloom is good, but note that this cultivar can be prone to mildew. The centers of the blooms are packed full of short petaloids that reflex back over the stamens. As the flowers mature, there is an occasional lighter streak of crimson, which later blackens in the sun. I find the scent of these blooms to be an enchantingly rich mix of fresh plums and a little bit of peach, mixed with a base of sweet rose potpourri.

Eugène de Beauharnais was the son of Joséphine by her first husband, Vicomte Alexandre de Beauharnais, who was guillotined during the Terror in 1794. Joséphine herself barely escaped the same end, but then her fate took a polar change when she met and then married Napoléon Bonaparte in 1796. In 1804, the two became Emperor and Empress of all France by Napoléon's decree, and in 1806 he adopted her two children, Eugène and Hortense.

HYBRIDIZER: Alexandre Hardy, Paris, France
SUITABILITY: all levels
AVAILABILITY: limited
STATURE & HABIT: warm climate, 3' × 3'; cool climate, 3' × 3'
FRAGRANCE: fruity, rose potpourri

USES: border, container, cutting
PARENTAGE: unknown
DISEASES: clean
HARDINESS: hot climate, very good; cold climate, tender
BLOOM: remontant

Eugène de Beauharnais

EXCELLENZ VON SCHUBERT

[*Polyantha, 1909*]

'Excellenz von Schubert' is a descendant of 'Gloire des Polyantha,' itself a child of 'Crimson Rambler,' a climbing Multiflora hybrid that was very popular around the turn of the century. Excellenz came out of the breeding program of the German hybridizer Peter Lambert and has as its other parent the white Hybrid Perpetual 'Frau Karl Druschki,' a rose for which Lambert is also justly famous. So even though introduced after 1900, you can see 'Excellenz von Schubert' manifests a fine Old Garden Rose pedigree.

Excellenz develops into a tightly growing, compact shrub of about 4 feet tall and 3 feet or so in diameter. The smooth, shamrock green canes brandish only a sporadic prickle or two and are covered with shiny, deep Lincoln green, lance-shaped foliage that is impervious to nearly all comers. Buds are produced in large panicles on taller-growing stems held above the level of the foliage. The buds' diminutive spheres open to deep royal pink to cardinal pompons, which age to vibrant crimson purple. There is not much fragrance, but the repeat bloom is strong and continuous.

Polyantha Roses were quite a novelty in their day, possessing good cold-hardiness combined with an almost ceaseless bloom. They were cherished as well for use as large mass plantings or as low hedges for edging beds. They require only the most perfunctory of prunings—simply remove the old and dead wood, and round off the shrub with hedge trimmers. Enjoy this one—he's a real gem.

HYBRIDIZER: Peter Lambert, Trier, Germany

SUITABILITY: all levels

AVAILABILITY: limited mail-order

STATURE & HABIT: warm climate, 4' × 4'; cool climate, 4' × 3'

FRAGRANCE: light at best

USES: border, low hedge, cutting, container

PARENTAGE: 'Mme. Norbert Levavasseur' × 'Frau Karl Druschki'

DISEASES: clean

HARDINESS: hot climate, good; cold climate, good

BLOOM: remontant

Excellenz von Schubert

FANTIN-LATOUR

[*Centifolia, Date Unknown*]

Although quite an old cultivar, 'Fantin-Latour' demonstrates a hybrid origin with its lustrous foliage. No one is quite sure where this cultivar originated, but its affinity to the Centifolia class is without question.

A loose-growing shrub attaining about 5 feet in height and diameter, Fantin is a bit of a sprawler, enjoying lots of air around the foliage. The smooth green canes, marked with an umber tone, have only a scattering of inconsequential prickles. The oval foliage is cobalt green and lustrous, with a polished oil-soap look. Round carmine buds are produced in small sprays and open to full, deeply cupped pink flowers. The petals are crowded in the center and brandish pale blush edges with deeper primrose tones in the folds. There is often a button-eye at the center of each flower, with just a hint of saffron stamens protruding through. Although smooth and shiny, usually a good indicator of strength, the foliage is somewhat prone to mildew, so precautions should be taken in areas where that problem exists. As the blossoms age, the outer guard petals reflex back, producing a petticoat effect that is altogether beguiling. The fragrance is strong of sweet Old Rose, matching the appeal of the flowers. Although strictly once-blooming, the flush is quite long for an Old Rose, extending several weeks past the time when other OGRs have finished.

Not many Centifolia Roses have survived the long years of indifference that this class has encountered. My first experience with this cultivar was when I planted a shrub on a low mound along a path in an uncle's garden. Fantin tumbled out over the walk in spring, thrusting deliciously fragrant blossoms into our unprepared faces, giving us quite a pleasant surprise.

Ignace Henri Joseph Théodore Fantin-Latour (1836–1904) was a French painter renowned for his sumptuous portraits of flowers.

HYBRIDIZER: unknown
SUITABILITY: all levels
AVAILABILITY: mail-order
STATURE & HABIT: warm
  climate, 5' × 5';
  cool climate, 5' × 5'
FRAGRANCE: strong of Old Rose
  attar

USES: border, cutting
PARENTAGE: unknown
DISEASES: mildew
HARDINESS: hot climate, good;
  cold climate, good
BLOOM: spring

Fantin-Latour

FÉLICITÉ PARMENTIER

[*Alba, 1834*]

Recognized by William Paul in the 19th century as "indispensable even in a small collection," 'Félicité Parmentier,' with her chic flower form and abundant bloom, is still one of the most popular OGRs today. There is speculation that Félicité has some Damask Rose in her background, but on the whole, she is pure Alba Rose. In our modern gardens, she is a dense, low-growing shrub, unlike her more typically tall-growing Alba sisters; this tendency makes her a useful candidate for the front of the border as well as for container planting in a patio garden.

At first Félicité's foliage is a washed-out, almost absinthe green with a lemon yellow tint, but at maturity the leaves take on the glaucous aquamarine tinge more in character with her Alba heritage. The twiggy gray-green canes are brimming with spiked scarlet prickles of diverse sizes and shapes. An uncommon feature is that the stout, flat-topped buds are yellowish at first, but open to a pale pink with deeper blush tones at their center. Mature blooms are a crisp peppermint pink, lighter on the edges; they are very fully petaled, and quartered, reflexing back to a pompon as they age. Fragrance is soft, sweet, and effervescent but not strong. Disease resistance is excellent in all areas of the country.

When simply provided with the horticultural necessities, Félicité will repay you with a bounty of elegantly sculpted blossoms. Take advantage of a strong old gal like this one, particularly if you have a lot of problems with plant diseases where you live.

Pale-colored roses like 'Félicité Parmentier' harmonize well with blue-flowered perennials such as fragrant, repeat-blooming, tall bearded irises, or the iridescent blue of Chinese delphiniums. Félicité was more than likely named for a member of the prominent 19th-century family of rose hybridizers and nurserymen, the Parmentiers of Enghiem, Belgium.

HYBRIDIZER: unknown
SUITABILITY: all levels
AVAILABILITY: wide
STATURE & HABIT: warm
climate, 4' × 4';
cool climate, 4' × 3'
FRAGRANCE: lightly
effervescent, soft and sweet

USES: border, low hedge,
cutting, container
PARENTAGE: unknown
DISEASES: clean
HARDINESS: hot climate, good;
cold climate, good
BLOOM: spring

Félicité Parmentier

FRANCIS DUBREUIL

[*Tea, 1894*]

Dark red Tea Roses are out of the ordinary, and thus have always been particularly prized and cherished by discerning gardeners. 'Francis Dubreuil' is one of the deepest reds of any I know, which makes him truly outstanding among the mostly pale pastel Teas.

Having a stocky, compact growth pattern for a Tea, this cultivar makes a low-mounding rose of only 3 feet or so. It's just possible, though, that over time the shrub will attain a bit more height, but in the five or six years I've had him in my garden, I've not seen any evidence of that on the horizon. New canes are thin and wiry, dark umber brown, with a sprinkling of small pale carnelian prickles. The vivid green oval foliage is relatively free of problems. Upon first opening, the buds are a deep, almost dusty maroon tone; these later open to an equally dark and bottomless Harvard crimson in the fully matured flowers. The color is even deeper at the center and base of the petals, approaching velvety black. The deep black-red petals are often embossed with a streak of white, a trait inherited from the cultivar's China Rose progenitor, 'Slater's Crimson China.' Until the shrub attains some size, flowers are produced on short stems; deadheading regularly will encourage better rebloom. The aroma is a rich blend of Damask and Tea Rose perfume.

Even under optimal conditions, Francis will appreciate a bit of extra effort toward his care. Deep mulching, regular watering, and fertilizing will make him very happy.

Francis Dubreuil was a tailor who dabbled in rose breeding and named this cultivar for himself. He was also the grandfather of another famous Francis, Francis Meilland, who produced the famous Hybrid Tea Rose 'Peace' around 1939.

HYBRIDIZER: Francis Dubreuil, Lyons, France

SUITABILITY: intermediate

AVAILABILITY: mail-order

STATURE & HABIT: warm climate, 3' × 3'; cool climate, 3' × 2'

FRAGRANCE: Damask and Tea Rose perfumes

USES: border, container, cutting

PARENTAGE: unknown

DISEASES: clean

HARDINESS: hot climate, very good; cold climate, tender

BLOOM: remontant

Francis Dubreuil

FRANÇOIS JURANVILLE

[*Rambler, 1906*]

The Barbier brothers spent some years experimenting with breeding *Rosa wichuraiana* and produced several Ramblers that are still seen in gardens around the world today. Ramblers attained the height of their popularity right around the turn of the 20th century. Their acclaim was due to two key traits: they were extremely cold-hardy climbers, and they came in a broad range of colors.

'François Juranville' throws gaunt, flexible, almost sinewy canes that scramble over structures and through trees to 15 feet or more. These wonderfully trainable canes are covered with lush, shiny, deep bottle green barbed foliage and only a few ruby prickles. New growth is coppery bronze, and the cultivar tends to bloom on the previous season's growth. Cream and cameo buds are produced in small clusters, opening to fully petaled, fragrant flowers of soft India pink with hints of coral. While the inner petals remain darker, the outer petals reflex back and fade to a pale mallow pink. I always smell a combination of a sweet gingerbread-like fragrance mixed with attar of rose—an engaging blend. The leathery foliage has good resistance to most incursions. François is a spring-blooming cultivar, but the bloom is extensive and lasts well, and the shrub possesses good winter-hardiness.

Ramblers like François should be pruned in midsummer, after the bloom is finished and new canes have started growing. Remove the older, previous year's flowering canes right down to the bud union, and begin attaching the new canes to their support structure. With his long, pliable canes, François can be easily attached to any type of garden accoutrement, and could even be trained nicely onto a catenary, adding wonderful dimensional texture to your space no matter the size. What a sight François creates when trained—as garlands of fragrant primrose-and-coral blossoms arch across your garden just at eye height.

HYBRIDIZER: Barbier Brothers, Orléans, France

SUITABILITY: all levels

AVAILABILITY: mail-order

STATURE & HABIT: warm climate, 15' × 15'; cool climate, 15' × 10'

FRAGRANCE: sweet gingerbread and attar

USES: climber, pillar, trained into trees, catenary

PARENTAGE: *R. wichuraiana* × 'Mme. Laurette Messimy'

DISEASES: clean

HARDINESS: hot climate, good; cold climate, good

BLOOM: spring

François Juranville

GREAT MAIDEN'S BLUSH

[Alba, Ancient]

The English, being the inhibited bunch they were, decided long ago to rename this rose in order to dodge any implications from the original, more descriptive and explicit French. "Cuisse de Nymphe" (Thigh of the Nymph) or "Cuisse de Nymphe Emue" (Thigh of the Passionate Nymph) became listed as 'Great Maiden's Blush' in English. Graced with other monikers, such as *Rosa alba incarnata,* "La Royale," "La Seduisante" (alluring, tempting), and "La Virginale," everyone seems to have caught a particular idea from this temptress of an Old Rose.

A rose so ethereal in coloring and perfume should, by nature, prove to be frail in lifespan, but nothing could be further from the truth. It turns out this is one tough old broad.

'Great Maiden's Blush' grows like a typical Alba: upright to around 6 feet, and as wide, with brownish puce-green canes, gray-green foliage that is whiter on the undersides, and dark caramel prickles. Large clusters of pale chartreuse buds, with exceedingly elaborate sepals, open to loosely formed blush pink, celestially fragrant flowers. The blush tone lingers at the center as the outer petals fade to creamy pearl with age, while the flowers retain a perfume reminiscent of sparkling wine with a pinch of pepper at the end. The shrub itself is somewhat loose and arching, principally at bloom time when the weight of the flowers pulls the canes over, making for a fountainlike effect. Although never completely free of disease, 'Great Maiden's Blush' nevertheless shrugs off most problems quite easily

Even though she's a bit more open in growth than some of her Alba sisters, the Maiden will fit right in among other shrubs and perennials in the border. Plant this beauty where her perfume will waft through the garden, seducing gardener and visitor alike to follow their noses to the source of her beguiling scent.

HYBRIDIZER: unknown
SUITABILITY: all levels
AVAILABILITY: mail-order
STATURE & HABIT: warm
  climate, 6' × 6';
  cool climate, 5' × 5'
FRAGRANCE: sparkling wine,
  peppery aftertaste

USES: border, tall hedge,
  cutting
PARENTAGE: unknown
DISEASES: some blackspot
HARDINESS: hot climate, good;
  cold climate, excellent
BLOOM: spring

Great
Maiden's
Blush

GREEN ROSE

[*China, 1845*]

Gaze not at this beauty with a jaundiced eye, shrink not away in disgust, but give a closer look to this horticultural debutante, all dressed up with no place to go. This is one of those few cases in botany when a flower is not a flower. The petals of the "flowers" have reverted back to leaves, substituting brightly colored wings for the green of chlorophyll. This China Rose has so changed itself that it has long since lost all ability to reproduce.

A typically low-growing, bushy shrub, 'Green Rose' develops into a convex mound of perhaps 3½ feet tall by 3 feet across. Characteristic China foliage is long and narrow, lance-shaped, lightly serrated, and deep forest green. Polished jade stems are straight with ruddy prickles, and terminate in large corymbs of bright green "flowers." Small aqua green pointed buds with long foliated sepals fold back to reveal small, deep turquoise green double flowers packed with short, pointed petals. The blooms last for a number of days on the bush, but as the flowers age, they take on cinnabar and russet tones along with the green. Like so many Chinas, 'Green Rose' has a peppery fragrance that remains on your hands for a long while after picking.

The history of 'Green Rose' seems to be lost in time. Most agree that it is a mutation, or sport, from a China Rose. Some date this rose back as far as 1743, but it first seems to have attracted attention in the mid 1850s in England, where it was offered for sale by the firm of Bembridge & Harrison around 1856. While doing research some time ago, I came across a novel by Helen Corse Barney entitled *Green Rose of Furley*, published in 1953. Her story is a semi-autobiographical account of a Quaker family living in mid-19th-century Baltimore and active in the Underground Railroad. The family were noted nurserymen whose home was called Furley, and who claimed possession of a horticultural novelty—you guessed it, a green rose. It would be wonderful to speculate that stationmasters along the Underground Railroad's Baltimore route might have used boutonnieres of 'Green Rose' as a covert sign to others transporting their perilous cargo northward.

HYBRIDIZER: unknown
SUITABILITY: all levels
AVAILABILITY: mail-order
STATURE & HABIT: warm
   climate 3' × 3';
   cool climate, 2' × 2'
FRAGRANCE: strong of peppers

USES: border, container,
   cutting, novelty
PARENTAGE: unknown
DISEASES: clean
HARDINESS: hot climate, very
   good; cold climate, tender
BLOOM: remontant

Green Rose

HARISON'S YELLOW

[*Species Hybrid, 1830*]

A rose with a true American pedigree, 'Harison's Yellow' is, along with 'Austrian Copper' and 'Persian Yellow,' a rose most often discovered growing out of weeds on abandoned home sites across the country. It roots so easily on its own that many a pioneer mother pulled up a piece and put it in a tin can with some dirt for the long trek westward.

'Harison's Yellow' grows to around 6 or 7 feet or more, and since it is usually cultivated as an own-root plant, it will in time colonize a large area by its own root runners. Canes are acorn brown with numerous sharp, straight prickles. The deep green foliage is unfortunately susceptible to blackspot, so it needs extra attention in areas prone to that fungal infection. The almost fully double flowers are produced in profusion from ornate, globular lemon yellow buds. As the blooms first open they are cupped, finishing off in a rather flat shape, deep goldenrod in tone with flaxen stamens at the center of the fully open flowers. The scent is like that of its parent 'Austrian Briar,' described by some as "fetid" but to me having nuances of musk and fresh green apples. Spring-blooming 'Harison's Yellow' is remarkably cold-hardy and a joy in the border.

This rose is presumed to have been raised by either George F. Harison or his father, Richard, both New York lawyers and gardeners at a time when there was still open land for farming and gardening on Manhattan Island. The date of introduction is usually given as 1830, but that may be a little late as I have studied an account of a Quaker household's move from coastal North Carolina to Indiana around 1800, and then on to North Dakota, with this rose moving with them from one homestead to the next, until it eventually ended up with two sisters in Los Angeles around 1930. As far as I'm concerned, forget whether or not this is "The Yellow Rose of Texas." What's important is that it's "The Yellow Rose of the Americas."

HYBRIDIZER: George Harison, New York City

SUITABILITY: all levels

AVAILABILITY: wide

STATURE & HABIT: warm climate, 7' × 4'; cool climate, 4' × 3'

FRAGRANCE: musk and fresh apples

USES: border, hedge, partial shade

PARENTAGE: 'Persian Yellow' × *R. spinosissima?*

DISEASES: blackspot

HARDINESS: hot climate, very good; cold climate, very good

BLOOM: spring

*Harison's
Yellow*

HEBE'S LIP

[Eglantine, Before 1846]

Pronounced "HEE-bee," this little beauty is named for the mytho-logical Goddess of Youth and Spring. Although she is sometimes listed as a Damask hybrid, my opinion is that 'Hebe's Lip' has a much closer affinity to the Eglantine group, with their uniquely fragrant green-apple-essence foliage. Hebe is a good candidate for the shrub bor-der, if anyone still has space for such a large garden room. For the rest of us, the back of the border is fine, where her thorny canes and toler-ance of less-than-optimum growing conditions will be a welcome relief of color. No need to coddle this goddess.

At her 4- to 5-foot diameter, the canes of 'Hebe's Lip' will bend over from the sheer profusion and weight of her flowers. The slender, absinthe green canes are profusely defended by hooked burgundy-colored prickles. The spring green, moderately apple-scented foliage demonstrates some Damask influence in that the leaves are folded along the midrib and are paler on the underside. Large clusters of round red buds open to cupped, semi-double, opaque alabaster flowers with a saf-fron boss of stamens. Lips of the milky cups are brushed with a delicate, pencil-thin stroke of cherry red. As they are exposed to sunlight, the buds are marked and mottled with lovely tones of buttercream and red, creating quite a distinctive impression. The scent is musky, and there is a good crop of bright scarlet hips in the fall.

'Hebe's Lip' should be placed where her uniquely enchanting blossoms can be savored up close. Even though she is tolerant of poor soils and will even survive light, high shade, she appreciates a little extra attention.

This Hebe should not be confused with 'Coupe de Hebe,' a some-what coarser-growing Bourbon from 1840. 'Hebe's Lip' is much older, and having fallen by the horticultural wayside for many years, was rein-troduced by the William Paul nursery in 1912.

HYBRIDIZER: J. Lee, Hammersmith, England

SUITABILITY: all levels

AVAILABILITY: mail-order

STATURE & HABIT: warm climate, 4' × 4'; cool climate, 4' × 4'

FRAGRANCE: musky, with lightly apple-scented foliage

USES: border, hedge, partial shade, poor soil

PARENTAGE: unknown

DISEASES: clean

HARDINESS: hot climate, very good; cold climate, very good

BLOOM: spring

Hebe's Lip

HENRI MARTIN

[*Moss, 1863*]

Frequently called "Red Moss" in this country, 'Henri Martin' is one of the few fully red Moss Roses. A Damask Rose was probably one of his parents—thus the coarser mossing on the stems and calyx. Moss Roses were extremely popular during the Victorian period but are often ignored today because of their limited color range and susceptibility to disease.

A moderately erect-growing shrub, Henri will reach 5 feet or a little more in height and about 4 to 5 feet in width. The Nile green canes are thoroughly and densely encrusted with both red and green prickles that extend right out to the buds, and the "moss" is more prickly than soft. The forest green, slightly jagged foliage and woolly stems will need protection from mildew wherever that fungus is a regular nuisance. The bright carmine, prickly, flat-topped buds are produced in large sprays that first open an intense blood red and progress to crimson double pompons with a sprinkling of bright lemon stamens poking out of the blooms. As the bloom ages, it takes on the deeper tones of maroon to almost black. Henri's fragrance is a strong mix reminiscent of milled soaps and spices.

This is an extraordinarily tough, cold- and heat-hardy rose, tolerating conditions that would cause many of his more modern cousins to curl up their leaflets. Henri is one of those gems that even relishes the stifling hot dryness of East Texas. But although he is reasonably drought-hardy and tolerant of poor soils, it's still a good idea to give him a decent site with plenty of compost in the planting hole.

Henri Martin (Bon-Louis-Henri Martin), born in 1810 in Saint-Quentin, remains most famous for his *Histoire de France,* a gargantuan, 15-volume tome glorifying the supposed Celtic and Druidic origins of the French race—with not quite as much attention to accuracy as one might hope.

HYBRIDIZER: Jean Laffay, Bellevue-Meudon, France
SUITABILITY: all levels
AVAILABILITY: mail-order
STATURE & HABIT: warm climate, 6' × 5'; cool climate, 5' × 4'
FRAGRANCE: strongly of milled soaps and spice

USES: border, hedge, poor soil, self-pegging
PARENTAGE: unknown
DISEASES: mildew
HARDINESS: hot climate, very good; cold climate, very good
BLOOM: spring

Henri
Martin

HERMOSA

[*Bourbon/China, 1840*]

'Hermosa' is a rose with a somewhat cloudy past. Many times during the 19th century, when sales of a particular cultivar fell off, a nurseryman would pull the cultivar from the market, wait a year or two, and then reintroduce it under a new name. This most likely accounts for the deluge of names under which 'Hermosa' is also known: "Armosa," "Mélanie Lemaire," and "Mme. Neumann," among them.

A dwarf, nicely compact-growing shrub, 'Hermosa' will create a mound 3 feet high by about as much across. The foliage is longer than broad, olive green, and grayer on the reverse; it remains reasonably clean, with only an infrequent bout with mildew. The skinny, medium green canes are on the wiry side but are supplied with broad-based, curved-saber vermilion prickles. Buds are produced in small clusters, at first opening red-pink; the fully petaled, cupped, small flowers are a soft and lovely lilac-pink. While bloom is produced almost continuously, the mace and pepper essence is more ephemeral—at times pronounced, but decreasing in intensity as the flowers age.

The bloom of 'Hermosa' is rather close in appearance to 'Old Blush,' differing only in having slightly larger and more fully petaled flowers. This is a rose frequently discovered in old gardens and cemeteries. I have collected specimens from a number of sites in the California gold rush country, and I'm constantly amazed at how different this cultivar can appear when growing under different conditions. From bush and flower size to color and shape, everything can vary so much that you'd not think it the same rose. Were you to root the cuttings back home and grow them on under your local conditions, lo and behold, they would all be 'Hermosa.' Just goes to show what a resilient and durable survivor this Old Rose truly is—and points out the dangers of making snap field identifications.

The word *hermosa* is Spanish for "beautiful" or "comely."

HYBRIDIZER: Marcheseau

SUITABILITY: all levels

AVAILABILITY: mail-order

STATURE & HABIT: warm climate, 3' × 3'; cool climate, 3' × 2'

FRAGRANCE: light, of mace and pepper

USES: border, low hedge, container, cutting

PARENTAGE: unknown

DISEASES: clean

HARDINESS: hot climate, good; cold climate, tender

BLOOM: remontant

Hermosa

ISPAHAN

[*Damask, 1832*]

Like the city for which it is named, this Damask Rose masquerades under a variety of noms-de-plume: "Pompon des Princes" and "Isfahan," to name two. The early 19th century was a time of widespread exploration by Europeans. Persia and the flora and fauna of the ancient Middle East fascinated many a traveler, who often brought back living treasures from adventures in the lands of the Thousand and One Nights. Not since the Crusades and Marco Polo had Europeans seen such delectable, fragrant roses.

'Ispahan' will reach 6 or 7 feet in warmer climes, with a 5- to 6-foot spread. The gracefully arching canes are papyrus green with small but sharp sabered prickles. The elliptical, textured, healthy avocado green foliage is silvery on its reverse, beautifully framing the small, pale moonlight pink buds, which are produced both singly and in small sprays all along the gently bending canes. The bloom form is best described as a pompon shape, with a relatively informal arrangement to the petals. Blossoms are soft, pure primrose pink with darker orchid tones at the center, while the petal edges fade to a pale seashell color, with an occasional hint of a green eye at the center of the bloom. Even though 'Ispahan' flowers only in spring, it has a longer blooming period than most other Damasks, and it is quite capable of covering itself with such a profusion of stunningly perfumed flowers that it can be impossible to get even a glimpse of green foliage! Its typically Damask fragrance is strong, rosy, and pervasive in the garden.

The ancient city of Aspadana, Persia—now Esfahan or Isfahan, Iran—has long been considered one of the most beautiful cities in the world. Situated almost equidistant between the Caspian Sea and the Persian Gulf, it has been an important medieval trade hub along a main caravan route, the capital of Persia, and a center for highly sophisticated silver filigree work and carpet weaving.

HYBRIDIZER: unknown
SUITABILITY: all levels
AVAILABILITY: wide
STATURE & HABIT: warm
climate, 7' × 6';
cool climate, 4' × 3'
FRAGRANCE: strong Damask

USES: border, tall hedge,
pegging, cutting
PARENTAGE: unknown
DISEASES: clean
HARDINESS: hot climate, good;
cold climate, good
BLOOM: spring

Ispahan

KÖNIGIN VON DÄNEMARK

[*Alba, 1826*]

'Königin von Dänemark' is one of the most beautiful roses ever produced. Also known as "Queen of Denmark," "Belle Courtisanne," "Reine du Danemark," and "Naissance de Venus," this enduring and endearing cultivar is cherished for the perfection of her blossoms and the delicious rosy perfume she purveys.

Königin is quite an open-growing shrub, permitting the sun to grace her every arm. She will reach nearly 6 feet in height and often as much or a little more in width. The long, lax canes are shrouded with long, large, pointed and dentate, dark malachite green foliage. Prickles are small but ample and sharp. Oval buds are produced in small clusters, and as they first open, are deep pink to fire red in color. The individual, pompon-shaped flowers are fully petaled, and as they age, reflex back into a ball. The central petals are dark carnation fading to blush, with the palest flushed cream to white on the outermost petals. Before they curl back, the flowers are clearly quartered and often show a green eye at their center. Like so many of her Alba sisters, the fragrance has a sweetness mixed into the light rose cologne that reminds me of a fruity sparkling wine. The clean foliage is reasonably free of most problems, and although only spring-blooming, 'Königin von Dänemark' has a reasonably long flowering season.

'Königin von Dänemark' was hybridized by James Booth of Flottbeck Nurseries near Hamburg. In those days, the province of Schleswig-Holstein, which included Hamburg, was still part of Denmark. Booth first introduced this rose around 1816, but it wasn't until 1826 that he could offer it in any numbers. At that point, he requested permission from the Danish crown to name the rose for the queen.

HYBRIDIZER: James Booth, Hamburg, Germany
SUITABILITY: all levels
AVAILABILITY: wide
STATURE & HABIT: warm climate, 6' × 5'; cool climate, 5' × 4'
FRAGRANCE: strong, sweet rose perfume

USES: border, pegging, cutting
PARENTAGE: unknown
DISEASES: clean
HARDINESS: hot climate, good; cold climate, very good
BLOOM: spring

Königin von Dänemark

LA BELLE DISTINGUÉE

[*Eglantine, 1837*]

A Sweetbriar, or Eglantine Rose of unknown origins, 'La Belle Distinguée' deserves more attention by modern suburban gardeners. Eglantines are best known for their green-apple-scented foliage, a trait not always passed along to their progeny. This Belle does have some of the crisp aroma, although not as strongly as her species parent. Some Sweetbriars will eventually climb as they mature, but Belle remains more demure in stature. In her life, she has also been known as "La Petite Duchesse," "Lee's Duchess," "Scarlet Sweet Briar," and "Double Scarlet Sweet Briar."

A dense little shrub, 'La Belle Distinguée' will usually reach no more than 4 feet in height with a slightly smaller spread. The almost olive-colored canes are festooned with thin, sharp prickles, of a café-au-lait hue, which continue right out to the flower buds, diminishing in size to hair-size growths as they go. The compound foliage is composed of five to seven leaflets, while individual toothed leaflets are small, ovoid, and a deep hunter green.

Scarlet buds are produced individually or in small clusters and are quite attractive either way. The flowers open as single to semi-double, bright poppy red blooms with a profusion of dazzling canary stamens prominently displayed at their centers. The foliage is clean and free of irritants. Flame red hips are occasionally set toward the end of the bloom cycle, but the real show is Belle's "coming out ball" in spring—truly an extravaganza of crimson and gold.

The apple-scented foliage of Sweetbriars is strongest on warm, moist mornings when their perfume drifts on the air and permeates the garden. In the hot, dry weather of summer, I sprinkle the foliage with water to revive the scent and clean off the dust and pollution. 'La Belle Distinguée' is a much more compact grower than many other Eglantines, so she would blend into the border nicely, while her larger growing sisters would have to be trained into a tree or over a wall.

HYBRIDIZER: unknown
SUITABILITY: all levels
AVAILABILITY: limited mail-
    order
STATURE & HABIT: warm
    climate, 4' × 3';
    cool climate, 4' × 3'
FRAGRANCE: light, rosy with
    green apples

USES: border
PARENTAGE: unknown
DISEASES: clean
HARDINESS: hot climate, good;
    cold climate, good
BLOOM: spring

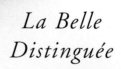

La Belle
Distinguée

LA FRANCE

[*Hybrid Tea, 1867*]

This is the very first Hybrid Tea Rose. Produced by the Lyons-based firm of Guillot, 'La France' caught the attention of the rose-growing public early on with its strong, sweet fragrance, cold-hardiness, and repeat bloom.

'La France' is reasonably tall, growing to 5 feet, stiff and upright—rather typical for a Hybrid Tea. New growth is lightly tinted with red, and the canes and flowering stems are polished and waxy with large, hooked, triangular red prickles. The deep forest green foliage is large and susceptible to most of the problems that can affect roses, so be prepared. The immense, globular pink buds are usually presented singly, one to each strong upright stem. The silvery pink conical blooms unfurl to tight globe-shaped flowers. Individual petals roll back distinctly at their tips and are deeper lilac-pink on the underside. The center petals also curl back, forming a star shape before opening completely. The fragrance is exceptional, combining a Damask-like Old Rose scent with a sweet, meadowy perfume. Rebloom is strong, and as with most modern Hybrid Tea Roses, there is bloom throughout the season. The huge globular flowers are unfortunately prone to balling in wet weather—petals stick together and the flowers fail to open, eventually turning gray from fungal infections. It's important to remove such affected blooms, and if external conditions improve, the next flowers shouldn't have the problem. 'La France' is a strong, vigorous grower and cold-tolerant in all but the wintriest zones of the country.

Although she may be the first Hybrid Tea, this rose is sterile, never setting seed for anyone in nearly 150 years. 'Mme. Leon Paine,' another Guillot rose from 1904, has been confused with and sold in North America as 'La France.' But the authenticity of 'Climbing La France,' which is a sport of the true bush form, has never been challenged. 'La France' is a charming shrub, well deserving of a spot in any garden.

HYBRIDIZER: Jean-Baptiste Guillot (Fils), Lyons, France

SUITABILITY: all levels

AVAILABILITY: wide

STATURE & HABIT: warm climate, 5' × 3'; cool climate, 4' × 3'

FRAGRANCE: strong of Damask and grassy meadows

USES: border, cutting, fragrance

PARENTAGE: 'Mme. Victor Verdier' × 'Mme. Bravy'

DISEASES: mildew; flowers often ball in wet weather

HARDINESS: hot climate, good; cold climate, moderate

BLOOM: remontant

La France

LA VILLE DE BRUXELLES

[*Damask, 1849*]

Beginning in the early years of the 19th century, hybridizers were utilizing the Damasks in their breeding programs. As a result, today almost every class of Modern Rose has some Damask in it. "The City of Brussels" is a late introduction as Damasks go, cherished nonetheless for her vivid allure and perfume. A stocky old girl with big bones, she requires proper placement in the garden for optimal growth where her ample, fragrant flowers will bestow nearly two months' worth of enjoyment.

'La Ville de Bruxelles' can easily reach 5 or 6 feet in height with a spread of 6 feet or more. Light green canes arc out from the center and are amply furnished with notched, oval celadon foliage and a dense covering of small brown prickles. Bright reddish pink buds with decorative, leaflike, foliate stamens are produced in medium to large clusters. The enormous, single-hued Pompeiian pink blooms reach up to 5 inches in diameter, and are at first shallow-cupped, flat, and distinctively quartered. The flowers are filled with small petals that swirl about the center, forming a button-eye. As the blooms mature, they progress into a sort of dome shape. The color remains a rich, clear, undeviating pink, which only lightens on the very outermost petals. A heady Damask aroma pervades the shrub, and resistance to disease is quite good.

A bush of 'La Ville de Bruxelles' in full glory is a sight not to be missed. Her lengthy, relaxed canes are pulled over by the extravagant weight of the flowers, which can best be described as a pavé of blossoms shrouding the canes. This bijou of the hybridizer's art is a prime example of what an Old Rose was meant to stand for.

'La Ville de Bruxelles' was named in the mid 19th century by her hybridizer for the capital city of Belgium.

HYBRIDIZER: Jean-Pierre
   Vibert, Angers, France
SUITABILITY: intermediate
AVAILABILITY: wide
STATURE & HABIT: warm
   climate, 6' × 8';
   cool climate, 5' × 3'
FRAGRANCE: strong Damask

USES: border, pegging, cutting
PARENTAGE: unknown
DISEASES: clean
HARDINESS: hot climate, good;
   cold climate, good
BLOOM: spring

La Ville de Bruxelles

LADY HILLINGDON

[*Tea, 1910*]

No book on Old Roses could rightly disregard this quintessential Tea Rose. Even in marginal zones, given a warm, protected spot in the garden, 'Lady Hillingdon' will astound you with her continuous crop of classically shaped, apricot-scented blossoms.

This rose stands tall. Ever an upright grower, in the milder regions she often reaches 6 feet in stature. New growth has a rich amethyst tone, maturing to a deep green; the canes are a polished bottle green, with a few large, ruddy prickles scattered along the stem. Globular-shaped buds are produced either individually or in small bouquets of up to three blooms per stem. These buds at first display a vibrant yellow-apricot tone, opening to classically shaped, high-centered, dazzling canary flowers with hints of deeper, more apricot centers. That color reference is fitting, actually, as her fragrance is a fascinating mixture, starting off with a combination of Tea Rose and apricots, then aging to a tobacco aroma, retaining a slighter blend of spice and fruit—truly wonderful in the border.

The luxuriant Lady continues blooming throughout the summer and deploys an even stronger second wave in autumn. Although her blooms are bright yellow in spring, the fall tone fits the seasonal mood by showing a flawless deep apricot. 'Lady Hillingdon' also spawned a climbing form, which is worth searching for if you have the space. She will reach nearly 20 feet and spill her nodding flowers down over passersby.

There is a story of dubious merit about the Lady. It is said that two English parsons, both of whom enjoyed gardening, were having dinner one midsummer evening. After their meal, the two parsons left their wives to women's talk and took their cigars and brandy while strolling the rose garden in the flush of twilight. As they walked, they swapped rose experiences, and the host pointed out the virtues of the various roses in his substantial garden. When they reached a glorious bush of 'Lady Hillingdon,' the host observed that in his rather cold part of the countryside, the Lady was "no good in bed but great against the wall."

HYBRIDIZER: Lowe & Shawyer, Uxbridge, England
SUITABILITY: all levels
AVAILABILITY: wide
STATURE & HABIT: warm climate, 6' × 4'; cool climate, 3' × 3'
FRAGRANCE: Tea Rose, apricots

USES: border, cutting
PARENTAGE: 'Papa Gontier' × 'Mme. Hoste'
DISEASES: mildew
HARDINESS: hot climate, very good; cold climate, tender
BLOOM: remontant

Lady Hillingdon

LAMARQUE

[*Noisette, 1830*]

A rose often discovered growing on or around old homesteads in the South and West, 'Lamarque' is a true antebellum rose. When the earliest bushy Noisettes were crossed with Tea Roses, a race of tender climbers was produced. Many modern authorities decry that the blooms of these Tea-Noisettes droop or hang on weak necks, but what could be more sensuous than walking under a pergola draped with exquisite clusters of 'Lamarque' blossoms, breathing in the nose-height exhilaration of his citrusy fragrance.

A vigorous climber, 'Lamarque' will eventually blanket a 20-foot-diameter spread. Smooth, burnished green canes hold clean, pointed, shiny, cobalt green foliage that frames clusters of frosty buds. The flat, doubled, nodding flowers open blond-white, with a hint of lemon yellow at the center. The blooms reflex back to large, flat pompons after opening. The overall health of this cultivar is very good, although it can be bothered by a spot of mildew from time to time—but nothing to worry about. The long, ropey canes will scale over obstacles using large, hooked red prickles to retain hold of surfaces along the way. Flower color will tend to the ivory side in the intense sun of the West, and a bit more to lemon and saffron-white in slightly cooler regions. 'Lamarque' is often listed as one of the hardier Noisettes, but remember that among the Tea and Noisette Roses, hardiness is a relative term. He should be hardy as far north as Washington, D.C., but a cold winter even there will cut him back to the ground. In the South and West, plants have survived for a century or more.

This cultivar was grown by a Monsieur Maréchal from seeds sown in a pot in his window garden in Angers. A cobbler by trade and an amateur rose hybridizer, he at first named this rose 'Thé Maréchal' for the marvelous Tea Rose fragrance (the French word *thé* means "tea"). 'Lamarque' commemorates Général Maximilien Lamarque (1770–1832), a Napoleonic commander and politician.

HYBRIDIZER: Maréchal, Angers, France
SUITABILITY: all levels
AVAILABILITY: wide
STATURE & HABIT: warm climate, 15' × 15'; cool climate, 15' × 8'
FRAGRANCE: strong, lemony citrus, meadow, Tea Rose

USES: climber, pillar, cutting
PARENTAGE: 'Blush Noisette' × 'Parks' Yellow Tea-scented China'
DISEASES: mildew
HARDINESS: hot climate, very good; cold climate, tender
BLOOM: remontant

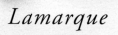
Lamarque

LÉDA

[*Damask, 1827*]

'Léda,' or "Painted Damask" as she is often called, may have originated in England around 1827; otherwise, little is known of the early history of this enchanting rose. A robust shrub, she will grow to around 6 feet tall and at least that wide in warm climates, staying somewhat smaller in the colder regions.

For a Damask, 'Léda' has rather atypical, round dusky green foliage. The leaflets are folded up along their midribs, and the stipules (leaflike growths) clasping the leaf stem are streaked with light red. Gray-green canes are covered with a mixture of both fine and sizable tawny brown prickles along their entire length. Flowers are produced in clusters at the ends of the canes. At first the buds are a deep black-red, but they open to full white flowers whose individual petals are delicately caressed with a filigree of fire red, giving the blooms a hand-painted look. Sweetly scented with Damask Rose attar and fine soap, the flowers reflex back to a ball, having a button-eye at the center.

Damask Roses resent any hard pruning by allowing the cut canes to simply die back completely, defeating the purpose of pruning altogether, and 'Léda' is no exception. However, pruning her back by about one half her size immediately after blooming will produce a larger-than-normal flush of flowers the following spring. Otherwise, it is only necessary to prune out all the dead or damaged canes, and then gently prune back the flowering shoots when she's finished her bloom. Damask Roses are winter-hardy in all but the coldest regions and will certainly bloom well in warmer regions that receive little to no winter chilling.

Occasionally, 'Léda' will sport back to a pink form. This "Pink Léda" is a soft, all-over primrose pink and is equally as fragrant as the painted form. So little is known of the origins of this rose that the pink form might be either a parent or merely a sport.

In Greek myth, Zeus disguised himself as a swan to seduce Leda, the Queen of Sparta. The child of this union was Helen, whose later kidnaping by Paris provoked the Trojan War.

HYBRIDIZER: unknown
SUITABILITY: intermediate
AVAILABILITY: wide
STATURE & HABIT: warm
    climate, 6' × 8';
    cool climate, 3' × 3'
FRAGRANCE: sweet of Damask
    attar and fine soap

USES: border, pegging, cutting
PARENTAGE: unknown
DISEASES: clean
HARDINESS: hot climate, good;
    cold climate, very good
BLOOM: spring

Léda

LOUISE ODIER

[*Bourbon, 1851*]

Often overlooked today, Bourbon Roses were at the peak of their glory in the mid 19th century. Bourbons are big, often growing to proportions that qualify them as climbing roses. 'Louise Odier,' or "Mme. de Stella" as she was sometimes called, is no exception. She will need some support by self-pegging, or training onto a tripod to control her vertical wanderlust, but this just helps to highlight the perfection of her tastefully cupped, fragrant blossoms—which will simply stun even the most jaded garden visitors.

'Louise Odier' will hit her stride at 6 to 7 feet or more, with an equal spread. Reddish new growth matures to olive green foliage, which is paler underneath. The canes are light grassy green with a plethora of large sienna-tinged, pyramidal prickles. The glossy foliage is somewhat vulnerable to disease, so take preventive measures if necessary in your region, particularly where mildew or blackspot can be a problem.

Small to medium-size clusters of three to five buds are produced on long, brawny stems. The orbs of buds are reddish at first, opening to deeply cupped and quartered, bright rose-pink blooms with a hint of lilac. The outer petals are lighter on the margins and reverse, and rebloom is good throughout the season. Louise's fragrance is strong and rich, to me a blend of Old Rose and ripe fruit. 'Louise Odier' is a perfect candidate for training, espalier-like, onto a wall or fence. The pliable, elongated canes are quite easy to control in this manner.

Little information about the names can be found—even whether Louise Odier and Mme. de Stella were the same person is now left to mystery and supposition. That hardly matters, though, when enjoying such a lovely addition to one's border.

HYBRIDIZER: Jacques-Julien Margottin, Bourg-la-Reine, France

SUITABILITY: all levels

AVAILABILITY: wide

STATURE & HABIT: warm climate, 6' × 6'; cool climate, 5' × 4'

FRAGRANCE: strong of Old Rose and ripened fruit

USES: bedding, cutting, pegging, low climber

PARENTAGE: unknown

DISEASES: mildew, blackspot

HARDINESS: hot climate, very good; cold climate, tender

BLOOM: remontant

Louise Odier

MADAME ALFRED CARRIÈRE

[*Noisette, 1879*]

A glimpse of 'Madame Alfred Carrière' scrambling through a low-growing fruit tree or over a garden shed is not soon forgotten. This rose is a large climber, to 18 feet or more and with an equal spread. New growth is light absinthe green, aging to large, oval-shaped gray-green leaflets. One of the earliest climbing roses to bloom in spring, the Madame's flowers are produced both individually and in clusters of two or three. The round buds open into pearl-white to pure white semi-double blooms with a distinct blush cast at their centers. At various times the flowers can have a flaxen cast to them. Petals are large and scalloped, and fold over to cover up the stamens. The fragrance is wonderfully strong and sweet, combining a heady rose attar with the lift of citrus. Probably one of the most widely grown Noisettes, the Madame is a bit more cold-tolerant than most others in this group. Mildew can be a slight annoyance at times, but even in the worst weather, it is never that much to worry about. Like so many white roses, though, this one can suffer heavily from thrips. In that case, you may have to resort to an application of a systemic fertilizer.

Allow Madame to do her thing, which will be to scamper up and through supporting structures or trees. She blooms almost entirely on established wood, so thin out only the oldest canes along with any dead-wood you may find every few years. Consider placing her where her camellia-shaped blossoms will be backlit by the late afternoon sun. There, each and every bloom will take on the aspect of a miniature Japanese lantern, glowing with an ethereal inner light.

The Madame was named in honor of the wife of a great devotee of roses.

HYBRIDIZER: Joseph Schwartz, Lyons, France
SUITABILITY: all levels
AVAILABILITY: wide
STATURE & HABIT: warm climate, 18' × 12'; cool climate, 12' × 10'
FRAGRANCE: rose attar, citrus

USES: climber, trained into trees, cutting
PARENTAGE: unknown
DISEASES: mildew
HARDINESS: hot climate, very hardy; cold climate, tender
BLOOM: remontant

Madame
Alfred Carrière

MADAME ERNST CALVAT

[*Bourbon, 1888*]

Like most Bourbon Roses, this Madame acts like a small climber or pillar rose in the garden. But if you're looking for maximum flower production, you may want to consider self-pegging, or bending the tall canes over and tying them back on themselves. A bush of 'Madame Ernst Calvat' so trained will simply flower her blooming head off. Bourbons are one of the quintessential Victorian roses—with their huge round buds and trusses of full flowers just reeking with perfume.

'Madame Ernst Calvat' produces plum-shaded foliage on her strong-growing, hazel brown new shoots. Mature foliage is ebony green with red underneath, quite luxuriant and profuse, covering the canes and providing a perfect foil for globular pale pink buds that are marked with deeper tones of cerise. These in turn unfurl into cabbagelike, soft, clear pink blooms with a dusky primrose reverse, while the outer guard petals fade to a blush pink. The outer petals tend to curl back, forming a petticoat effect. The mouthwateringly sweet-scented flowers have a deep, fully cupped shape and are quartered.

Somewhat bushier than other Bourbons, this cultivar will grow to 6 or 7 feet and can be easily trained as a low climber. Flower production is constant throughout the growing season, and the deliciously fragrant blooms cut well for the house.

'Madame Ernst Calvat' is a sport discovered growing on a plant of 'Madame Isaac Pereire' in the Lyons nursery of Vve. (widow) Schwartz. This rose is named for the wife of Ernst Calvat, a glover and amateur horticulturist most active in growing chrysanthemums around the turn of the last century.

HYBRIDIZER: Veuve Schwartz, Lyons, France
SUITABILITY: all levels
AVAILABILITY: wide
STATURE & HABIT: warm climate, 7' × 7'; cool climate, 5' × 4'
FRAGRANCE: strong, sweet rose

USES: border, climber, pegging, cutting
PARENTAGE: sport of 'Mme. Isaac Pereire'
DISEASES: mildew
HARDINESS: hot climate, very good; cold climate, very good
BLOOM: remontant

*Madame
Ernst Calvat*

MADAME HARDY

[*Damask, 1832*]

If perfection can be achieved at all, then 'Madame Hardy' may just be it. Yet the supreme quintessence of her outer beauty is often faulted for hiding something of a cold, haughty heart. Nothing, however, could be further from the truth. The reserve of her lovely blossoms warms and nourishes the soul of any gardener fortunate enough to share a garden with this Madame.

Back when I was a novice rose grower, one of the first Old Roses I cultivated was 'Madame Hardy.' I remember bringing one of the first flowering sprays she produced to a local rose society meeting and positioning her on the show table next to the more gaudy Hybrid Teas. The exhibitors and judges simply ignored her because she wasn't "show quality." But I had simply wanted to share a beautiful Old Rose with my fellow rose lovers, not challenge them for their precious trophies.

A moderately tall- and strong-growing shrub, 'Madame Hardy' will reach 6 feet in height and about the same in width. The thin Lincoln green canes are covered with a mixture of prickles of all sizes, from bristlelike hairs to formidably hooked hazelnut thorns. Five to seven matte green, egg-shaped, compound leaflets are rough and barbed along their margins, and flowers are produced in small, delicate clusters of three to five buds. Each unopened bud is attired with long decorative sepals that peel back to reveal a dark claret red bud. Then each individual bloom opens to the purest, heart-melting white—never is there any other tone or hue marring the rare perfection of these blossoms. Fully-petaled, flat flowers are meticulously quartered and show an emerald green eye of styles at the center. The strong, sweet, rosy Damask perfume is intoxicating. The frosty, patinated foliage remains reasonably free from most invaders.

This beauty was named for Félicité Hardy, wife of the hybridizer Alexandre Hardy, the superintendent of the Luxembourg Gardens in Paris who received his horticultural apprenticeship at Malmaison.

HYBRIDIZER: Alexandre Hardy, Paris, France
SUITABILITY: all levels
AVAILABILITY: wide
STATURE & HABIT: warm climate, 6' × 5'; cool climate, 5' × 5'
FRAGRANCE: full Damask attar

USES: border, cutting
PARENTAGE: unknown
DISEASES: clean
HARDINESS: hot climate, good; cold climate, very good
BLOOM: spring

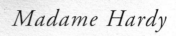
Madame Hardy

MADAME ISAAC PEREIRE

[*Bourbon, 1880*]

Often said to be the most fragrant rose in history, 'Mme. Isaac Pereire' has nevertheless both admirers and detractors. Her color is a bit strident for many, and disease is not unknown to her, but it is her powerful perfume that is most worshiped.

The spring canes will sprawl and climb to 8 feet or more with an equal spread. Canes are outfitted with garnet red prickles, while the toothed oval foliage is jade green, edged with chestnut. The foliage is, unfortunately, often afflicted with fungal diseases like mildew and blackspot, so be forewarned and ready to spray in those areas where such problems exist. Scarlet buds are produced in large clusters and open to intensely pink-to-magenta, deeply cupped and quartered flowers. The enormous blossoms are incredibly scented of powerful Old Rose and a rich, ripe fruit perfume. Early bloom is often not the best, but later in the year, flowers of fine form come again and are produced in abundance.

'Madame Isaac Pereire's' propensity to disease is enough reason for some to decide not to grow her, especially in regions of the country where she will suffer. But there are many zones, such as the warm, dry Southwest, where she can be truly outstanding. It should be noted that this Madame is frequently susceptible to "proliferation," which means that a new flower bud is produced right out of the center of an existing flower. If this happens, simply deadhead the affected bloom and the next flower to form should be fine.

Margottin purchased the rose, originally known as "Le Bienheureux de la Salle," or "Blessing of the Bower," from its developer. He named her 'Mme. Isaac Pereire' for the wife of a prominent Paris banker.

HYBRIDIZER: Garçon, Rouen, France

SUITABILITY: all levels

AVAILABILITY: wide

STATURE & HABIT: warm climate, 8' × 8'; cool climate, 6' × 6'

FRAGRANCE: Old Rose mixed with ripening fruit

USES: cutting, self-pegging, climber

PARENTAGE: unknown

DISEASES: mildew, blackspot

HARDINESS: hot climate, good; cold climate, good

BLOOM: remontant

*Madame
Isaac Pereire*

MADAME PIERRE OGER

[*Bourbon, 1878*]

One of the most popular Old Roses ever, 'Madame Pierre Oger' is a flawless representative of her class, and even today, with so much improvement in the family, few roses can hold a candle to her ethereal, translucent beauty and delicious fragrance. Introduced at the height of the Belle Époque, she summons memories of the age of Monet and Degas. And like one of their paintings, she is full of radiance from a warm afternoon's glow.

'Madame Pierre Oger' is a bit more open-growing than some of the other Bourbons, reaching 6 to 8 feet in height and spread. New growth is vigorous and upright, arching out only after the shrub attains full height. The pastel green, pointed, and plentiful foliage is borne on red-brown canes with small carnelian prickles. Plump, oval buds are produced both individually and in small clusters at the ends of the short side-branches. The pearl white base color of the deeply cupped, fragrant flowers offsets bright orchid pink flushes that escalate toward the edges of each petal, creating a blushing-cheek appearance. In warm weather, the blooms take on ever more shocking pink and often suntan in the hottest weather to a brilliant, all-over carmine red. It is, however, in the cool of the spring or fall that the Madame takes on her most alluring look.

The fragrance is sweet and powerful, with strong undertones of fresh berries and pear, and rebloom is strong throughout the season. This Madame is only occasionally bothered by disease, but in some zones it will be necessary to protect her from blackspot.

A sport of 'Reine Victoria,' 'Madame Pierre Oger' is named in honor of the mother of the hybridizer.

HYBRIDIZER: Arthur Oger, Caen, France; introduced by Charles Verdier, Paris, France

SUITABILITY: all levels

AVAILABILITY: wide

STATURE & HABIT: warm climate, 8' × 8'; cool climate, 4' × 4'

FRAGRANCE: sweet, powerful mix of berries and pear

USES: border, climber, pegging, cutting

PARENTAGE: sport of 'Reine Victoria'

DISEASES: blackspot

HARDINESS: hot climate, very good; cold climate, very good

BLOOM: remontant

Madame
Pierre Oger

MADAME PLANTIER

[*Alba, 1835*]

'Madame Plantier' is a rose often found growing on an old homestead—or even more often, in a cemetery—where she competes with weeds for sun and water. I have seen her growing amid tombstones and pine trees, where her Alba heritage allows her to thrive and bloom in the worst of conditions, often as a low- to medium-size mound of foliage, which in season transforms into a bounteous bevy of pure white bloom.

'Madame Plantier' creates a large mound of growth that frequently throws out elongated, sweeping canes to as much as 12 feet. The medium green canes are almost thornless and shrouded with dark green, elliptical, seven-leaflet compound foliage. Petite orbs of buds are produced in rouged bundles, and at first opening, display bright flame pink. As the flowers open further, they transform to immaculate white with only a hint of red at the base of some petals. The flowers are sweetly fragrant of champagne and fruit and bloom over six to eight weeks. Disease is not a problem.

A Michigan report raves that 'Madame Plantier' is one tough rose: extremely cold-hardy and with no disease problems. Take advantage of her natural toughness and lasting qualities by planting her under high trees, training her up and through them to cascade out the other side. Another good possibility would be to consider planting a hedge of this cultivar where no other rose seems to want to grow for you. Poor soil, high shade, drought—none of these problems will keep Madame from blooming and flourishing. True, she will do better with a little tender loving care, but then who wouldn't?

'Madame Plantier' is listed as an Alba, but she shows definite signs of hybridization with either a Noisette or a Musk Rose. Named by the hybridizer for a family member, this is another of those roses our pioneer mothers carried with them when they settled the Wild West.

HYBRIDIZER: Plantier, La Guillotière, Lyons, France

SUITABILITY: all levels

AVAILABILITY: wide

STATURE & HABIT: warm climate, 12' × 12'; cool climate, 12' × 8'

FRAGRANCE: champagne and fruit

USES: climber, ground cover, pillar

PARENTAGE: *R. alba* × *R. moschata*

DISEASES: clean

HARDINESS: hot climate, good; cold climate, good

BLOOM: spring

*Madame
Plantier*

MAGNA CHARTA

[*Hybrid Perpetual, 1876*]

The middle years of the 19th century were halcyon days for Hybrid Perpetuals, with something like 4,000 roses of this class alone being introduced before 1900. The English took them to their hearts and to their rose shows. Exhibiting Hybrid Perpetuals became such a craze—not entirely dissimilar to the tulipomania of 250 years before—that the gardening public almost turned off growing roses. It also happened that many of the best exhibition-grade Hybrid Perpetuals were simply not good garden roses. 'Magna Charta' is one of the good ones, though, with strong vigor and excellent garden demeanor.

A stout, vertically growing rose, 'Magna Charta' will often reach 5 or 6 feet in height while remaining between 3 and 4 feet in breadth. Canes are light green with small red, triangular-shaped prickles widely spaced along the canes. The dusky green, oval foliage is thick and leathery, with few problems, and the blooms are produced individually or in small clusters. Dark maroon red buds are corpulent and round and have pepper-scented sepals. Flowers are large and fully petaled, cupped, with just a hint of yellow stamens showing at the center. The color at full bloom is rich crimson pink, with darker crimson tones at the center and a silvery cast to the outer petals. The soft fragrance is of sweet Old Rose potpourri, and fall rebloom is good.

'Magna Charta' is a rather typical mid-century Hybrid Perpetual in that it blooms well in spring, then gives only a scattering of flowers until it goes back into full fall production. Because of the light summer crop, many gardeners shy away from growing this entire class, but that is truly a shame.

This rose's name commemorates the "Great Charter" that King John was forced to sign at Runnymede in 1215.

HYBRIDIZER: William Paul, Waltham Cross, England

SUITABILITY: advanced

AVAILABILITY: mail-order

STATURE & HABIT: warm climate, 6' × 4'; cool climate, 5' × 3'

FRAGRANCE: soft Old Rose potpourri

USES: border, container, cutting

PARENTAGE: unknown

DISEASES: mildew

HARDINESS: hot climate, good; cold climate, tender

BLOOM: remontant

Magna Charta

MAMAN COCHET

[*Tea, 1893*]

I have stumbled upon 'Maman Cochet' in the California gold rush country, as well as in Bermuda, New Zealand, and Australia—happily growing in abject abandonment amid tombstones and weeds. Ever the hardy survivor, Maman fills that role wonderfully in moderate-climate gardens.

A medium-size shrub, 'Maman Cochet' will, in milder climes, eventually reach 4 feet or so in height and diameter. Triangular red prickles are scattered along strong, upright-growing grass green canes with verdant, reasonably problem-free foliage that frames large, bulbous flowers. Individually formed, corpulent strawberries-and-cream buds are held upright on the strong canes until the weight causes them to nod. They open to mammoth pink blossoms that display a parfait of pink, eggshell, strawberry, lavender, and even soft lemon yellow, but the overall coloration is dusky lavender-pink. The outer two rows of guard petals often flare widely, revealing a spherical dome of overlapping petals at the center. 'Maman Cochet' is strongly redolent of peach and apricot with a hint of raspberries and an earthy attar. The large, fully petaled flowers will ball in wet weather, but the repeat bloom is strong and the fall flowers are truly outstanding.

Maman produced several important sports over the years, and at least one has been misidentified in the trade. The white sport of 'Maman Cochet' came out in 1896 and has an all-over white to pale lemon yellow cast with hints of pink. The rose most often confused with Maman is 'Niles Cochet,' which was introduced in 1906 by the California Nursery Company of Niles, California. 'Niles Cochet,' or as it is sometimes called "Red Maman Cochet," has a decidedly more sanguine cast and none of the soft lavender of its parent rose.

"Mother" Cochet was named in honor of the hybridizer's mother and grandmother.

HYBRIDIZER: Scipion Cochet, Grisy-Suisnes, France
SUITABILITY: all levels
AVAILABILITY: mail-order
STATURE & HABIT: warm climate, 4' × 4'; cool climate, 3' × 2'
FRAGRANCE: peach, apricot, raspberries, earthy attar

USES: border, container, cutting
PARENTAGE: 'Marie van Houtte' × 'Mme. Lombard'
DISEASES: mildew
HARDINESS: hot climate, excellent; cold climate, tender
BLOOM: remontant

Maman Cochet

MARBRÉE

[*Portland, 1858*]

"M arbled" is how this name translates, and marbled is the best description for this cultivar. Streaked, speckled, striped, and otherwise marked roses were very popular before the advent of incandescent lighting—the deep rich tones took on a romantic look under the flickering candles or gas lighting of the age. The changeover to incandescent electric lights at the end of the 19th century, as well as a perception that these roses were old-fashioned and out of style, led to their decline in popularity.

A typical Portland Rose, 'Marbrée' will top out at around 4 feet and grow almost as wide. The light red-to-green canes are covered with small, hairlike prickles right up to the flowers. The spring green foliage is long and pointed and continues up the stem, so that the bloom seems to rest in a nest of leaves. Leaf stalks are bright red with green stipules clasping the stem, and you'll have few if any foliage problems. Spherical ruby buds are held in small, tight clusters and open to flat, bright primrose pink flowers that are speckled with a lighter shell pink. Golden stamens liven up the center of the semi-double blooms.

The fragrance is a mixture, strongly of lime and spice and more lightly of Old Rose attar, like that used in rose perfumes. The repeat bloom is very good, and a decent crop of long, narrow, Damask-like hips dusted with fine hairs will be produced in autumn if you discontinue deadheading in late summer. Portland Roses like 'Marbrée' are good choices for a low border or even planting in containers.

Rose hybridizers quickly incorporated Portland Roses, first into the Hybrid Perpetuals in order to reinforce the H.P.'s cold-hardiness and repeat bloom, and through them, into our modern Hybrid Teas and Floribundas. It is easy to overlook this class as there were so few Portlands introduced, but they still are a dependable, hardy group that deserve to be considered for a place in the garden.

HYBRIDIZER: Robert et Moreau, Angers, France
SUITABILITY: all levels
AVAILABILITY: mail-order
STATURE & HABIT: warm climate, 4' × 4'; cool climate, 4' × 3'
FRAGRANCE: lime and spice, lighter of Old Rose

USES: border, container, cutting
PARENTAGE: unknown
DISEASES: clean
HARDINESS: hot climate, good; cold climate, good
BLOOM: remontant

Marbrée

MARIE PAVIÉ

[*Polyantha, 1888*]

The first Polyantha Roses were crosses of dwarf seedling forms of *Rosa multiflora* and Chinas, and although 'Marie Pavié' (sometimes spelled "Marie Pavič" or "Marie Parvie") is true to that form, little information is available about her parentage. Marie is found all over the South and West, persisting in old gardens, abandoned home sites, and cemeteries.

Low-growing and compact, this rose never exceeds 4 feet by about the same in width. The thornless dark green, bifurcated canes are camouflaged by emerald green, pointed, five- to seven-leaflet compound foliage. The waxy foliage is strongly resistant to disease. Small pale yellow buds are displayed in large corymbs atop the foliage, then they open to small, double, Hybrid Tea-shaped alabaster and cream blooms that occasionally flash a hint of shell pink in addition to a lovely strong, peppery fragrance. The overall effect is a mound of green with an airy display of white blossoms waving in the breeze. The repeat bloom is nearly continuous, simply needing occasional deadheading to keep the shrub clean looking.

Marie is about as close to perfection as any rose in this class comes. Uncomplicated in her demands, hardy and tough, she will prosper with the minimum of care. Pruning need be nothing more than taking hedge shears and rounding her off each spring, although she will benefit from the judicious removal of old, dead, and diseased wood if you come across any.

What little I've been able to discover about Marie Pavié leads me to believe she was the daughter of a wealthy family, possibly a woman who lived a saintly and devout Catholic life, also probably one whose husband was important in the region's political hierarchy as she was both married and buried at Nôtre Dame. Marie was born about 1637 at Le Château D'Oléron in Saintonge, France.

HYBRIDIZER: Alphonse Alégatière, Lyons, France

SUITABILITY: all levels

AVAILABILITY: wide

STATURE & HABIT: warm climate, 4' × 4'; cool climate, 4' × 2'

FRAGRANCE: strong pepper

USES: border, container, hedge, cutting

PARENTAGE: unknown

DISEASES: clean

HARDINESS: hot climate, good; cold climate, good

BLOOM: remontant

Marie Pavié

MRS. JOHN LAING

[Hybrid Perpetual, 1887]

Henry Bennett was an experienced breeder of livestock long before he took up rose breeding. His experience with horses and cattle confirmed the value of keeping accurate parentage records. Up until his day, no one in the rose world had bothered to keep any records to speak of—often, parentages were surmised after the fact by comparing the new seedling to existing roses. Bennett not only recorded the mother (seed parent), but also which rose provided the pollen (father). Even though Gregor Mendel had published his principles of inheritance in 1866, they were for the most part ignored by the scientific community, so Bennett was truly ahead of the curve, and this is one of his most enduring roses.

'Mrs. John Laing' is a moderate- to tall-growing, upright shrub—in other words, a typical Hybrid Perpetual. The bottle green canes are strong and fastigiate, with triangular-shaped, small red prickles. The healthy, deep green, waxy foliage is egg-shaped, jagged along the margins and hairy below. Flowers and buds are usually produced individually, one to a stem. The tall, pointed, conical buds are deep pink opening to deeply cupped, globular, fully petaled, heavily perfumed flowers of an all-over jejune rose-pink, with a lilac flush to the pink; the reverse side of the petals exhibits a silvery sheen. The flowers are seldom if ever adversely affected by rain or mildew, and the fragrance is a cheery mix of rose and citrus.

In her day, 'Mrs. John Laing' was every bit as ubiquitous as 'Peace' or 'Charlotte Armstrong' were in their day. The color is a rather dull, unimposing pink, but the fragrance and the strength of rebloom created a niche in just about every garden of the period.

The name commemorates the wife of a famous British horticulturist. It is reported that Bennett sold the rights for this cultivar in the United States for $45,000, an enormous sum at the time.

HYBRIDIZER: Henry Bennett, Shepperton, England
SUITABILITY: all levels
AVAILABILITY: wide
STATURE & HABIT: warm climate, 6' × 6'; cool climate, 5' × 5'
FRAGRANCE: rose, citrus

USES: border, hedge, cutting
PARENTAGE: 'François Michelon' seedling
DISEASES: clean
HARDINESS: hot climate, good; cold climate, moderate
BLOOM: remontant

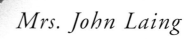

Mrs. John Laing

MUTABILIS

[*China, 1894*]

A shrub of 'Mutabilis' in full bloom can only be described as a congregation of scarlet, pink, and yellow butterflies taking up residence on a big bush, warming their outstretched wings in the late afternoon sun before taking to flight at twilight. No other single-petaled rose elicits as many comments as this one. 'Mutabilis' is a large shrub, often attaining climbing stature if left on its own; with a little judicious pruning, it is an accommodating low mound enwrapped with kaleidoscopic bloom.

This adaptable shrub can grow anywhere from 3 feet to more than 6, with an equal spread. The strong, twiggy, buffed mahogany red canes are peppered with massive, hooked crimson prickles. New growth is burgundy-violet and altogether appealing. Narrow, lance-shaped, glossy jade green foliage provides a framework for displaying the crisp, vermilion red buds that first open peachy yellow with just a hint of apricot, transforming with the day to cameo pink, and concluding the following day as crimson. This color change is induced by sunlight acting upon pigments in the petals, causing a chemical reaction that results in this unfolding sequence of colors, each one spanning a single 24-hour period. The fragrance is just as fickle as the rest of this rose, starting off candy sweet, aging with spice to finish as a slight peppery nuance. 'Mutabilis' is seldom bothered by disease, and the rebloom is endless.

A large, fully grown specimen of 'Mutabilis' is a sight to behold—the suntanning effect will take your breath away. Plant the shrub where it can grow to full size, even placing a pair at the entrance to a secret garden, or allow it to scamper over a low wall. You'll not be disappointed.

'Mutabilis' was originally collected on a botanical expedition to Réunion, in the Indian Ocean, sponsored by the Italian prince Ghilberto Borromeo. We do know that by the late 1890s, the prince was growing 'Mutabilis' in his famous island garden in Lago Maggiore in the north Italian lake district.

HYBRIDIZER: unknown
SUITABILITY: all levels
AVAILABILITY: wide
STATURE & HABIT: warm climate, 6' × 6', cool climate, 3' × 2'
FRAGRANCE: slight candy sweetness, spice and pepper

USES: border, hedge, small climber, container
PARENTAGE: unknown
DISEASES: clean
HARDINESS: hot climate, very good; cold climate, tender
BLOOM: remontant

Mutabilis

OLD BLUSH

[*China, 1752*]

'Old Blush' is one of the most influential roses of all time, and a key player in the creation of modern reblooming roses. "Common Monthly," "Old Pink Daily," and "Parsons' Pink China" are names often applied to this "stud." Before the introduction of this cultivar, only two roses were known in Europe that bloomed more than the one traditional spring flush, those being 'Autumn Damask' and the 'Musk Rose.' Both of these Old European Garden Roses were combined with the "new kid on the block" (which had been around for centuries in its own homeland far to the east). These days in the California gold rush country, a cemetery isn't a cemetery without at least one bush of this ubiquitous Old Rose.

Usually grown as a low, condensed shrub, given space and time 'Old Blush' can create a large mound of 3 or 4 feet in height and at least that, if not a little more, in width. The coppery red new growth contrasts nicely with the thin, leek green canes. Cordovan prickles are small and few, and the avocado green, lance-shaped foliage suffers mildew only occasionally. Small flowers are produced in medium-size clusters from diminutive, peaked sanguine buds, and upon opening, the China pink flowers are fully cupped. The blossoms then open completely to rather informally shaped, blowsy roses. The outer or upper surfaces of individual petals gain much deeper pink tones as they're exposed to the sun, while the inner petals, which receive less sunlight, remain a silvery pink. Fragrance is light when compared to the more traditional perfumes of the Old European Roses, but may best be described as a spicy, peppery tea scent. Disease resistance is quite good and rebloom is almost continuous, while small orbs of strawberry red hips are produced in the fall.

'Old Blush' is the "Last Rose of Summer" celebrated by the Irish poet Thomas Moore: "'Tis the last rose of summer/Left blooming alone;/All her lovely companions/Are faded and gone . . ."

HYBRIDIZER: unknown
SUITABILITY: all levels
AVAILABILITY: wide
STATURE & HABIT: warm climate, 3' × 4'; cool climate, 2' × 2'
FRAGRANCE: spicy, peppery

USES: border, hedge, container
PARENTAGE: unknown
DISEASES: mildew
HARDINESS: hot climate, very good; cold climate, tender
BLOOM: remontant

Old Blush

PAUL NEYRON

[*Hybrid Perpetual, 1869*]

Looking for humongous roses? You've come to the right place. Sometimes described as more peony-like than rosy, 'Paul Neyron' produces some of the largest blooms among the Old Rose group.

A tall, fastigiate shrub, 'Paul Neyron' will grow to 6 feet and about half as wide. The new growth is a shiny, citron green edged with red. The light Kelly green canes are often described as thornless, but I would find it more accurate to say that most canes carry a smattering of barbs, with an occasional stem completely armed. Foliage is large, glaucous green, leathery, and somewhat prone to rust in areas where that problem is commonplace. The plump buds are usually produced one to a stem, and first appear a primrose pink with silvery pink reverses, opening to enormous, fully petaled, shocking pink, lilac-tinted blossoms. When open, the flat, quartered flowers are simply crammed with petals—no room for propagation of any kind. The receptacle, which sits just below the bud, is relatively long, narrow, and tubelike, and the leafy sepals are long and quite appealing. It is the fragrance, though, that will astound you. Deep and pervasive, Paul's scent is the essence of rose distilled from a thousand crisp, dewy petals. A constant repeat bloom is relatively good in warm zones, but in cooler regions, the shrub will bloom strongest in spring and fall with only an intermittent bloom between. In cool, wet weather, disease can be a concern, so preparation is essential.

'Paul Neyron' was and is known as the "Cabbage Rose" in gardens where his true identity is lost or clouded. He was widely planted in his day and then shared from garden to garden, where, while his name may have occasionally been forgotten, his scent ensured a following.

This rose is named for a medical student who died in 1872 during the Franco-Prussian War while helping the sick.

HYBRIDIZER: Antoine Levet, Lyons, France

SUITABILITY: all levels

AVAILABILITY: wide

STATURE & HABIT: warm climate, 6' × 3'; cool climate, 3' × 2'

FRAGRANCE: intense distilled rose attar

USES: border, hedge, cutting, pegging

PARENTAGE: 'Victor Verdier' × 'Anna de Diesbach'

DISEASES: mildew, rust

HARDINESS: hot climate, very good; cold climate, good

BLOOM: remontant

Paul Neyron

PERLE D'OR

[*Polyantha, 1884*]

O ften found labeled as "Yellow Cécile Brünner," 'Perle d'Or' is a completely satisfying shrub. The soft apricot-colored bloom is almost unique among Old Garden Roses, and the fact that there were, until recently, few commercial sources for her made her a very desirable rose for the connoisseur. Thankfully, obtaining this cultivar today is no longer a challenge as a number of nurseries regularly catalog 'Perle d'Or' among their prized offerings. In every way, Perle is so similar to that other great Polyantha, 'Mlle. Cécile Brünner,' that it would be almost impossible to say which is which except for the difference in color.

'Perle d'Or' creates a low-mounding shrub to 3 or 4 feet in height and diameter. New growth is bronze with red canes. The narrow, elliptical-shaped foliage is verdant green, burnished, and angular, with not the slightest proclivity to pest or fungal troubles. Mature canes are light green to almost yellow-green, with the sporadic large, hooked, claret red prickle. Buds are produced on tall, upright, twiggy flowering stalks that branch out well above the foliage. Enormous clusters of apricot-orange, Hybrid Tea-shaped buds open to soft apricot-pink flowers. Individual flowers are small and chock-full of narrow, straplike petals, opening to flat, loosely formed blooms. Perle's aroma is a cornucopia if you keep your nose close: starting with a strong pepper and tobacco scent, becoming a sweeter spice after a few seconds, and finishing as a light peachy essence. The flowering spikes rise high above the foliage, giving the bush a light, airy appearance, and rebloom is quite strong.

'Perle d'Or' truly is a "Golden Pearl" for your garden. Plant her as a hedge along a walk or to define a bed, or plant her in containers to accent a sunny patio garden. Perle was developed by Rambaux and introduced by his mother-in-law, the widow of Francis Dubreuil.

HYBRIDIZER: Rambaux; introduced by Veuve Dubreuil, Lyons, France

SUITABILITY: all levels

AVAILABILITY: wide

STATURE & HABIT: warm climate, 3' × 3'; cool climate, 2' × 2'

FRAGRANCE: pepper, tobacco, spices, peach

USES: border, low hedge, container, cutting

PARENTAGE: Polyantha × 'Mme. Falcot'

DISEASES: clean

HARDINESS: hot climate, very good; cold climate, moderate

BLOOM: remontant

Perle d'Or

PERSIAN YELLOW

[*Species Hybrid, 1837*]

Originating as a double sport of *Rosa foetida,* 'Persian Yellow' has proved to be a very influential parent of Modern Roses. Working over a number of years, Joseph Pernet-Ducher used the pollen of 'Persian Yellow' to produce the very first repeat-blooming yellow rose, 'Soleil d'Or.' That's the good news. The bad news is that it is also responsible for the preponderance of blackspot among so many Modern Roses today.

The thin, hazel brown canes of 'Persian Yellow' will reach 6 to 7 feet in height and will fountain outward, from their own weight, to nearly as wide. The umber canes are bedecked with spiny, needle-sharp gray prickles spaced just below the leaflets at the nodes. The delicate foliage is small, oval, serrated, and edged thinly with reddish brown tones. Flowers are produced individually on squat, shamrock green shoots that form off the main canes. The cupped double blooms are a brilliant chrome yellow. The fragrance of the *R. foetida* species is often described, just as the Latin word indicates, as "smelling of rotten flesh," but this one reminds me more of spice and apples. 'Persian Yellow' habitually blooms earlier than most other roses, so its brilliant yellow flowers are especially welcome in the garden even though it only blooms that one time. This cultivar is also a real survivor, existing for decades with little or no special care. Even the disease blackspot, for which it is the notorious carrier, isn't all that much of a problem for this shrub.

'Persian Yellow' is a double form of what is usually listed as the species *Rose foetida persiana.* But the pollen fertility is so low with 'Persian Yellow' that it's difficult to see just how this "species" could have survived and propagated itself from seed without our help.

HYBRIDIZER: unknown; introduced by Sir Henry Willock, England

SUITABILITY: all levels

AVAILABILITY: wide

STATURE & HABIT: warm climate, 6' × 6'; cool climate, 6' × 4'

FRAGRANCE: sometimes fetid, often more of spice and apples

USES: border, partial shade, cutting

PARENTAGE: sport of 'Austrian Briar '

DISEASES: blackspot

HARDINESS: hot climate, very good; cold climate, excellent

BLOOM: spring

Persian Yellow

PETITE DE HOLLANDE

[*Centifolia, 1800*]

Introduced to France from Holland around the end of the 18th century, this is another compact-growing Old Rose that will blend nicely into our smaller modern gardens and still be capable of adding verticality to an area planted with low-growing perennials or other plants. The bloom and foliage are also well-proportioned to the size of the shrub. 'Petite de Hollande' is an accommodating shrub, tucking nicely into a corner where her spring bloom will be a pleasant surprise.

A modest shrub, 'Petite de Hollande' will attain 4 feet in height with age, and about the same in reach. The wrinkled, holly green foliage is serrated, and in all aspects similar to that of other Centifolias except in size—this cultivar's leaves are slightly smaller. Canes are bottle green and bejeweled with Vandyke brown prickles of assorted sizes and shapes. Bouquets of bloom are formed in clusters along the stems, while the carmine buds are ornamented with decorative, leafy sepals that give the opening flowers a fresh, airy appearance. The small, fully petaled, carnation flowers remain cupped at first and later mature to flat rosettes. The diminutive blooms are scaled beautifully in proportion to the size of the foliage. The fragrance is sweet and strong with hops and Old Rose perfume. Disease resistance for this spring-blooming cultivar is good. 'Petite de Hollande' is ranked as having very good cold- and drought-tolerance in the Pacific Northwest.

If the garden space is available, consider planting a cluster of three plants of this dainty shrub at a focal point, where her luxuriant spring display and fragrance will create a sensation in your garden. A light pruning in summer, right after the shrub has finished blooming, will be enough to keep this delicate rose under control.

Like so many of her older sisters, 'Petite de Hollande' has been given a number of names: "Petite Junon de Hollande," "Pompon des Dames," and "Normandica" are a few. Essentially, they all refer to her being a "daughter of Holland."

HYBRIDIZER: unknown
SUITABILITY: all levels
AVAILABILITY: mail-order
STATURE & HABIT: warm
    climate, 4' × 4';
    cool climate, 4' × 3'
FRAGRANCE: strong of hops and
    sweet Old Rose

USES: border, low hedge,
    cutting
PARENTAGE: unknown
DISEASES: clean
HARDINESS: hot climate, good;
    cold climate, excellent
BLOOM: spring

Petite de Hollande

POMPON BLANC PARFAIT

[*Alba, 1876*]

For me, this rose simply radiates an ethereal charm that almost defies description. For such a large plant, the individual flowers are small and not always perfectly formed, but it's actually the fragrance that dazzles me. The closest I can approach it in words is to say it reminds me of how a soft, fruity, sparkling wine should taste. And not any sparkling wine, but the finest vintage of Asti Spumante from Italy.

Pompon will often reach heights of 6 or 7 feet in my garden, somewhat less in cooler climes. She is rather unbranching in her tall, upright, columnar growth. The new aqua green foliage is small, roundish, and jagged-edged. Canes are only lightly dusted with hooked, emerald green prickles, and the foliage is resistant to most fungal problems. Diminutive, pompon-shaped rosette flowers are displayed individually and in tight clusters amid mature glaucous green foliage. Tiny orbed buds open white, and then form tight pompons that are flushed with pale shell pink, aging to ivory white. The blooming season is noticeably longer than that of many other roses in this class.

Plant Pompon where her upright growth and height will fountain out of the border and allow her intense perfume to mesmerize you. The canes of this cultivar are a bit too stiff to either train onto a structure or self-peg, but the shrub could be splayed out over a fence or wall in a fan-like shape; maybe a trellis would be a fitting home for her in your garden.

The small flowers and stiff, fastigiate growth of 'Pompon Blanc Parfait' are somewhat atypical for an Alba Rose, and probably indicate a hybrid origin with some other class of Old Rose. That aside, for pure olfactory pleasure, I can think of no other rose that emits such a sweet distillation.

HYBRIDIZER: Eugène Verdier, Paris, France

SUITABILITY: intermediate

AVAILABILITY: mail-order

STATURE & HABIT: warm climate, 7' × 3'; cool climate, 4' × 3'

FRAGRANCE: strong of fruity sweet wine

USES: border, hedge, partial shade

PARENTAGE: unknown

DISEASES: mildew, rust

HARDINESS: hot climate, very good; cold climate, very good

BLOOM: spring

Pompon
Blanc Parfait

PRINCESSE LOUISE

[*Rambler, 1829*]

Rambling roses were popular through the latter portion of the 19th and early part of the 20th centuries, primarily because they were among the first true climbing roses of the age, and because they were exceptionally cold-tolerant. 'Princesse Louise' was listed by the breeder as a seedling, most likely from *Rosa sempervirens,* a nearly evergreen species from southern Europe. Monsieur Jacques was gardener to the Duc d'Orléans and introduced several other Ramblers; among the best known are 'Adélaïde d'Orléans' (1826) and 'Félicité Perpétue' (1827).

'Princesse Louise' will reach 12 feet or more with little coaxing and spread nearly as wide, rambling up and over trees or whatever gets in her way. The shiny, nearly evergreen foliage is pointed, deeply veined, and exceedingly healthy. Bloom is produced in large terminal clusters at the ends of long, ropelike, supple canes. Rotund, cameo pink buds open to fully petaled flowers in blush pink to ivory white. Individual rosettes are nicely shaped, with the shorter inner petals often forming a button-eye at the center. The soft primrose fragrance is slight at best. A once-bloomer, 'Princesse Louise' blooms a little late in spring and continues on into early summer.

Ramblers like the Princesse are perfectly suited for training over arches and covering pergolas, where her flexible canes and deep green foliage create a perfect foil for the lovely June display of blossoms. She also is quite amenable for training into trees where she will spill out, brandishing her charms to passersby lucky enough to stroll your garden.

Antoine Jacques continued as gardener to King Louis XVIII's grounds at Neuilly and developed some of the first repeat-blooming roses. Princesse Louise was one of the king's daughters.

HYBRIDIZER: Antoine A. Jacques, Neuilly, France

SUITABILITY: all levels

AVAILABILITY: mail-order

STATURE & HABIT: warm climate, 12' × 12'; cool climate, 12' × 12'

FRAGRANCE: slight, of primrose

USES: climber, trained into trees

PARENTAGE: *R. sempervirens* hybrid

DISEASES: clean

HARDINESS: hot climate, good; cold climate, good

BLOOM: spring

Princesse Louise

REINE DES VIOLETTES

[*Hybrid Perpetual, 1860*]

Down through the years there have been many a "Queen of Roses," but this "Queen of the Violets" reigns supreme. Her deep purple-pink blooms, almost approaching a shade of blue, have long been cherished for their color, complexity of texture, and appropriately violet-like perfume. For me, the best Hybrid Perpetuals are among the very earliest introductions, but this Queen is the exception to that rule.

Often reaching 6 feet or more in height, Reine is an upright grower, with a relatively short spread. New growth is absinthe green edged with bronze, and the long, thin, knobby glaucous green canes are nearly thornless with puce-purple mottling. The toothed, seven-leaflet compound aquamarine foliage is elliptical in shape; it is clean and reasonably free of pests. Bloom is often produced singly or in small, tight clusters on the stem. Flattish scarlet buds open to fully petaled cerise flowers, which later take on alluring amethyst-purple hues mottled with white and lavender on the reverse. The perfume is delicate and sweet of violets, with an undertone of the finest milled French soap, while the foliage has a peppery scent to me. Rebloom is strongest at the height of spring and fall, but there can often be a scattering of bloom throughout the season.

There is a strong sense of the Gallica Rose about 'Reine des Violettes,' and the way the flowers are tightly underlaid by the foliage is very reminiscent of the Portland class. This grand old dame will tolerate some shade, and in fact, the color of her blooms will be much improved when protected from the hottest sun. As she tends to be a large grower, she can be trained onto a pyramid of garden stakes or some other structure to increase flowering. I do find that this cultivar appreciates a firm hand at pruning time, and suggest that you prune her back a bit more severely than I have suggested for other Old Roses.

HYBRIDIZER: Millet-Malet
SUITABILITY: all levels
AVAILABILITY: wide
STATURE & HABIT: warm climate, 6' × 6'; cool climate, 5' × 3'
FRAGRANCE: strong of milled soaps and delicate violets; peppery foliage

USES: border, low climber, cutting
PARENTAGE: 'Pius IX' seedling
DISEASES: rust
HARDINESS: hot climate, very good; cold climate, very good
BLOOM: remontant

Reine des Violettes

REINE VICTORIA

[*Bourbon, 1872*]

For ages hybridizers have named roses to honor the rich and famous in hopes of garnering a cachet of celebrity for their creation. The survival and continued garden popularity of 'Reine Victoria' is a testament to the developer's confidence in his production. Often listed in catalogs as "La Reine Victoria," the "La" was added some time after the rose's introduction by catalog writers and is incorrect.

'Reine Victoria' is quite capable of reaching 8 feet or more in warm zones with an equal spread, so caution should be taken as to her placement. Canes are forest green and smooth with the occasional scattered, hooked ruby prickle. The seven-leaflet compound foliage is on the smallish side, and is a glossy deep green on the top with a duller tint on the reverse; it possesses good resistance to disease. The pointed buds are produced in large terminal clusters and are at first revealed in cerise to red hues. The opened, fully petaled, silvery pink blooms are first cupped, later opening to flat rose madder flowers, often with well-organized quartering. Spring bloom is best but you will have flowers throughout the season. As with all Bourbons, the fragrance is sweet and powerful—this one full of ripening pears and stone fruits.

Many gardeners have abandoned this Queen for her more delicately colored daughter, 'Mme. Pierre Oger,' but in my opinion, both warrant a place in the garden as their colors and aromas blend and complement each other. I have seen Bourbons like 'Reine Victoria' trained onto an 8- or 10-foot-tall pyramid or similar structure, taming her exuberant growth. In this manner, you'll be able to maximize bloom production and minimize the amount of valuable garden space used.

Victoria became Queen of England in 1837 on the death of her uncle, William IV. She remains the longest-reigning monarch in the history of the United Kingdom, continuing to rule for 63 years until her death at the age of 82 in 1901.

HYBRIDIZER: Joseph Schwartz, Lyons, France
SUITABILITY: all levels
AVAILABILITY: wide
STATURE & HABIT: warm climate, 8' × 8'; cool climate, 5' × 3'
FRAGRANCE: strong and sweet

USES: border, short climber, pegging, cutting
PARENTAGE: unknown
DISEASES: mildew
HARDINESS: hot climate, very good; cold climate, good
BLOOM: remontant

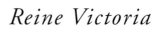

Reine Victoria

ROSA BANKSIAE LUTEA

[*Species Hybrid*]

This "Lady Banks' Rose" is not one of the true species, but a double yellow-flowering sport of the wild form, which has been in cultivation for so long in Asia that no one is quite sure how it originated. For those who have the space and climate, Lady Banks is one of the most spectacular shrubs in the spring garden.

A large, rambling rose, Lady Banks will clamber over a wall or up into trees, often to 20 feet or more. Almost thornless, the lengthy, slender flowering canes are a burnished olive green, and blanketed with small, shiny, lance-shaped, moss green foliage. The three- to seven-leaflet compound leaves are disease-resistant. The large, older canes are covered with chestnut brown, flaky bark. Small clusters of primrose yellow buds open to chrome yellow, popcorn-size and -shaped blooms. Each flower cluster is produced on short stems at the leaf nodes of mature canes. As the petals of each flower reflex back, they surprisingly reveal the most lovely green centers and saffron yellow stamens. The scent of this double form is very slight, but the single white species, *Rosa banksiae banksiae,* is resplendent with the fragrance of violets. The species and double forms are spring bloomers, with an occasional second blooming in fall as the plants mature.

The delicacy of the bloom is matched by no other rose, so care should be taken to avoid excessive pruning of this Lady as she only blooms on mature wood of one year or older.

'Lady Banks' was named for the wife of the director of Kew Gardens, Sir Joseph Banks. Sir Joseph had sailed on the *Endeavour* with Captain Cook during his first voyage to Australia.

ORIGIN: central and western China

SUITABILITY: intermediate

AVAILABILITY: limited

STATURE & HABIT: warm climate, 20' × 15'; cool climate, 15' × 8'

FRAGRANCE: very slight

USES: climber, pillar, pegging, cover for hillsides and banks

PARENTAGE: species

DISEASES: clean

HARDINESS: hot climate, very good; cold climate, tender

BLOOM: spring, occasionally repeats

Rosa
banksiae lutea

ROSA GLAUCA

[*Species*]

Also known as *Rosa rubrifolia,* this Species Rose originated in the mountain wilds of central to southern Europe, where it was introduced into cultivation prior to 1830. Most often grown for its handsome gray-purple foliage, *R. glauca* can create quite a stir in the border when its leaves are set against the much brighter greens of contrasting shrubs.

R. glauca is an open-growing shrub that can range from 3 to 12 feet or so in circumference, depending on placement and climate; usually, though, it remains a pendant shrub, arching out to around 6 feet at most. The lustrous mahogany-colored new canes are quite delicate and slender to their tips, with narrow, pointed, small gray-green to amethyst-purple new foliage that is darker on its reverse. This shrub produces its new growth on thin, wiry branches with few prickles. Leaflets are lance-like and finely serrated along their margins. The ligules, which clasp each leaf stem, are often reddish purple and beautifully ornamental as well. Small clusters of dark pink buds, with delicate ornamental sepals, open to tiny, five-petaled, lightly fragrant, mallow pink flowers with a white inner circle and bright yellow stamens. Like many Species Roses, this shrub seems to be remarkably resistant to most diseases. A spring-flowering species, *R. glauca* produces small clusters of striking, roundish red hips in the fall, so do yourself a double favor and don't bother to deadhead.

The red, fuzzy ball in our portrait is a gall, commonly called "robin's pincushion," caused by a minute wasp that stings the young stems in the process of laying her eggs. The female wasp's sting injects a chemical to force the growth, providing a haven for the growing larvae she'll never see.

ORIGIN: mountains of central and southern Europe
SUITABILITY: intermediate
AVAILABILITY: mail-order
STATURE & HABIT: warm climate, 3' × 3'; cool climate, 6' × 5'
FRAGRANCE: light rosy scent

USES: border, cutting, hips
PARENTAGE: species
DISEASES: clean
HARDINESS: hot climate, poor; cold climate, excellent
BLOOM: spring

*Rosa
glauca*

ROSA
MULTIFLORA CARNEA

[*Species*]

osa multiflora carnea, the double form of *R. multiflora cathayen-sis,* was introduced from China to Britain around 1804. This is one of the longest-blooming OGRs I grow—some years back, it extended its bloom in my garden clear through August. A thorny, sprawling plant that needs discipline and a good deal of thought as to placement in the garden, *R.m. carnea* can be tamed by training into an old fruit tree or over an unsightly outbuilding. In full bloom, this rose will simply take your breath away.

The olive green, 10- to 12-foot canes are sprinkled with tiny, needlelike garnet prickles, while the small, oval, downy gray-green foliage is a little sparse. Tiny pink buds are produced in small bouquets on short flowering stems; the diminutive, flat double blooms open cameo pink aging to white, often displaying a jade green point at their center. Each cluster will exhibit all the color stages of bloom from rosy pink through milky pink, and in good weather, this rose will bloom for six weeks and often much longer. The exquisite blossoms exhale a soft, sweet spicy scent, with nuances of rose and cinnamon. The parent of this form is a species from eastern China, and as such is reasonably winter-hardy in our coldest zones. The velvety textured foliage is seldom afflicted with disease.

Ask any Midwestern Boy Scout from the '50s and he will remember planting hedgerows of *R. multiflora* as a windbreak and habitat for native wildlife. The scouts planted miles of these hedgerows though, unfortunately, this species reproduces itself easily by seed and became a noxious weed in those areas where it had been planted extensively.

Carnea comes from the Latin *carneus,* for "flesh-colored."

ORIGIN: eastern Asia

SUITABILITY: intermediate

AVAILABILITY: mail-order

STATURE & HABIT: warm climate, 12' × 12'; cool climate, 12' × 12'

FRAGRANCE: soft spices, rose and cinnamon

USES: climber, hedge, trained into trees

PARENTAGE: species

DISEASES: clean

HARDINESS: hot climate, good; cold climate, very good

BLOOM: spring

Rosa multiflora
carnea

ROSA MUNDI

[*Gallica, 1581*]

The first mention of this "Rose of the World" was in *The Garden Book* of Sir Thomas Hanmer, published in 1659, where it is listed as a sport of 'Apothecary's Rose' that had been found in a Norfolk garden a few years before. Few Old Roses evoke more memories and history than 'Rosa Mundi.'

As a typical Gallica, this cultivar will reach 3 feet or so, and on its own roots, will create a spreading colony that may need to be pruned back with a shovel from time to time to contain the shrub. The emerald green canes are thin and arching, enwrapped with numerous small, dark brown prickles. The matte bottle green foliage is oval and lightly serrated. The terminal leaflet is often folded along the midrib and points downward. Bloom is produced in small clusters at the ends of the canes from pointed, deep pink buds. The five-petaled to semi-double flowers open fully and are striped and streaked with cameo pink on a deep cerise pink to carmine base. There is a flamboyant boss of golden yellow stamens at the center of the lightly perfumed blooms. Spring-blooming only, this tough shrub is hardy in the coldest of climates. 'Rosa Mundi' will often sport back to 'Apothecary's Rose,' so do not be surprised to find a solid-colored nugget among the striped gems.

In my mild Southern California winters, this cultivar is a far more dependable bloomer than her solid-colored sister, though there is little fragrance to speak of. Reports from all over the country confirm that 'Rosa Mundi' is dependably cold- and drought-tolerant, though she may be bothered by a bit of mildew and blackspot from time to time—but she doesn't seem to mind and neither should you.

Some books state emphatically that this rose was named for Jane Clifford, "Fair Rosamund," mistress of Henry II. Although apocryphal, it's still a good story.

HYBRIDIZER: unknown
SUITABILITY: all levels
AVAILABILITY: wide
STATURE & HABIT: warm climate, 3' × 3'; cool climate, 3' × 3'
FRAGRANCE: none to light Old Rose

USES: border, low hedge, cutting
PARENTAGE: sport of 'Apothecary's Rose'
DISEASES: mildew
HARDINESS: hot climate, very good; cold climate, very good
BLOOM: spring

Rosa Mundi

ROSA ROXBURGHII NORMALIS

[*Species*]

While the 'Chestnut Rose,' the double form of this species, has been in European gardens since at least 1814, the true species wasn't discovered and introduced into cultivation until sometime around 1909.

Rosa roxburghii normalis can become quite a large shrub given time. The tall canes are covered with unusual straight prickles that point upward, unlike any other rose with which I'm familiar. These prickles are often paired just below each leaf. The taupe brown canes have unusual bark that as the plant matures, peels off in long, thin ribbons, revealing leek green bark underneath. This deciduous bark gives the old plant an interestingly shaggy look. Leaves are also unusual in that each compound leaf has from seven to nineteen tiny leaflets, giving the stem a fernlike look. Before opening, the Kelly green flower buds are covered with sharp, spiny growths that resemble a horse chestnut—thus the more common name. These burrs open to bright pink buds, which then reveal cameo pink, five-petaled flowers with a lovely central boss of golden stamens. The flowers can range from bright coral pink to lilac pink to silvery pink to alabaster white, while the petal reverse is always a much darker pink. Flowers are quite ephemeral, blooming only in the spring, but after the petals fall, the hips form into large green, round, spiny fruits that eventually turn red-orange, a charming seasonal addition. The single form is much more winter-hardy than the double form, making it more reliable in colder regions.

The English botanist John Lindley first described the double form in 1820 upon viewing a Chinese painting. He named it *R. microphylla,* but as that name had already been given by someone else to another rose, this one was eventually named for its discoverer, Dr. William Roxburgh (1751–1815).

ORIGIN: eastern and southern China, Japan
SUITABILITY: all levels
AVAILABILITY: limited
STATURE & HABIT: warm climate, 10' × 8'; cool climate, 8' × 8'
FRAGRANCE: light rose

USES: border, hedge
PARENTAGE: species
DISEASES: clean
HARDINESS: hot climate, good; cold climate, good
BLOOM: spring

Rosa roxburghii
normalis

ROSE DE MEAUX

[*Centifolia, 1789*]

A miniature Centifolia in every way, 'Rose de Meaux' can be compared to the other surviving diminutive Centifolias, 'Petite de Hollande' and 'Pompon de Burgogne,' for it too is a charming little rose when tucked into a cozy corner of the garden. Unlike so many modern miniature roses, De Meaux's foliage, growth habit, and blooms are all in perfect harmony with each other.

A low-growing, compact, shrubby plant with thin, upright, absinthe green canes, 'Rose de Meaux' may with time reach 3 feet in height and width. The new growth is light green, edged with red, while the canes are blanketed with numerous, small, pinlike, red-green prickles. Foliage is jade green, oval to pointed, and serrated. Tiny blossoms, hardly 1 inch across, are produced in small clusters from pale pink buds with handsome ornamental sepals. The cameo pink flowers are cupped at first, opening to flattish rosettes, while the outer petals pale to almost white. The mature flowers, while small, are fully petaled and often quartered. At best they emit a light, clean rose and pepper fragrance—it's usually almost nonexistent. The shrub is, in general, free of most diseases and is quite cold- and drought-tolerant in the Pacific Northwest.

Tough and hardy in all zones, this diminutive charmer can be planted as a low hedge, or in a container used to brighten the spring patio. I hardly ever see more than a little mildew on my plants from time to time, but there is a form in The Huntington's study collection that we christened "Mildewy de Meaux"—I don't think that you will be seeing it in commerce anytime soon. There is also a "White de Meaux" listed in a few catalogs.

The origins of this rose are obscure. Some say it was first discovered by a man named Sweet in 1789. Others claim it was named for Domenique Séguier, Bishop of Meaux, in whose garden it was reportedly found. The town of Meaux is about 20 kilometers northeast of Paris.

HYBRIDIZER: unknown
SUITABILITY: all levels
AVAILABILITY: mail-order
STATURE & HABIT: warm
   climate, 3' × 3';
   cool climate, 2' × 2½'
FRAGRANCE: slight, of roses and
   pepper

USES: border, low hedge,
   container
PARENTAGE: unknown
DISEASES: mildew
HARDINESS: hot climate, good;
   cold climate, very good
BLOOM: spring

Rose de Meaux

ROSE DE RESCHT

[*Autumn Damask, Ancient*]

Miss Nancy Lindsay collected this shapely old cultivar from a garden in the ancient caravan town of Rescht, in Persia, sometime before the Second World War. The upright, bottle green canes reach 3 feet or more with an equal circumference, and they are veiled with curved, needlelike prickles. Oval, rugose jade green foliage blankets the plant so that the flowers appear to float just above the leaves. Round red buds are formed either in small, tight clusters or individually. Flowers open dark crimson and quartered, seemingly choked with swirling, blood red petals. The blooms take on shades of slate gray and purple as they fade. The perfume is a light, perfect distillation of attar of Damask, but occasionally more dense. The tough foliage is seldom bothered by problems. This beauty's rebloom is continuous—a great boon in the summer shrubbery.

Not all Old Roses are rampant shrubs, fit only for an estate or wild garden. This little cultivar will blend nicely into a modern entrance garden, and can be grown quite easily in a container with annuals or perennials. When cut at the fully open stage, the flowers will not last long in a bouquet; instead, try cutting the bud just before the half-open stage, and condition it with hot water. Deadheading will further improve repeat bloom.

Some books list this rose as a Portland, and it does share a number of Portland traits, but 'Rose de Rescht' fits more closely with the Autumn Damasks, which were used to breed repeat-bloom into a number of classes of Old Roses in the 19th century.

HYBRIDIZER: unknown
SUITABILITY: all levels
AVAILABILITY: wide
STATURE & HABIT: warm
    climate, 4' × 4';
    cool climate, 3' × 3'
FRAGRANCE: distillation of
    light rose attar, sometimes
    stronger

USES: border, cutting
PARENTAGE: Portland × China
DISEASES: clean
HARDINESS: hot climate, very
    good; cold climate, good
BLOOM: remontant

Rose de Rescht

RUGOSA RUBRA

[*Hybrid Rugosa, Ancient*]

Rugosa roses originated along the coastal regions of northern Japan, Korea, and Manchuria, where they were discovered and brought into cultivation long before the first European ever saw them; they're still there today. These extremely cold-hardy, tough, remontant roses are true garden jewels, for few roses will take the conditions these roses can survive. Plant them on a coastal sand dune for erosion control and they will grow, lapping up the salt spray to spread into a formidable colony.

Described as "tough as nails" in Michigan, 'Rugosa Rubra' will create a large shrub of 7 feet and nearly as wide in just about any cold climate. In a warmer, drier zone, it doesn't seem to want to exceed 3 or 4 feet in height. The thin, arching Kelly green canes are defended by a wall of needlelike, hooked, green and brown prickles around which you'll practically need body armor. The wrinkled jade green compound foliage is long and narrow, and often produced with seven to nine leaflets. The foliage is impervious to all diseases, and bloom is produced in small, open clusters of three or more fragrant flowers. Blood red, elongated buds open to single, crinkled, five-petaled deep crimson flowers with a dusting of golden yellow stamens and a greenish eye. A fine crop of hips is produced right along with a constant supply of flowers, so there is really no need to deadhead. The turban-shaped hips, when mature, turn a stunning orange-red, and additional color is provided when the foliage turns red and gold in the fall.

Plant 'Rugosa Rubra' wherever you need an extremely cold-hardy, drought-tolerant shrub. The only problem listed for this cultivar seems to be that of Japanese beetles in areas where they are an absolute menace to gardening.

This hearty soul is usually listed among the species roses as *Rosa rugosa rubra,* but here we include it among the cultivars, as it is a selected form of the species. There is a white form, 'Rugosa Alba,' which is almost identical to 'Rugosa Rubra' except that the flowers are white.

HYBRIDIZER: unknown
SUITABILITY: all levels
AVAILABILITY: wide
STATURE & HABIT: warm climate, 4' × 5'; cool climate, 7' × 6'
FRAGRANCE: strong Old Rose

USES: border, container, erosion control, cutting, hips, fall color
PARENTAGE: species hybrid
DISEASES: very clean
HARDINESS: hot climate, good; cold climate, very good
BLOOM: remontant

Rugosa Rubra

RUSSELL'S COTTAGE ROSE

[*Rambler, 1837*]

My first foray into the world of rose rustling some years back brought me into contact with 'Russell's Cottage Rose' in the heart of the California gold rush country. Although this is a Rambler of unknown origins, it does appear to have a strong dash of *Rosa multiflora* in its blood. 'Russell's Cottage Rose' will reach 20 feet in height with an equal spread, so find either space for it to ramble or the time to train it.

The thin, ropelike Lincoln green canes are covered with abundant, tiny-but-adequate ginger-colored prickles. The forest green, seven-leaflet compound foliage is lance-shaped, finely serrated, and often folded along the midrib. As is usual for Ramblers derived from Multifloras, the stipules (the structures clasping the stem at the base of the leaf) have comblike or hairy growths along their edges. The spring blooms are found at the ends of the ropey canes and produced in luxurious large clusters. The small scarlet buds are round, with flat tops, and have attractive sepals that curl out and above the opening buds. There is a progression of color in the bloom cycle—from cerise pink, deepening to dark crimson with purple highlights, finally aging to amethyst purple. At their best, the crimson-purple flowers open out flat, displaying a bright boss of yellow stamens and often a white eye at their centers. The fragrance is strong of Old Garden Rose. The textured foliage can suffer from mildew in regions where that problem is prevalent, but it really isn't much of a problem.

Russell's is also listed under the names "Russelliana," "Old Spanish Rose," and "Souvenir de la Bataille de Marengo." No matter what you call him, 'Russell's Cottage Rose' is a flower in search of the right garden, and beautiful once planted there.

HYBRIDIZER: unknown
SUITABILITY: intermediate
AVAILABILITY: mail-order
STATURE & HABIT: warm climate, 20' × 20'; cool climate, 15' × 15'
FRAGRANCE: Rose attar

USES: climber, tall hedge, trained into trees, cutting
PARENTAGE: unknown
DISEASES: mildew
HARDINESS: hot climate, good; cold climate, good
BLOOM: spring

Russell's Cottage Rose

SAFRANO

[*Tea, 1839*]

The Tea Roses have always evoked a visceral response from me. Among the most cold-tender of roses, and seemingly delicate in both nature and growth pattern, their ephemeral charms evoke a calmer age. My plant of 'Safrano' came—with a history—from rosarian Ralph Moore, the father of modern miniature roses. He was in his nineties at the time, and his plant had been growing in his own father's garden. 'Safrano' is one of the earliest Teas still in general cultivation, and deservedly so.

An open-growing shrub of 5 feet or so, 'Safrano' has the typical Tea Rose habit of producing bloom on remarkably thin, twiggy wood. The smooth, almost polished plum green new canes are almost thorn-free; cinnamon brown prickles are reserved for the older canes. New leaves are red-bronze and mature to shiny, oval, smooth olive green, serrated foliage. The pointed apricot buds open to typically Tea-shaped, loosely petaled, straw yellow to apricot blooms. The scent is a mix—certainly more astringent, spicy, and fruit-scented than the classic Old Rose scent, but appealing nonetheless. Blossoms are produced individually or in small clusters at the ends of thin, branching stems. The "weak neck syndrome" one hears about so often as a criticism of Teas gives this plant a rather nodding appearance. The foliage can be susceptible to mildew, so if that can be a problem in your area, you may want to try one of the new environmentally mindful fungicides on the market.

Like all Teas, 'Safrano' will take some time to build up to its full size. Prune only lightly, remembering that bloom is on the thinnest wood. It's best to give only the lightest trim in spring, and then it may only be necessary to tip back the flowering branches and remove dead or damaged canes. Believe me, this rose will repay you with much more abundant bloom the easier you are with the shears!

Sometimes cataloged as "Aimé Plantier," 'Safrano' receives its name from the soft saffron yellow to apricot color of its bloom.

HYBRIDIZER: Beauregard, Angers, France

SUITABILITY: all levels

AVAILABILITY: mail-order

STATURE & HABIT: warm climate, 5' × 4'; cool climate, 4' × 3'

FRAGRANCE: spices and fruits

USES: border, cutting

PARENTAGE: unknown

DISEASES: mildew

HARDINESS: hot climate, very good; cold climate, tender

BLOOM: remontant

Safrano

SLATER'S CRIMSON CHINA

[*China, 1790*]

So much history and controversy revolves around this insignificant little rose, it's hard to know where to begin. Given names like *Rosa chinensis semperflorens,* "Chinese Monthly," and "Old Crimson China," one could expect some huge-flowered, constantly blooming, imposing shrub. The controversy revolves around just exactly which of the many disparate, small-flowered, red China Roses one finds is truly *the* 'Slater's Crimson China.' Our candidate, from Bermuda (grown there as "Belfield"), has been heavily promoted as the true rose of this name.

A runt of a stick-filled shrub to start with, 'Slater's Crimson China' will over time build itself up into a substantial bush of 5 feet or more with a spread of equal proportions. The slight, twiggy growth is shiny moss green with the occasional hooked ruby prickle. The jade green foliage is long and narrow, lightly serrated, and pointed at the tips. Small, loosely petaled blooms are produced in clusters on thin, knobby stems held atop the foliage. Upon first opening, the buds are pale pink, darkening later to crimson. The petals darken perceptibly with prolonged exposure to sunlight—in other words, they suntan. Individual petals are narrow at the base and wider, with a notch at the tip. There is often a vein of white, called a quill, running from the base up the length of some of the petals. The fragrance is strongly redolent of pepper, with an astringent undertone. A slight susceptibility to mildew is about this bush's only problem, while rebloom is continuous until the first frost stops all growth.

'Slater's Crimson China' is one of the stud roses that created our modern repeat-blooming roses. William Ker is credited with introducing this rose into England around 1789, where it was grown at Kew Gardens. The rose is named in honor of Gilbert Slater, who had connections with the British East India Company.

HYBRIDIZER: unknown
SUITABILITY: all levels
AVAILABILITY: mail-order
STATURE & HABIT: warm climate, 5' × 5'; cool climate, 3' × 3'
FRAGRANCE: strong, peppery

USES: border, low hedge, container
PARENTAGE: unknown
DISEASES: mildew
HARDINESS: hot climate, very good; cold climate, tender
BLOOM: remontant

Slater's Crimson China

SOLEIL D'OR

[*Hybrid Tea, 1900*]

To call 'Soleil d'Or' the seminal rose of the 20th century, as well as the first modern rose, is actually no exaggeration. So revolutionary in color was this "golden sun" that it was snapped up by hybridizers the moment it came on the market, and so assimilated into the bloodlines of contemporary roses that one would be hard-pressed to find a Modern Rose without 'Soleil d'Or' as a distant parent. At first it was given a class of its own, Pernetiana, in honor of the hybridizer, Joseph Pernet-Ducher. Eventually, though, the early roses of the class were recognized as Hybrid Teas. After 'Soleil d'Or,' roses would never be the same—its genes spread to every corner of the world where roses were grown in less than a decade.

A tall, lusty, upright shrub, 'Soleil d'Or' will reach 6 feet in height and diameter. The new canes and growth are a shiny, light leek green and dusted with long, needlelike red-brown prickles. The oval, moss green foliage is heavily serrated, with prominent ribbing. Flowers are produced individually on short stems along the bending canes. Buds are elegantly pointed, deep yellow to orange, and decorated with beautiful foliated sepals. Each cup-shaped bloom is somewhat loosely petaled, dazzling orange-apricot with highlights of yellow and burnt orange at the petals' base. The scent is tangy and not at all fetid, as so often reported, with a strong overlay of apples. Blackspot will be a problem in regions prone to that problem, so be prepared with one of the new, less damaging fungicides. The rebloom is good, if a bit spotty.

Soleil does not do well in the hot sun of our dry Southwest, so place it where it will receive some protection from the most direct midday sun. The shrub does seem to do quite well with dappled sun, so if you've a tall, spreading tree, site Soleil nearby—and the filtered sunlight will play across the spectacularly colored blossoms.

HYBRIDIZER: Joseph Pernet-Ducher, Lyons, France

SUITABILITY: intermediate

AVAILABILITY: limited mail-order

STATURE & HABIT: warm climate, 6' × 6'; cool climate, 3' × 3'

FRAGRANCE: tangy fruit and spice

USES: border, cutting

PARENTAGE: 'Antoine Ducher' × 'Persian Yellow'

DISEASES: blackspot

HARDINESS: hot climate, good; cold climate, moderate

BLOOM: remontant

Soleil d'Or

SOMBREUIL

[*Climbing Tea, 1850*]

No book on Old Garden Roses could be considered complete without mentioning 'Sombreuil.' That said, what we now grow as 'Sombreuil' may actually be a rose introduced originally in the 1950s as 'Colonial White.' It little matters if this cultivar is 'Sombreuil' or something else—the fact remains it's so outstanding, so popular, and so entrenched in the psyche of the rose-growing public that it will forevermore be known as our 'Sombreuil.'

A tall, elegantly proportioned climber, 'Sombreuil' will climb to 12 feet or more. The long, supple new canes are a gleaming deep green, easily trained, and furnished with abundant, hooked, claret red prickles. The oval, shiny jade green foliage narrows to a point just at the tips. Bloom is produced in open clusters of three or more alabaster white, plump, pointed buds. Individual blooms have a classic Hybrid Tea shape upon first opening, then mature to creamy white, flat-topped, fully petaled and quartered, sweetly Tea-scented flowers. The waxy foliage is exceptionally resistant to most problems in most areas of the country, but blackspot and some slight mildew have been noted in Texas. Deadhead regularly to encourage rebloom.

My 'Sombreuil' at home is trained up a liquidamber tree, with the canes curving around the trunk in a barber pole pattern. The flowers are produced along the canes on splendid flowering shoots and at the tips of the canes as well. This creates an absolutely stunning pillar of creamy white going 15 feet up the tree, and never fails to stop passersby in wonder. It later blankets the triangular pink garden underneath with a snow shower of falling petals.

This treasure was named in honor of Mademoiselle de Sombreuil, a heroine of the French Revolution who, during the Terror, stopped the mob from executing her father and herself by her supplications.

HYBRIDIZER: Robert, Angers, France
SUITABILITY: all levels
AVAILABILITY: wide
STATURE & HABIT: warm climate, 12' × 12'; cool climate, 8' × 5'
FRAGRANCE: strong Tea Rose

USES: climber, pillar, cutting
PARENTAGE: 'Gigantesque' seedling
DISEASES: mildew, blackspot
HARDINESS: hot climate, very good; cold climate, somewhat tender
BLOOM: remontant

Sombreuil

SOUVENIR DE LA MALMAISON

[*Bourbon, 1843*]

The survival of Old Roses is due to a number of factors: health, fragrance, garden worthiness, and sometimes, simple serendipity. All these qualities come together in this cultivar, which is sometimes known as "Queen of Beauty and Fragrance."

'Souvenir de la Malmaison' is a relatively low-growing, compact shrub, hardly ever exceeding 3 feet in circumference. The fresh green and mottled brown young canes are covered with emerald prickles and long, pointed grass green foliage that is only lightly serrated along the margins. Large, globular, pale pink buds are produced singly or in small, tight clusters on short stems just above the foliage. Sweetly scented blooms open to very double, shallow-cupped, shell pink to white flowers. For me, this one has a panoply of fragrance—from a touch of cold cream to the strongest odor of freshly peeled peaches to a lighter rose attar. As the petals reflex, the blooms take on a flat-topped shape and remain strongly quartered, and the repeat bloom is as continuous as that of any Modern Rose. The foliage can suffer from blackspot in areas such as Texas, and all areas report a problem with mildew, so be forewarned. Malmaison's flowers do ball in wet weather, but in dryer, warmer seasons, nothing can match the alluring charms she imparts to your garden.

'Souvenir de la Malmaison' produced a climbing sport in 1893 that is identical to the bush form except for size. A less double sport ('Souvenir de St. Anne's') occurred in Ireland in the 1950s.

Malmaison was Joséphine's residence outside Paris. 'Souvenir de la Malmaison' was named in honor of her and the renowned collection of roses she established in her garden there, most of which were immortalized in Redouté's magnificent work *Les Roses*.

HYBRIDIZER: Jean Béluze, Lyons, France
SUITABILITY: all levels
AVAILABILITY: wide
STATURE & HABIT: warm climate, 3' × 3'; cool climate, 3' × 3'
FRAGRANCE: peaches and rose

USES: border, low hedge, container, cutting
PARENTAGE: 'Mme. Deprez' × Tea Rose
DISEASES: mildew
HARDINESS: hot climate, very good; cold climate, moderate
BLOOM: remontant

Souvenir de la Malmaison

SOUVENIR DU DOCTEUR JAMAIN

[Hybrid Perpetual, 1865]

A much overlooked selection, this Docteur catches both the eye and nose with its unusual deep color and superb perfume when in bloom. 'Souvenir du Docteur Jamain' is equally good as a shrub or trained onto a support as a climber. The bendable canes lend themselves to training onto a pillar or tripod, and you get a more easily contained shrub along with the added benefit of increased bloom. Whoever the good doctor was, he is remembered by a fine rose.

The thin canes of 'Souvenir du Docteur Jamain' will arch out to 8 feet or more, with a nearly equal spread, and when given support they can attain 12 feet. New canes are plum-colored with oval, pointed chartreuse green foliage edged with antique bronze. The smooth gray-green mature canes carry only the occasional small red-green prickle. Round, blood red buds are produced in small clusters and open to fully petaled, ruffled, velvety crimson-to-plum, cupped flowers with bright yellow stamens at their centers. There is an occasional white streak, known as quilling, which tags the velvety texture of the petals. The fragrance is strong and sweet of Cabbage Rose perfume. Rebloom is good in spring and fall, though only intermittent the rest of the season. The foliage is prone to problems such as mildew, so be on the alert if that's a concern in your area.

The deep burgundy tones of the loosely petaled flowers will suffer without some protection from the hottest direct sun. Try planting the good Docteur where he will spill over a whitewashed brick wall. The contrast between the wall and the deep claret and crimson colors of this cultivar will cause your garden visitors to gasp in amazement.

HYBRIDIZER: François Lacharme, Lyons, France

SUITABILITY: all levels

AVAILABILITY: mail-order

STATURE & HABIT: warm climate, 8' × 8'; cool climate, 8' × 8'

FRAGRANCE: strong, sweet Old Rose

USES: border, hedge, climber, cutting

PARENTAGE: 'Général Jacqueminot' × 'Charles Lefèbvre'

DISEASES: mildew

HARDINESS: hot climate, good; cold climate, good

BLOOM: remontant

*Souvenir du
Docteur Jamain*

SYDONIE

[*Portland, 1846*]

Sometimes listed as a Hybrid Perpetual, or among the Damask Perpetuals, and often seen spelled "Sidonie," our 'Sydonie' seems to me to have more in common with the Portlands than any other class. A popular rose in its day, 'Sydonie' continues to have a loyal following for her deep, pervasive perfume and generous rebloom.

This Portland, like all others, remains a condensed yet upright bush of 3 to 4 feet with a diameter of around 3 feet. 'Sydonie' produces strong-growing gray-green canes fortified with ruby red hooked prickles and patina green new foliage edged in cinnamon red. The long, pointed-to-oval forest green foliage is narrowly serrated and somewhat prone to blackspot. Marble-shaped cherry red buds are produced in large clusters with long, leafy ornamental sepals. Small, fully petaled blooms open carnation rose, are often quartered, and display a button-eye at their centers. 'Sydonie' is redolent of grapes ripening on the vine, combined with soft, sweet Old Rose and a soupçon of black pepper.

The open flowers sit atop the foliage in the typical Portland Rose manner, and the frequency of rebloom is superb. 'Sydonie' does have a problem with blackspot in regions where that disease can be insidious, so be prepared with one of the new biocompatible fungicides.

This rose often takes hits for her alleged lack of proper form from those of us more attuned to Modern Rose shapes. But 'Sydonie' is from an age that hadn't yet developed rules and regulations for exhibition. The simple charms, strong repeat bloom, and wonderful Damask perfume of this cultivar were enough for gardeners of the time to cherish this fine Old Garden Rose. The hairs on the back of my neck bristle when I hear someone at a rose show condemn a rose for not having "form"; the form was there long before we developed our silly rules and corseted our sense of aesthetics with such narrow and ignorant criteria.

HYBRIDIZER: Dorisy; introduced by Jean-Pierre Vibert, Angers, France

SUITABILITY: all levels

AVAILABILITY: limited mail-order

STATURE & HABIT: warm climate, 4' × 3'; cool climate, 3' × 2'

FRAGRANCE: ripe grapes, Old Rose, hint of pepper

USES: border, container, cutting

PARENTAGE: unknown

DISEASES: blackspot

HARDINESS: hot climate, good; cold climate, very good

BLOOM: remontant

Sydonie

TRICOLORE DE FLANDRE

[Gallica, 1846]

'Tricolore de Flandre' was introduced right as the popularity of the Gallicas waned. By the time she came out, her repeat-blooming sisters, the Bourbons and the Hybrid Perpetuals, were seducing gardeners with their copious and nearly continuous bloom. I must admit I have never been a fan of striped Modern Roses, but flamboyant excess seems to fit these grande dames like crinoline and brocade, and is very endearing and not a little nostalgic.

As is usual for Gallica Roses, Tricolore grows to 3 or 4 feet in height and width, although it will colonize a much larger circumference when grown on its own roots. The thin canes are polished pale green mottled with chestnut and only an occasional small prickle. The oval moss green foliage is shinier than usual, somewhat rugose in texture, with smooth margins. Plump claret red buds are produced in large clusters. Blooms open shallow-cupped, with a button-eye, and are shell pink to milk white with shocking pink to scarlet striping and mottling. Occasionally, a bloom will sport to a solid deep pink tone, which may be the original form of this cultivar. The foliage is handsome and quite free of most problems, and the fragrance is light but crisp with sharp, rosy undertones.

Striped roses were a hot item in the 19th century, and are enjoying a renaissance today. Try planting Tricolore where the contrast of her flashy blossoms will work against a deeper-toned rose such as 'Velvet,' or a mass of soft blue nepeta as an underplanting. Or plant her along a path at the front of the border, where the unique individual blossoms can be seen at their best. Gallica Roses are hardy almost to the absolute extremes of our coldest zones with no protection needed.

HYBRIDIZER: Louis Van Houtte, Grand, France
SUITABILITY: all levels
AVAILABILITY: limited mail-order
STATURE & HABIT: warm climate, 4' × 3'; cool climate, 3' × 2'
FRAGRANCE: light, crisp, rosy

USES: border, hedge, container, cutting
PARENTAGE: 'Belle des Jardins' × seedling
DISEASES: clean
HARDINESS: hot climate, good; cold climate, very good
BLOOM: spring

Tricolore
de Flandre

VARIEGATA DI BOLOGNA

[*Bourbon, 1909*]

Bourbon Roses have a reputation for becoming large shrubs, and 'Variegata di Bologna' is no exception. Given some support, this striped rose will easily reach climbing proportions, but don't let its size deter you. Its spring display is a carnival sideshow of color and scent that any gardener would be proud to share.

Depending on location and climate, Variegata will grow 6 to 8 feet or more with at least an equal or larger spread. The supple, spring green canes are lightly supplied with small red prickles and celery green, lance-shaped, pointed foliage that is lighter on the reverse. Clusters of round, deep burgundy buds appear at the ends of the long canes. Flowers open to fully double, bulbous, fragrant blooms with a cream to oystershell base and are striped with crimson-magenta. The globular cupped flowers are quartered and heavily scented of Old Rose. Pale green foliage is not as resistant to diseases as one could hope, so prepare for an onslaught where blackspot and mildew are troublesome. The best bloom production is always in spring, although some experts report that they sometimes have a fall bloom. I must say, however, that this Variegata has never bloomed past spring for me.

Large-growing Bourbon Roses such as Variegata need careful consideration as to siting in the garden. This old girl needs room in which to show off, so consider her a prime candidate for self-pegging.

Since the reported repeat bloom of this cultivar has never happened for me, my thought is that Variegata may prefer cooler climes to bestow a second go-round. She does occasionally sport back to a purple rose, which seems to be her parent.

HYBRIDIZER: A. Bonfiglioli and Son, Bologna, Italy
SUITABILITY: all levels
AVAILABILITY: wide
STATURE & HABIT: warm climate, 8' × 8'; cool climate, 6' × 6'
FRAGRANCE: Old Rose

USES: border, climber, hedge, cutting
PARENTAGE: unknown
DISEASES: blackspot, mildew, rust
HARDINESS: hot climate, good; cold climate, very good
BLOOM: spring

*Variegata di
Bologna*

VELVET ROSE

[*Gallica, 1597*]

An enigmatic rose that will most often be found under the name "Tuscany," 'Velvet Rose' far outdates that name. In his landmark work *Herball,* or *Generall Historie of Plantes,* John Gerard listed "Velvet" among the eight or nine roses he grew in his garden in 1597—and it is probably much older than that. This cultivar hides its historical face among many other names: "Old Velvet," "Gerard's Velvet," "La Belle Sultan," even "Meheka." Boasting none of the sovereignty of the double-flowered Centifolias of later years, or the media-hungry flamboyance of the striped Gallicas, this superb rose unveils a simple, uncorrupted nature in its semi-double, wide-open form.

Short but upright in growth, the chestnut brown canes of 'Velvet Rose' are rather thin and bristly, covered with a mixture of small hairs and sharp tawny prickles. Foliage is that of a typical Gallica, unpolished holly green, lightly toothed along the edges, with a rough, crinkled texture. The individual leaflets are folded along the midrib, with the terminal leaflet poised downward. Stipules clasping the leaf stalk, or petiole, are streaked with cherry red down the center. Small, oval, pointed crimson buds sit atop round green ovaries rather like a turban on top of a maharaja's head. The wine red, velveteen-textured flowers open flat, revealing two or three rows of petals. Fully opened flowers expose a whitish inner eye with a ring of bright golden yellow stamens when fresh. Flowers are produced individually or in small clusters, and the essence they purvey is an alluring combination of bell peppers and spice with just a nuance of rose attar.

The later appellation of 'Tuscany' to this rose probably refers to its origin, or possibly to its Tuscan wine red color. 'Tuscany Superb,' or more correctly, 'Superb Tuscan,' is a more double-flowered, deeper-colored sport of 'Velvet Rose,' with much larger blooms. The color ages to an enchanting, deep claret to purple. Many gardeners prefer this double form, but for me, nothing surpasses the unencumbered charm of the original.

HYBRIDIZER: unknown
SUITABILITY: all levels
AVAILABILITY: wide
STATURE & HABIT: warm climate, 4' × 3'; cool climate, 3' × 3'
FRAGRANCE: bell peppers, spice, rose attar

USES: border, hedge, container, cutting
PARENTAGE: unknown
DISEASES: clean
HARDINESS: hot climate, good; cold climate, very good
BLOOM: spring

Velvet Rose

WILLIAM LOBB

[*Moss, 1855*]

"Old Velvet Moss" and "Duchesse d'Istrie" are just two of the names under which you might find this durable cultivar listed. The 19th century marked the high tide of Moss Roses, when a garden just wasn't a garden without a compliment of these fragrant treasures. From bud to bloom, few roses of any class transcend the Mosses for their gentility of form and refinement. Dark-colored Moss Roses are scarce these days, so we tend to cherish those we still have.

Best described as a tall, vigorous-growing shrub, 'William Lobb' will easily attain dimensions of 6 to 8 feet in height and often an equally wide diameter. The curving olive brown canes are enshrouded from ground to bud with abundant, small-to-large russet prickles. The ragged, oval moss green foliage is comparatively smooth for an Old Rose. Egg-shaped buds are produced in clusters and draped with fleecy olive green moss from the flowering stem right out to the tips of the calyx. As the sepals pull apart, they reveal a deep Venetian red tone. The fully open blooms are choked with narrow, quartered petals that commence Tyrian crimson, aging to regal purple, and finish with undertones of gray. The underside of the petals is a muted lilac pink. Ruffled blossoms expel a strong but velvety Old Rose perfume, with a strangely tinged aftertaste of citrus rind. Mildew is often a problem with these roses, so be ready with an appropriate deterrent.

William Lobb worked as a plant collector for Veitch & Co., one of the most famous British family nurseries of the 19th and early 20th centuries. He set out to catalog unknown species within the still young and largely unexplored United States, settling at the end of his life in California. He is probably most noted for having introduced the *Sequoia gigantea,* which at the time was incorrectly christened *Wellingtonia gigantea* to honor the Duke of Wellington. We of course know them as our great Sequoia redwoods.

HYBRIDIZER: Jean Laffay, Belevue-Meudon, France
SUITABILITY: all levels
AVAILABILITY: wide
STATURE & HABIT: warm climate, 8' × 6'; cool climate, 6' × 6'
FRAGRANCE: strong Old Rose

USES: border, hedge, cutting
PARENTAGE: unknown
DISEASES: mildew
HARDINESS: hot climate, good; cold climate, very good
BLOOM: spring

William Lobb

YOLANDE D'ARAGON

[*Portland, 1843*]

This Spanish beauty has been seducing gardeners for over a century and a half. Sometimes seen as "Iolande" or "Jolanda d'Aragon," this rose is best described as sensuous. First introduced as a Perpetual Damask, it best conforms to the Portland class. Portlands are among the most free-flowering and dependable of all roses, and at the same time, they manifest a strong Damask Rose perfume.

A lanky, vertical shrub, Yolande will reach 6 feet in height but only around 3 feet in diameter. The burnished jalapeño green canes bear infrequent carnelian prickles. The emerald toothed foliage is oblong and pointed. Pudgy orbs of buds are burgundy at first, opening to flat, quartered, very fully petaled amaranth to lilac-pink blooms. The outer petals, fiesta pink on their margins, reflex back on themselves while the crowded inner petals take on deep crimson tones at the base. Bloom is strong in spring and intermittent throughout the summer, but there is an ardent fall bloom. Her essence is that of raspberries and sweet, fruity apples mixed into a base of Damask. The foliage is resistant to most problems, but some protection from mildew may be in order in regions subject to that nuisance.

Yolande looks best at the center of the border where her leggy canes will be hidden by lower shrubs or tall perennials. The Portland Roses are reasonably winter-hardy, so this one can be grown in most regions of the country.

Yolande was the wife of Louis II, the ruler of Provence and Aragon, Duke of Anjou, and later, King of the "Two Sicilies," which combined for the first time the island kingdom of Sicily with the region of Naples. At the close of the Hundred Years War, this ruling couple owed much of the return of their French power to the efforts of a young girl from Domremy named Jeanne, later canonized as Jeanne d'Arc, our Joan of Arc.

HYBRIDIZER: Jean-Pierre
  Vibert, Angers, France
SUITABILITY: all levels
AVAILABILITY: mail-order
STATURE & HABIT: warm
  climate, 6' × 3';
  cool climate, 4' × 3'
FRAGRANCE: raspberries, apples,
  Damask Rose

USES: border, hedge, cutting
PARENTAGE: unknown
DISEASES: clean
HARDINESS: hot climate, very
  good; cold climate, moderate
BLOOM: remontant

Yolande d'Aragon

YORK AND LANCASTER

[*Damask, 1551*]

With 'York and Lancaster,' we traverse that line between history and fiction. The name alone conjures up images of the Wars of the Roses and Shakespeare's *Richard II*. The interesting problem here is that Shakespeare created the idea of 'York and Lancaster' from a rose that did not exist when the actual events occurred. In Shakespeare's day, our rose was a new cultivar with no relationship to the events of the historical 15th-century Wars of the Roses.

'York and Lancaster' is a typical Damask, growing to 6 or 7 feet high and almost as wide. The cobalt green canes are defended by sharp ruby prickles while the downy bluish green foliage is lightly serrated and wrinkled. Bouquets of pale pink and cream buds open to flat, fully petaled flowers of blush pink to Dutch white, sprinkled with yellow stamens. Most blooms are pink, but an occasional striped royal pink bloom will show up, and sometimes the bloom is divided, half pale and half royal pink. The shrub is a strong, vigorous grower, but like all Damask roses, it resents any hard pruning of the main wood. Its bouquet starts off a sweet rose scent, and turns strongly into the aroma of cloves. Some protection against mildew may be necessary in regions where that problem exists, though it's safe to say that 'York and Lancaster' is rock hardy in most areas of the country.

This fine old cultivar is often listed in catalogs as *Rosa damascena versicolor* or just plain "Versicolor." Earlier in the resurgence of the popularity of Old Roses, 'York and Lancaster' was confused with another striped rose, 'Rosa Mundi.' The chaos was caused by eager nurserymen, unfamiliar with the two roses, rushing to introduce them in their catalogs. No such confusion should exist today. 'York and Lancaster' is a tall, open-growing shrub that only occasionally stripes, and 'Rosa Mundi' is a compact growing shrub that is always strongly striped.

HYBRIDIZER: described by Monardes, 1551

SUITABILITY: intermediate

AVAILABILITY: wide

STATURE & HABIT: warm climate, 7' × 5'; cool climate, 5' × 4'

FRAGRANCE: sweet rose turning to strong cloves

USES: border, hedge, partial shade

PARENTAGE: unknown

DISEASES: mildew

HARDINESS: hot climate, good; cold climate, excellent

BLOOM: spring

York and Lancaster

ZÉPHRINE DROUHIN

[Bourbon, 1866]

A few years back, a major retail supplier of roses illustrated the cover of their catalog with a sumptuous photograph of 'Zéphrine Drouhin,' and the nursery industry hasn't been able to keep up with the demand since. I have never quite seen what all the commotion is about, but the popularity of this rose continues to grow and I must admit I have seen superb examples in gardens that have caused me to rethink my judgment.

Zéphrine is a lofty, somewhat spindly growing Bourbon that is more a climbing shrub than a bush, growing easily to 7 or 8 feet or more in height. Her waxed, supple, brownish green canes are completely devoid of thorns. The sparse bronzy purple of the new leaves matures to forest green, lance-shaped, lightly serrated, five-leaflet foliage. Garnet buds are produced in large clusters and open to loosely petaled, semi-double blooms of a deep, rich shocking pink. The petals reflex at their margins and pull back to reveal custard yellow at their base and a dusting of amber stamens. The foliage will need some protection against both mildew and blackspot if those problems affect your area. The other outstanding feature of this rose is the fragrance—sweetly perfumed and pervasive with Old Rose and citrus, wafting on a warm breeze to enchant all who come near. The rebloom is best in the spring, and somewhat sparse the rest of the year.

Placement of this rose in the garden must be done with a delicate eye for color. Her strong cerise pink tones will dominate the color scheme if you don't watch out. Train her over a wall or through a low-growing fruit tree, and you'll enjoy sprays of perfumed blossoms spilling into the garden. This cultivar will tolerate some shade and still bloom.

There is a softer, mallow pink sport named 'Kathleen Harrop,' which was introduced in 1919 and is identical in all but color. All in all, both can be happy additions to the garden border.

Zéphrine was named for the wife of a noted horticulturist who lived on the French Côte d'Or.

HYBRIDIZER: Bizot, France

SUITABILITY: intermediate

AVAILABILITY: wide

STATURE & HABIT: warm climate, 7' × 5'; cool climate, 5' × 4'

FRAGRANCE: strong of Old Rose and citrus

USES: border, hedge, partial shade

PARENTAGE: unknown

DISEASES: mildew, blackspot

HARDINESS: hot climate, good; cold climate, moderate

BLOOM: spring

*Zéphrine
Drouhin*

Appendix A

NORTH AMERICAN MAIL-ORDER SOURCES *for* OLD ROSES

Τ he retail mail-order sources listed herein specifically grow and offer Old Roses for sale, among other classes of roses. Each offers a catalog and ships their roses at the appropriate season for your region.

THE ANTIQUE ROSE EMPORIUM
9300 Lueckemeyer Road
Brenham, TX 77833
PHONE: 800-441-0002
FAX: 409-836-0928
CATALOG: free
❋ *Own-root and container-grown plants*

ARENA ROSE COMPANY
PO Box 3096
Paso Robles, CA 93447
PHONE: 805-227-4094
FAX: 805-227-4095
COLOR CATALOG: $5.00
❋ *Grafted and own-root field-grown plants*

HEIRLOOM OLD GARDEN ROSES
24062 Riverside Drive N.E.
St. Paul, OR 97137
PHONE: 503-538-1576
FAX: 503-538-5902
COLOR CATALOG: $5.00
❋ *Own-root plants*

HORTICO, INC.
723 Robson Road
Waterdown, Ontario L0R 2H1,
Canada
PHONE: 905-689-6984
FAX: 905-689-6566
COLOR CATALOG: $3.00
❋ *Grafted and some own-root plants*

PICKERING NURSERIES INC.
670 Kingston Road
Pickering, Ontario L1V 1A6, Canada
PHONE: 905-839-2111
FAX: 905-839-4807
CATALOG: $3.00
❋ *Grafted plants*

ROSES UNLIMITED
363 North Deerwood Drive
Laurens, SC 29360
PHONE: 864-682-7673
FAX: 864-682-2455
CATALOG: free
❋ *Own-root plants*

VINTAGE GARDENS
2833 Old Gravenstein Highway
    South
Sebastopol, CA 95472
PHONE: 707-829-2035
FAX: 707-829-9516
CATALOG: $5.00
❋ *Own-root plants*

WAYSIDE GARDENS
1 Garden Lane
Hodges, SC 29695-0001
PHONE: 800-845-1124
FAX: 800-817-1124
COLOR CATALOG: free
❋ *Grafted and some own-root plants*

Appendix B

LIST *of* PUBLIC GARDENS DISPLAYING OLD ROSES

Here is a state-by-state guide to various gardens across the country that have Old Roses on display. A visit to a collection of Old Roses growing in a gardening zone similar to your own will help you make informed and intelligent decisions as to which Old Rose will be best suited to your garden.

ALABAMA

BIRMINGHAM BOTANICAL GARDENS
2612 Lane Park Road
Birmingham, AL 36223
PHONE: 205-414-3900
HOURS: Dawn to dusk
ADMISSION: No charge

ARIZONA

SCOTTSDALE ROSE GARDEN
North West Corner of Goldwater
   & 5th Avenue
Scottsdale, Arizona
HOURS: Dawn to dusk
PHONE: 602-234-2700
ADMISSION: No charge

CALIFORNIA

DESCANSO GARDENS
1418 Descanso Drive
La Cañada Flintridge, CA 91011
PHONE: 818-952-4396
HOURS: 9:00 A.M. to 5:00 P.M.
ADMISSION: Charge

MENDOCINO COAST BOTANICAL GARDENS
18220 North Highway 1
Fort Bragg, CA 95437
PHONE: 707-964-4352
HOURS: 9:00 A.M. to 5:00 P.M.
ADMISSION: Charge

THE HUNTINGTON LIBRARY, ART COLLECTIONS, AND BOTANICAL GARDENS
1151 Oxford Road
San Marino, CA 91108
PHONE: 626-405-2264
HOURS: Tuesday through Thursday
   12:00 P.M. to 4:30 P.M., Saturday
   and Sunday 10:30 A.M. to
   4:30 P.M., closed Monday
ADMISSION: Charge

SAN JOSE HERITAGE ROSE GARDEN
Guadalupe River Park & Garden
Between Highway 87 and
   Coleman Avenue
San Jose, CA 95110
PHONE: 408-277-5998
HOURS: Dawn to dusk
ADMISSION: No charge

COLORADO

DENVER BOTANIC GARDEN
909 York Street
Denver, CO 80206
PHONE: 303-331-4000
HOURS: Wednesday through
   Friday 9:00 A.M. to 5:00 P.M.,
   Saturday through Tuesday,
   9:00 A.M. to 8:00 P.M.
ADMISSION: Charge

CONNECTICUT

ELIZABETH PARK ROSE GARDEN
150 Walbridge Road
West Hartford, CT 06119
HOURS: Dawn to dusk
PHONE: 860-722-6543
ADMISSION: No charge

DISTRICT OF COLUMBIA

UNITED STATES NATIONAL ARBORETUM
National Herb Garden
3501 New York Avenue, NE
Washington, DC 20002
PHONE: 202-225-8333
HOURS: 8:00 A.M. to 5:00 P.M.
ADMISSION: No charge

FLORIDA

RINGLING MUSEUMS
5401 Bayshore Rd.
Sarasota, FL 34243
PHONE: 941-351-1660
HOURS: 10:00 A.M. to 5:30 P.M.
ADMISSION: Charge

GEORGIA

ANTIQUE ROSE EMPORIUM
Cavender Creek Road
Dahlonega, GA 30533
PHONE: 800-441-0002
HOURS: Monday through Saturday
    10:00 A.M. to 5:30 P.M.,
    Sunday 12:30 P.M. to 5:30 P.M.
ADMISSION: No charge

IDAHO

IDAHO BOTANIC GARDEN
Jane Falk Oppenheimer Heirloom
    Rose Garden
2355 Old Penitentiary Road
Boise, ID 83706
PHONE: 208-383-0583
HOURS: 9:00 A.M. to 5:00 P.M.
ADMISSION: Charge

ILLINOIS

CHICAGO BOTANIC GARDENS
Lake Cook Road
Glencoe, IL 60022
PHONE: 847-835-5440
HOURS: Dawn to dusk
ADMISSION: Charge

KANSAS

E.F.A. REINISCH ROSE GARDEN
4320 West 10th St.
Topeka, KS 66604
PHONE: 785-272-6150
HOURS: 6:00 A.M. to 11:00 P.M.
ADMISSION: No charge

LOUISIANA

AMERICAN ROSE CENTER
8877 Jefferson-Paige Road
Shreveport, LA 71119
PHONE: 318-938-5402
HOURS: Monday through Friday
    9:00 A.M. to 5:00 P.M., Saturday
    and Sunday 9:00 A.M. to 6:30 P.M.
ADMISSION: Charge

MARYLAND

WILLIAM PACA GARDEN
1 Martin Street
Annapolis, MD 21401
PHONE: 410-267-6656
HOURS: March 1 through
    December 31, Monday through
    Friday 10:00 A.M. to 5:00 P.M.,
    Sunday 12:00 P.M.to 5:00 P.M.
ADMISSION: Charge

MASSACHUSETTS

ARNOLD ARBORETUM OF HARVARD UNIVERSITY
125 Arborway
Jamaica Plain, MA 02130
PHONE: 617-524-1718
HOURS: Dawn to dusk
ADMISSION: No charge

MISSOURI

JACOB L. LOOSE MEMORIAL PARK
52nd Street at Pennsylvania Avenue
Kansas City, MO 64112
HOURS: Dawn to dusk
ADMISSION: No charge

MISSOURI BOTANICAL GARDEN
3444 Shaw Boulevard
St. Louis, MO 63110
PHONE: 314-577-5111
HOURS: 9:00 A.M. to 8:00 P.M.
ADMISSION: Charge

NEW MEXICO

ALBUQUERQUE ROSE GARDEN
Wyoming Regional Library
Wyoming and Menaul
HOURS: Dawn to dusk
ADMISSION: No charge

NEW YORK

BROOKLYN BOTANIC GARDEN
The Cranford Rose Garden
1000 Washington Avenue
Brooklyn, NY 11225
PHONE: 718-622-4433
HOURS: 9:00 A.M. to 5:00 P.M.
ADMISSION: Charge

NEW YORK BOTANICAL GARDEN
The Peggy Rockefeller Rose Garden
200th Street and Southern Boulevard
Bronx, NY 10458
PHONE: 718-817-8047
HOURS: Tuesday through
    Sunday 10:00 A.M. to 6:00 P.M.
ADMISSION: Charge

OLD WESTBURY GARDENS
71 Old Westbury Road
Old Westbury, Long Island,
NY 11568
PHONE: 516-333-0048
HOURS: 10:00 A.M. to 5:00 P.M.,
    closed Tuesday
ADMISSION: Charge

NORTH CAROLINA

BILTMORE ESTATE
One North Pack Square
Asheville, NC 28801
PHONE: 828-274-6202
HOURS: 9:00 A.M. to 6:00 P.M.
ADMISSION: Charge

OREGON

HEIRLOOM OLD GARDEN ROSES
24062 Riverside Drive NE
St. Paul, OR 97137
PHONE: 503-538-1576
HOURS: 9:00 A.M. to 5:00 P.M.
ADMISSION: No charge

**INTERNATIONAL ROSE TEST
GARDEN**
400 Southwest Kingston Avenue
Portland, OR 97201
PHONE: 503-823-3636
HOURS: 9:00 A.M. to 5:00 P.M.
ADMISSION: No charge

PENNSYLVANIA

HERSHEY GARDENS
Hotel Road
Hershey, PA 17033
PHONE: 717-534-3492
HOURS: 9:00 A.M. to 6:00 P.M.
ADMISSION: Charge

SOUTH CAROLINA

BOONE HALL
1235 Long Point Road
Highway 17 North
Mount Pleasant, SC 29464
PHONE: 843-884-4371
HOURS: Summer 8:30 A.M. to 6:30 P.M.
ADMISSION: Charge

**RIVERBANKS ZOOLOGICAL PARK
AND BOTANICAL GARDEN**
500 Wildlife Parkway
Columbia, SC 29202
PHONE: 803-779-8717 ext 1220
HOURS: 9:00 A.M. to 5:00 P.M.
ADMISSION: Charge

TENNESSEE

MEMPHIS BOTANIC GARDEN
Audubon Park
750 Cherry Road
Memphis, TN 38117
PHONE: 901-685-1566
HOURS: 9:00 A.M. to dusk
ADMISSION: Charge

TEXAS

THE ANTIQUE ROSE EMPORIUM
9300 Lueckemeyer Road
Brenham, TX 77833
PHONE: 800-441-0002
HOURS: Monday through Saturday
9:00 A.M. to 6:00 P.M.,
Sunday 12:00 P.M. to 5:30 P.M.
ADMISSION: No charge

VIRGINIA

WOODLAWN PLANTATION
9000 Richmond Highway
Mount Vernon, VA 22309
PHONE: 703-780-4000
HOURS: 10:00 A.M. to 4:00 P.M.
ADMISSION: Charge

WISCONSIN

BOERNER BOTANICAL GARDENS
5879 South 92nd Street
Hales Corners, WI 53130
PHONE: 414-425-1130
HOURS: 8:00 A.M. to sunset
ADMISSION: Charge

CANADA

BUTCHART GARDENS
900 Benvenuto Avenue
Victoria, British Columbia, Canada
PHONE: 604-652-4422
HOURS: 9:00 A.M. to 11:00 P.M.
ADMISSION: Charge

**EDWARDS GARDENS AND
CIVIC GARDEN CENTER**
777 Lawrence Avenue East
Toronto, Ontario, M3C 1P2 Canada
PHONE: 416-397-1340
HOURS: 9:00 A.M. to 5:00 P.M.
ADMISSION: No charge

MONTREAL BOTANICAL GARDEN
4101 Sherbrooke Street East
Montreal H1X 2B2 Québec, Canada
PHONE: 514-872-1400
HOURS: Dawn to dusk
ADMISSION: Charge

ROYAL BOTANICAL GARDENS
680 Plains Road West
Hamilton, L8N 3H8 Ontario,
Canada
PHONE: 905-527-1158
HOURS: 9:30 A.M. to dusk
ADMISSION: Charge

Appendix C

INDEX *of* OLD GARDEN ROSES *by* COLOR

The following is a complete listing, by color, of all the Old Garden Roses included in the Field Guide of this book. Notations on flower florm, size of shrub, and type of rose are also given.

RED-PURPLE

BELLE DE CRÉCY: *button-eye, low, Gallica*

BIZARRE TRIOMPHANT: *quartered, low, Gallica*

CARDINAL DE RICHELIEU: *reflexed, thornless, tall, Gallica*

EUGÈNE DE BEAUHARNAIS: *cupped, low, Bourbon/China*

REINE DES VIOLETTES: *cupped, thornless, tall, Hybrid Perpetual*

RUSSELL'S COTTAGE ROSE: *flat, tall, Rambler*

WILLIAM LOBB: *quartered, button-eye, tall, Moss*

DARK RED

BARON GIROD DE L'AIN: *deeply cupped, edged white, medium, Hybrid Perpetual*

FRANCIS DUBREUIL: *reflexed, low, Tea*

HENRI MARTIN: *quartered, tall, Moss*

VELVET ROSE: *single/semi-double, medium, Gallica*

CRIMSON RED

DR. HUEY: *flat, tall, Climber*

DUCHESS OF PORTLAND: *semi-double, low, Portland*

LA BELLE DISTINGUÉE: *semi-double, low, Eglantine*

ROSE DE RESCHT: *quartered, low, Autumn Damask*

RUGOSA RUBRA: *single, hips, medium/tall, Hybrid Rugosa*

SLATER'S CRIMSON CHINA: *shallow-cupped, low, China*

SOUVENIR DU DOCTEUR JAMAIN: *cupped, quartered, tall, Hybrid Perpetual*

DARK PINK

APOTHECARY'S ROSE: *single, low, Gallica*

BARONNE PRÉVOST: *quartered, medium, Hybrid Perpetual*

CHESTNUT ROSE: *spiky hips and buds, medium, Species Hybrid*

MADAME ISAAC PEREIRE: *cupped, tall, Bourbon*

MAGNA CHARTA: *cupped, tall, Hybrid Perpetual*

MARBRÉE: *flat, low, Portland*

MRS. JOHN LAING: *cupped, tall, Hybrid Perpetual*

PAUL NEYRON: *reflexed, tall, Hybrid Perpetual*

ROSA GLAUCA: *single, low, Species*

ROSA MUNDI: *semi-double, striped, low, Gallica*

ZÉPHRINE DROUHIN: *semi-double, thornless, tall, Bourbon*

LILAC PINK

EXCELLENZ VON SCHUBERT: *pompon, low, Polyantha*

HERMOSA: *cupped, low, Bourbon/China*

MAMAN COCHET: *cupped, medium, Tea*

YOLANDE D'ARAGON: *flat, quartered, tall, Portland*

MEDIUM PINK

AUTUMN DAMASK: *flat, informal, tall, Damask*

BELLA DONNA: *quartered, medium, Damask*

CELESTIAL: *semi-double, tall, Alba*

COMMON MOSS: *quartered, medium, Moss*

COMTE DE CHAMBORD: *cupped, medium, Portland*

CRESTED MOSS: *cupped, tall, Moss*

EMPRESS JOSÉPHINE: *quartered, medium, Species Hybrid*

KÖNIGIN VON DÄNEMARK: *cupped, medium, Alba*

LA VILLE DE BRUXELLES: *button-eye, tall, Damask*

LOUISE ODIER: *cupped, tall, Bourbon*

OLD BLUSH: *cupped, low, China*

REINE VICTORIA: *cupped, tall, Bourbon*

LIGHT PINK

AMÉLIA: *semi-double, medium, Alba*

BELLE ISIS: *button-eye, low, Gallica*

BLUSH NOISETTE: *pompon, medium/tall, Noisette*

CATHERINE MERMET: *pointed bud, medium, Tea*

CÉCILE BRÜNNER: *tea-like, low, Polyantha*

CELSIANA: *semi-double, medium, Damask*

COMTESSE DE MURINAIS: *button-eye, tall, Moss*

DUCHESSE DE BRABANT: *cupped, medium, Tea*

ENFANT DE FRANCE: *cupped, low, Hybrid Perpetual*

ISPAHAN: *pompon, tall, Damask*

LA FRANCE: *pointed bud, medium, Hybrid Tea*

MADAME ERNST CALVAT: *cupped and quartered, tall, Bourbon*

PETITE DE HOLLANDE: *pompon, low, Centifolia*

ROSA MULTIFLORA CARNEA: *pompon, tall, Species*

ROSE DE MEAUX: *pompon, low, Centifolia*

SYDONIE: *flat, low, Portland*

TRICOLORE DE FLANDRE: *flat, quartered, striped, low, Gallica*

BLUSH PINK

BLUSH MOSS: *cupped, medium, Moss*

FANTIN-LATOUR: *quartered, medium, Centifolia*

FÉLICITÉ PARMENTIER: *reflexed, low, Alba*

GREAT MAIDEN'S BLUSH: *quartered, fragrant, tall, Alba*

MADAME PIERRE OGER: *cupped, edged pink, tall, Bourbon*

POMPON BLANC PARFAIT: *flat, tall, Alba*

PRINCESSE LOUISE: *pompon, tall, Rambler*

ROSA ROXBURGHII NORMALIS: *single, burr-like hips, tall, Species*

SOUVENIR DE LA MALMAISON: *flat, quartered, low, Bourbon*

YORK AND LANCASTER: *flat, striped, tall, Damask*

WHITE

ALBA SEMI-PLENA: *semi-double, tall, Alba*

BLANC DOUBLE DE COUBERT: *semi-double, medium, Hybrid Rugosa*

BLANCHEFLEUR: *button-eye, tall, Centifolia*

HEBE'S LIP: *semi-double, tipped red, medium, Eglantine*

LAMARQUE: *nodding, tall, Noisette*

LÉDA: *pompon, edged red, tall, Damask*

MADAME ALFRED CARRIÈRE: *semi-double, tall, Noisette*

MADAME HARDY: *flat, green eye, medium, Damask*

MADAME PLANTIER: *quartered, tall/climbing, Alba*

MARIE PAVIÉ: *pompon, low, Polyantha*

SOMBREUIL: *flat, tall, Climbing Tea*

VARIEGATA DI BOLOGNA: *cupped, striped, tall, Bourbon*

GREEN

GREEN ROSE: *novelty, low, China*

BLUSH YELLOW

ALBÉRIC BARBIER: *flat, informal, tall, Rambler*

ALISTER STELLA GRAY: *pompon, tall, Noisette*

MEDIUM YELLOW

HARISON'S YELLOW: *flat, tall, Species Hybrid*

DARK YELLOW

AUSTRIAN COPPER: *single bicolor, medium, Species Hybrid*

PERSIAN YELLOW: *cupped, tall, Species Hybrid*

ROSA BANKSIAE LUTEA: *pompon, tall, Species*

YELLOW-APRICOT

CRÉPUSCULE: *Tea-like, sprays, tall, Noisette*

LADY HILLINGDON: *cupped, medium, Tea*

MUTABILIS: *single, changeable, medium, China*

SAFRANO: *loosely cupped, medium, Tea*

SOLEIL D'OR: *cupped, tall, Hybrid Tea*

ORANGE

COMTESSE DU CAYLA: *semi-double, low, China*

PINK-APRICOT

PERLE D'OR: *pompon, low, Polyantha*

SALMON PINK

BELLE OF PORTUGAL: *nodding flowers, tall, Climber*

FRANÇOIS JURANVILLE: *pompon, tall, Rambler*

Appendix D

OLD ROSE ORGANIZATIONS *and* PUBLICATIONS

I f you find yourself wishing to expand your own knowledge of Old Garden Roses, or dream of sharing your own experiences of, and love for, growing OGRs, you may want to contact one or more of the following and join in with those who continue to foster this divine obsession.

THE AMERICAN ROSE SOCIETY
PO Box 30,000
Shreveport, LA 71130-0030
Publishes a monthly magazine and annual.
MEMBERSHIP: $32.00

THE CANADIAN ROSE SOCIETY
c/o Anne Graber
10 Fairfax Crescent
Scarborough, Ontario M1L 1Z8
    Canada
MEMBERSHIP: $25.00 (U.S. funds)

HERITAGE ROSES GROUP
Beverly R. Dobson, Secretary
1034 Taylor Avenue
Alameda, CA 94501
Publishes a quarterly journal.
MEMBERSHIP: $6.00

THE COMBINED ROSE LIST
An essential publication for any lover of Old Roses. The 1999 edition lists 274 nurseries worldwide, as well as a total of 11,571 rose species and cultivars listed alphabetically and cross-referenced as to where they can be purchased.
Order from:
Peter Schneider
PO Box 677
Mantua, OH 44255
The 2000 Edition is $20.00 postpaid in the U.S.